# THE MANDORLA AND TAU

The Secrets and Mysteries of Freemasonry Revealed

## KEVIN L. GEST

For:

Emma, Matthew, Alexander,
Jasmine, Jordan, Reuben.

Other books by **Kevin L. Gest**

*The Secrets of Solomon's Temple*

*Chivalry – the Origins and History of Orders of Knighthood*

# THE MANDORLA AND TAU

The Secrets and Mysteries of Freemasonry Revealed

## KEVIN L. GEST

The Mandorla and Tau
Kevin L. Gest

First published 2011

ISBN 978 0 85318 385 3

Published by Lewis Masonic

an imprint of Ian Allan Publishing Ltd, Hersham, Surrey KT12 4RG.
Printed in England by Ian Allan Printing Ltd, Hersham, Surrey KT12 4RG.

Distributed in the Unites States of America and Canada by BookMasters Distribution Services.

Visit the Lewis Masonic website at
**www.lewismasonic.com**

# Contents

# List of Illustrations

## Charts and Diagrams:

# Acknowledgements

This book started with an innocent enquiry, twenty years ago. I expected to gain an answer to that enquiry, but when one wasn't forthcoming, I started my own investigation. In that twenty-year period, I've spoken to, and communicated with, numerous people; visited many libraries and archives, famous buildings and historical sites, around the world. Along the way, I have gathered a little information from each person I've met. The sum total of that accumulated knowledge has been encyclopaedic. I am indebted to all those people I have met or contacted, who have helped and advised, even in a small way.

For this book, I wish to thank the librarians and archivists at the Guildhall Library, City of London; Medway Archives and Libraries in Rochester and Strood; Kent archives, Maidstone; City Library and County Archives, St. Albans, Hertfordshire; The British Library, London; The Library of the City of Cambridge; The National Maritime Museum Library, Greenwich; The Library of the Royal Institute of British Architects, London; the Victoria and Albert Museum, London; County archives in Lincolnshire; The library and museum at Freemasons Hall, London; The Friends at, St Albans, St. Pauls, Rochester, Canterbury, Salisbury, Durham, Lincoln, Lichfield, Peterborough, Chichester and Winchester cathedrals, and Romsey Abbey Church, Hampshire; and many others.

My thanks also go to Nick at Ian Allan, whose patience I have sorely tried over the past few two years, and to the editorial and production team who have been so helpful.

My agent, Fiona, deserves a huge vote of thanks. She has had such a calm but encouraging approach that has been very beneficial to me, and the finished project.

I also thank Mr Kenneth E. Thomas, who, at the time of writing, is the Provincial Grand Master for the Masonic Province of Sussex. Over ten years ago I produced a short paper about some of the things my enquiries and research had revealed. I expected that to be the end of the matter. Instead, I received a handwritten letter in response, the contents of which were encouraging me to keep going with my research. I'm sure he never expected to hear from me again, but that encouragement, and the research and enquiries I have made since, has resulted in this book, as well two others, *The Secrets of Solomon's Temple* and *Chivalry – the Origins and History of Orders of Knighthood*. And then there is Reg Barrow, curator of the Masonic museum and library in Sussex, whom I also thank. He has not always found my ideas to be agreeable, has cherry-picked the bits he has liked – and used them, has always been most supportive, and provided me with copies of books and other items of memorabilia I have asked for.

And not forgetting my long suffering wife, Lois, who has put up with, though not always silently, the piles of paper and books that have been strewn around rooms in the house, as I've tried to piece together an enormous jigsaw puzzle of facts.

My sincere thanks to you all.

## Disclaimer
The background research and enquiry that supports the information contained in this book, was collected over a protracted period approaching twenty years. Every effort has been made to ensure that no copyrights have been infringed. If anyone feels that rights have been infringed, then please accept my sincere apologies; notify the publishers so that corrections can be made in any future editions.

K. L. Gest
Sussex
2011

# Chapter 1

# SOMETHING DIFFERENT

**And now, for something different.**

**The mandorla is a symbol with a secret.**
Windsor Castle, nestling close to the banks of the River Thames, the waterway that had once been the major highway for the transport of kings and nobles, is just to the west of the urban sprawl of London. Originally built as a fortress many centuries ago, its grey stonewalls radiate a cold, forbidding aura.

Since the fourteenth century Windsor Castle has been the home of the Most Noble Order of the Garter, and still is. Within the grounds of the castle stands what, to all appearances, is a rather ordinary-looking stone church, with architectural features as might be found in many churches across England. Step inside, however, and one is met by a cavernous interior of breath-taking proportion and architectural splendour. It is St George's Chapel, the spiritual home of the Knights of the Garter. At one end of the chapel is the quire and the stalls of the current knights, their individual banners hung above the stalls to denote where each knight will be seated. There is something else there which the majority of visitors will never notice, and if they do, they will have no idea what it is.

As a church, and one with a long historical connection with the Christian faith, one would expect to find a large cross in gold or silver, the traditional symbol of Christianity, prominently displayed where the knights will have it continuously before their eyes. Not so. There is another symbol. Elliptical in shape it is the symbol known as the *mandorla, almond* or *vesica*.

For thousands of years it has been regarded as most sacred, even more so than the cross. The symbol also appears in the church founded by the Emperor Charlemagne around 800 CE, at Aachen, Germany. It can be found in other prominent positions; above the main west door to Chartres Cathedral, France; in a church at the castle in Prague, a city that was once the centre of the Holy Roman Empire; and in close proximity to the grave of Leonardo da Vinci, in the Loire Valley in France, to name but a few. These are all visible settings. But sometimes it can be revealed or have had an influence in places that one would least expect.

What brought it to prominence? What does it signify? What secrets does it hold?

### Is anybody out there?

Christmas Eve, 24th December 1968, may well have been the day that God's hitherto robust health of many centuries, started to decline, or so historians may record when they reach the greater depths of the twenty-first century.

For thousands of generations of the development and evolution of man on planet Earth, the wonders of nature, predictability of the seasons, the birth and rebirth of the sources of food, the regular and routine passage across the sky of the sun, the moon and the myriad stars in the firmament of heaven, were wonders to behold. They were seen as the fruits of creation of an unknown and supreme being, for how else could all these wonderful things have come into existence?

So what happened in December 1968? That was the month of the USA's NASA Apollo 8 mission to the moon. Although man had mastered the sciences that enabled him to leave the surface of planet Earth and circle it at a distance of a few hundred miles in the earlier years of that decade, December 1968, was the first time that man had left the relative safety of Earth and voyaged into space. The mission involved travelling around 300,000 miles to the far side of the moon (the dark side, as it was known, an area previously not seen by man) then re-emerging and returning to Earth. It was as the Apollo 8 spacecraft emerged from its journey of circumnavigating the moon, that the astronauts gained their first view of the Earth from such a distance. One of the astronauts, William Anders, quickly grabbed a camera and took an unscheduled photograph of what they saw. Transmitted back to Earth, the picture was flashed around the world. Man had already used expressions like sunrise and moonrise, now another was added to the repertoire – *Earthrise*.

Apollo 8 astronaut, William Anders, is quoted as having said of the impact of that image of *Earthrise*:

*"We came all this way to explore the moon, and the most important thing is that we discovered the Earth."*[1]

Earthrise photograph taken by William Anders. Reproduced by kind permission of NASA

The beauty the astronauts witnessed had a profound effect on many people. It made so many who witnessed that event realise that, at that point in time, Earth, our home, was and remains, unique in the universe; one precious small round dot of blue, brown, green and white against the background of the blackness of the infinity of space. Since that time, the depths of space, measured in tens, hundreds or thousands of light years, have been probed by radio-telescopes like that at Manchester University - Jodrell Bank, England, or the Green Bank Telescope in West Virginia, USA. Optical telescopes launched into space, like Hubble, have sent back wonderful images of the universe. Special probing satellites have been sent to venture far out into space, some venturing way beyond our own solar system, recording information and transmitting it back to Earth. There have been probes and robots sent to the planets, to look at their structure and assess if any life forms could exist there. For all the probing and looking that has taken place for over half a century, there has been no sign of life, in any other form, elsewhere in the universe.

Scientists now believe that the universe was created by particles of matter that came together in such a way that they created a massive explosion, a big bang, that fused particles together to create solid masses, whilst hurtling these masses far out across the universe to create galaxies and stars that we can view from Earth.

Despite all this knowledge and investigation there are no grand or immortal mansions for God to reside in, yet found. To the best of our knowledge we, the inhabitants of planet Earth, are unique and alone in the entire universe.

These startling revelations raise some interesting and worrying consequences for religions that promoted the residence of God in a heaven above the Earth; for prophets that *came down to Earth* from heaven; for the concept that we all, when we are no more, will rise up to heaven and live for eternity. And, in the longer term, it will cause difficulty for many of our national and international institutions who have built their foundations on the concepts espoused by the various religions. For example, kings and royal dynasties have seized power and maintained it by implying that they have a right to rule by virtue that they, and their blood-line, were chosen by God – *mon dieu, mon droit – my God, my right.*

Through several thousand years, the lot of our ancestors changed very little, generation to generation. In Europe, from around 500 CE, organised religion began to permeate every aspect of life, but the lot of ordinary people changed little. Wealth was measured more by the land controlled by a few nobles, rather than money. The 1700s saw the rise of the period known as the enlightenment, when experimental science became the basis for the study of the world about us, and some of the views about the origins and cycles of life and nature, as espoused through religion, were questioned; some things started to change; wealth was largely in the hands of the merchant adventurers and nobility and measured in money and land and possessions. The 1800's saw the rise of the industrial revolution; trades, crafts, products, living places and standards changed; wealth was now in the hands of the landed nobility – and industrial barons. Then came the twentieth century, when, by its conclusion, hardly anything was the same as it was at the start; change had been dramatic; personal freedom of expression increased; the nobility and influence of religion, marginalised; science had made massive advances creating new products, skills and customs; wealth moved to the those that owned and managed the vast industrial and financial institutions that had developed through the century; links with the knowledge of our ancestors, had been all but abandoned.

Amongst the institutions that face a difficult challenge without a heaven or deity, or connection with the knowledge of our ancestors is freemasonry; an institution whose ceremonies embrace many of the attributes of organised religion, because during its evolution over the centuries, the political and religious climates then prevailing dictated such adherence in the absence of any other knowledge. Yet, at its core there is a different knowledge and understanding that was developed by our ancestors through hundreds of past generations; knowledge that provided the foundations on which our modern world has been created.

The *mandorla* is an integral element of that ancient knowledge.

**The *mandorla* is a symbol with a secret.**

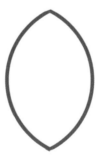

# Chapter 2

## THE GIFT OF LIFE

It is humbling to think that every one of us alive today is, and can only be so, because we have a continuous chain of ancestors that extends back in time to the very origins of human life on this planet, and whatever went before the process that led to the evolution of man.  Most people will have known their parents. A high number will have known their grandparents. Some may even have known their great-grandparents. But, only a few can trace their ancestral line back in time for more than a few generations. Yet, our ancestors lived, survived childhood, loved, and begat children. Those children also survived in their time, and begat children that have provided that unbroken chain of the ancestral line. Most of us are so caught up with living our own lives, coping with our own difficulties, trying to survive and prosper in our own age that we hardly give a thought to the thousands of men and women who went before us, where they came from, how they survived, how long they lived, what fears and difficulties they had to endure, what skills and knowledge they accumulated in their lifetime. Through what they endured, they gave us a very precious thing – an accumulation of knowledge and wisdom, that we in our generation have used. Thanks to them we have the gift of life.

As we plough ever deeper into the twenty-first century, for most of the peoples of the world, wherever we live on the planet, the condition of our lives is far more sophisticated than it was for previous generations. We are only able to experience and enjoy that sophistication because our ancestors acquired knowledge about a range of subjects, from the passing of the seasons, what foods to grow and cultivate and where to find them, what not to eat as it was harmful, animal husbandry; a deep understanding of the natural world, its cycles and the connections that sustained it. They leant how to take natural materials, like stones and wood, and make them into tools and weapons. They noted which materials floated on water, then fashioned canoes and small boats to take to the seas. They discovered materials that melted in fire, like gold and silver, and they learnt how to fashion that molten material into intricate jewels. They noticed that if they picked a certain berry, crushed it so that the juices flowed, left those juices for a period of time and filtered them, the result was a very agreeable drink – wine. They learnt to make cloth and fashion clothes instead of only wearing the skins of dead animals.  They learnt that the sea provided an abundance of food and that some of that food could also be crushed and boiled to release fluids that became dyes for the cloth they made. They noted the stars in the night sky above and that some of them moved in regular cycles – the planets. Our ancestors of thousands of years ago did all these things without the aid of expensive and complex instruments that we might use today. They did it by simple observation of things and events that occurred around them.

They observed the cycles of life.

They also did something else that has been extremely important to us. They found ways and means to ensure that the knowledge and experience they had gained was passed from generation to generation, father to son, mother to daughter. Some of these ways and means were seen to be so important to survival that it was collected and retained in the minds and experience of the older members of tribal groups - the tribal elders. As small scattered tribes grew into civilisations, so the collective knowledge was built on and embodied in organisations that we might call traditions and religions, and the role of the tribal elders changed to priests and sages. It is believed by some academics, that as certain of those civilisations in various parts of the world became more sophisticated, elected elders or priests within those traditions and religions, selected young men and women who showed intellectual ability, educated and passed on to them much of the knowledge then known. It has even been suggested that specific young men and women who clearly demonstrated high intellectual abilities, would be encouraged into tribal or arranged marriages with the objective of producing highly intelligent off spring. If this did indeed happen, it would have been an attempt at gene manipulation, the sort of science that has only recently been the subject of dedicated study. These same tribal groups understood that there needed to be a code of conduct that all should follow for people to live in reasonable harmony together. The codes of living they evolved ultimately became the types of rules that we find in the Ten Commandments of the Old Testament of the Bible. Not only were they a set of rules to live life by, but also they provided a basis for agreed punishment of those who offended those rules. Thus, the tribal elders were the lawmakers and high courts of their day and the collection of rules was a code for behaviour in an organised society. These same rules became the cornerstone of religious belief and teaching for thousands of years and still underpin many of the laws in our modern civilisations.

Interestingly, in the ancient world, the Greeks, for example, appear to have known nothing about the existence on the planet of the areas we know today as South America, Australia and sub-Saharan Africa. Yet within these widely separated geographical regions, isolated from each other by vast oceans, groups of people developed different cultures and civilisations, in almost every case, influenced by the environment in which they lived. Despite their apparent isolation these disparate cultures developed the same type of community rules that are included in the Ten Commandments; a set of laws that were supposedly conveyed by a deity to a man by the name of Moses, as he camped on a remote mountaintop in the Sinai desert.

Without the ability to write down their knowledge as we might do today, knowledge was probably passed on in the verbal tradition through tribal ceremonies and stories, told and retold around fires as families rested at night. In later eras some specific knowledge was built into the fabric of temples and other stately edifices. It is that accumulation of knowledge, passed on through the ancestral generations, added to and refined with the passing of time, that has provided the stimulus that we, now in our time, are able to live the sophisticated lifestyles we enjoy, by comparison with the elementary lifestyles of our ancient ancestors.

There are however, many intellectuals who believe that as a consequence of the industrial and technological era of the twentieth century, we have become removed so far from our ancestral roots that much of the knowledge that every one of us needs to know to be able to survive, without the aid of modern technology, has been lost to the majority of people; civilisation, they tell us, could collapse, with life on Earth being inherited by those tribes and people that we sometimes regard as *primitive*. At the start of the twentieth century almost everyone knew where food came from, and how to harvest and store it during the long winter months. At the start of the twenty-first century in the highly urbanised culture of the western world, there are many who believe that food is made in factories and have little understanding about where it grows, or is husbanded. The trades and skills that existed prior to the industrial revolution had been developed by our ancestors over the preceding centuries and passed down the generations with very little change. In the space of a few decades of the twentieth century, many of those trades and skills ceased to exist, except amongst a few academics and individuals who are keen to see the knowledge preserved. Each passing decade, however, sees fewer and fewer of such old skills surviving.

There are organisations that exist where some of that ancestral knowledge remains and is passed on in much the same way as it was in earlier times, by verbal tradition. One such organisation is freemasonry.

Freemasonry is a progressive fraternity that encourages, charity and morality through its symbols and ceremonies. That morality. An allegory is a means of presentation which obscures the main feature. In other words, what you see is not necessarily what you get.

## A Reflection on Freemasonry

> *"I've long been of the opinion that when you look at Masonic ceremonies, the words and actions, at the symbols and procedures, across all the degrees, then whoever put all this together three hundred years ago, with the objective of creating a so-called gentleman's club, was definitely one wheel short of a trolley. It must have a meaning that we've lost sight of in our modern world. The question is – What is that meaning?"*

> The Author in *The Secrets of Solomon's Temple*

# Section 1

## Chapter 3

# HERE IS THE KEY!!

**Author's Introduction**

The early years of my Masonic career passed all too quickly. I could remember that on the evening of my initiation, I was impressed by the way that those with whom I came into contact conducted the ceremony without the need for a prompt from the wings. It was like being a guest character in a specially scripted play. The main actors knew their words and actions well and presented both with a high degree of precision. When it was revealed to me on that first evening, I was equally impressed by the décor of the room where the lodge held its meetings. It was referred to as a Masonic Temple.

Unlike many Lodge rooms, that, over the past few hundred years have been built into small converted barns, disused village halls, old houses, or created in hotel rooms temporarily set out for the purpose, the Masonic Temple in which I was initiated was purpose-built. It was quite large, measuring some sixty feet long, forty feet wide and twenty feet high. The walls were covered with a fine oak wood panelling, from the top of which the lighting emitted from behind a floral pelmet to give an even and diffused illumination to the room. But the most impressive feature was a zodiac measuring nearly forty feet in diameter, that dominated the ceiling in the centre of the room directly above a black and white chequered pavement that was encased in a tessellated border. As well as the impressive zodiac, other areas of the ceiling were adorned with an array of symbols, some that I could recognise but many that conveyed no meaning to me at that time.

During the first ten years of my Masonic career, I had visited this room on many occasions and its setting became such a familiar backdrop to our proceedings that I didn't give the decor another thought. Then, in a short period of time, a series of events occurred that led me to question the reason why the room was so elaborately decorated, why the zodiac was there, what the symbols on the ceiling were meant to convey and why certain items of furnishings in the temple existed. On one evening, I took a visitor into that room who was so impressed with the décor that I was asked a lot of questions about their meaning, especially the zodiac. I was somewhat acutely embarrassed in having to admit that I didn't know. Through this encounter I realised that I had been so involved with getting my part in the ceremonies right, that I had not taken due stock of what was around me, what it was there for, why it was there or what it meant. Before long, I realised that all our members were in the same boat, we were taking these wonderful facilities for granted. It didn't stop there. I realised that, like many generations before me, men had learnt the ceremonies, and some were so accomplished at performing them that they were held up as great exponents of the art of delivering the Masonic ritual. Praise was heaped on them. There were aspects of these ceremonies that I too performed well, and for which I received some acclaim. Then came the day when I realised that I had learnt the words, knew the actions associated with them, but I hadn't got a clue what it all actually meant. In a short space of time I found myself not only seeking answers about the reasons behind the temple furnishings, but also asking:

- *What are we doing?*
- *Why are we doing it?*
- *Where did it come from?*

Every lodge holds what are known as *Lodge Instruction* evenings at which ceremonies are rehearsed and some of the lesser known facts about freemasonry are meant to be conveyed. As I looked back over the years I realised that on each such *instruction* evening, we had rehearsed parts of forthcoming ceremonies but I could not remember an occasion when other facts about the Order had been conveyed, or the significance of the prominent items of furnishings or décor that surrounded us. I asked the elders of our lodge what the significance was of that splendid zodiac on the ceiling of the temple. I was amazed to find that none of them knew. A couple of members of very long standing, commented that our Deputy Provincial Grand Master, a very senior officer in local freemasonry, had once been heard to remark that he too had often wondered at its significance. I was astonished. Among these senior members of the lodge there were a few that had regularly attended for thirty to forty years. I estimated that some of them had been into the temple and had this magnificent decoration before their eyes, on at least one thousand occasions during their membership. I found it bewildering that these highly intelligent, and in some cases, intellectual men, could not provide me with an answer. If nothing else, it suggested that they hadn't even given the matter any thought themselves. I even sought out the curator of the temple for his opinion, only to find out that he didn't know either. I was even more astonished. How, I wondered, could such a prominent feature reside in that room and nobody have any idea why it was there.

From this experience with our Masonic elders, I soon came to the conclusion that we were committing considerable effort into learning and perfecting our ceremonies but devoted no time at all to understanding what we were doing, why we were doing it, or had any idea where it came from. If that same situation was common to other lodges then, as an entire organisation, we were in serious danger of losing any vestige of understanding about the basis of our ancient institution and, in consequence we would end up as a society which was an empty shell devoid of meaning. To me, this seemed an extraordinary set of circumstances. After all, freemasonry is an ancient organisation with a documented history for at least the past three hundred years, and there are isolated references to it that stretch back to at least the medieval period. As none of my fellow masons seemed able to provide the information I was seeking, I decided to try and gain some understanding for myself, at least. But as time progressed I found that there were other people, masons and non-masons alike, who found the results of my enquiries, equally of interest.

Over the next fifteen years, I did find answers, but not as I had originally imaged they might be, and the revelations were not always welcomed by the Masonic hierarchy. As I began searching I found I was led down an intricate path that crossed the boundaries of religion, history, ancient cultures, geometry, temple building and celestial mechanics. The revelations enabled me to come to conclusions about the significance of specific features of Masonic culture and ceremonies, such as, references to Solomon's Temple, Solomon's Seal - more usually known as the Star of David, and the pentagram. The details of that journey of discovery, what I found and my interpretations of the significance, I have revealed in an earlier book - *The Secrets of Solomon's Temple*[2].

Today, in many lodges, efforts are made to ensure a high standard of ceremonial enactment which brings a feeling of great satisfaction to those who have participated or undertaken the coaching. Sadly, however, members have little understanding about the meaning of the ceremonies they enact or the history associated with it. As the generations pass, new members have less understanding for the uniqueness of the institution and the part they are playing in it.

So, what about the ceremonies? Are they empty shells devoid of meaning? The answer, I suggest is a resounding - No!! They are filled with information if we know how to look behind them.

The purpose of this book is to try and shine a light into the somewhat darkened corners of Masonic ceremony and life. And, to get a better feeling for explanations, it will be necessary to cast our net in search of knowledge outside of the Masonic institution to understand the context of some of the ceremonial contents and unravel their *secrets and mysteries*.

This book is the result of over twenty years of enquiry and research. I have tried to present answers to the questions - What?  Why? Where? When? How?

Some of the information is considerably at variance with the positions adopted by eminent men of title and letters that wrote on a range of Masonic subjects in the one hundred year period of 1850 – 1950. I make no apology for that. They did not have the advantages of research and information tools at their disposal that we have today. In some cases, their experience of life was very narrow and they looked at freemasonry from the paradigm they were trapped in, and the social position they were conditioned to conduct their lives within.

I have presented the information I have gathered, as I have found it. I trust this book will, by the end, meet with your favour.  I leave you to make up your own mind.

*Si talia jungere possis sit tibi scire satis*
*Nil nisi clavis deest*

If thou canst comprehend these things, thou knowest enough
Nothing is wanting but the key

I now hand you - the key.

*"Now every mason has taken several very solemn obligations not to divulge [their] secrets; and the way in which the promise has been kept by the hundreds of thousands of brethren who are spread all over the world is not only a credit to the Order but commands the respect of all right-minded people."*

*Printed in a popular magazine in London, March 1888.*[3]

# Chapter 4

# THE OPENING

**What?  Why?  When?  Where?  How?**
**Behind each question, there rests an interesting story.**
Throughout the past two hundred years, there have been many claims made about freemasonry and the secrets it is supposed to harbour. Yes, it does have secrets, but there is no evidence that they are of the type that will lead to buried treasure, the holy grail, centres of conspiracy, or new world orders. These claims have largely been made by:

- individuals who have had no connection with the organisation but found it an easy target for sensationalised rants based on anachronistic interpretations of old hoaxes and religious fanaticism;

- individuals who have joined the organisation specifically to claim membership whilst publishing innuendo and distorted facts merely for the purpose of making profit by so doing;

- individuals who have presented theories as if based on fact, but whose knowledge has been very wide of the mark and more fitting to be included in the domains of fantasy and fiction;

- used in works of fiction to create plot-lines of intrigue and suspicion, and presented as if material quoted, represents fact.

In addition, there have been periodic claims that those who participate in Masonic ceremonies are actually undertaking rituals that are blasphemous and irreligious. Yet, despite the tirades of religious and political fervour that have periodically engulfed this institution, not to mention a flow of mocking and unfavourable banter, in its current form it has existed for nearly 300 years, has grown in membership and become an internationally respected institution. Members of royal families, nobility, bishops and clergymen, high-ranking government officials, diplomats and ministers of state, scientists, artists, entertainers, doctors, lawyers and a plethora of other professions and trades have been members in past years, and still are.

Some of the observations made in this book will be considerably at variance with previous works by other authors. In the seventy years between the end of the Second World War (1939 – 1945), and the second decade of the twenty-first century, huge strides have been made by an international army of academics in locating, translating and researching events from history, and with the aid of advanced scientific practices, various aspects of historical events have been revealed that presents some previously held interpretations and theories, considered in their time as absolute fact, in a new light. Even new disciplines of research and study have been created. When freemasonry was first organised into a structured manner in the year 1717, resulting in the organisation we know today, archaeology was still one hundred and fifty years from gaining its first academically credible steps into the world of our ancestors, whilst the science known as astro-archaeology only appeared towards the end of the twentieth century. Even religion has not escaped scrutiny as parchments discovered in the area hitherto known as the *Holy Land,* has forced a reappraisal of some long-held and preached doctrines and dogmas, and threatened to turn established concepts on their head. From this wholly new perspective, there is an opportunity to try to answer the questions that form the header for this chapter, by asking:

1.  What do the ceremonies mean?
2.  Why are they done?
3.  When did it all start?
4.  Where did it come from?
5.  How has it reached us today?

## An introduction to the Masonic World

As an institution, freemasonry has a documented history that is nearly 300 years old and roots that extend back further in time. Yet, it is not an easy organisation to understand. It is really a collection of individual cells, called lodges which together make up the entire institution. This is not unlike the monastic communities of the mediaeval period which were often divided into cells in remote locations but came together as a religious Order, be it the Benedictines, Cistercians, Augustinians, and others. If it is a regular lodge, operating within the constitutions of, and recognised by the United Grand Lodge of England, one cannot merely roll up to a meeting, fill in a prepared application form and be declared a member from that day forth, as happens with many social or sporting clubs. Instead, one is proposed for membership of a lodge by an existing member who must have known the candidate for some six months prior to nomination and ideally for at least three years. There are annual fees that must be paid; there is regalia to buy; and one is encouraged to make an annual charitable commitment. A meeting is completed by the lodge members dining together, accompanied in the time-honoured tradition of proposing toasts to the honour and wellbeing of members of the institution and beyond. And, last but not least, the institution is organised in a hierarchical manner where every new member starts his Masonic career on the bottom rung of a very long ladder.

Masonic meetings are undertaken in a ceremonial context throughout, rather like enacting a series of short plays, the contents of which encourage the pursuit of a good and wholesome lifestyle, being benevolent and charitable, and in so doing make a positive contribution to the community of which one is a part, and the world at large. All this requires some commitment in time and effort so it is not an organisation that will appeal to those of strained financial means, are not prepared to spend some time learning the play-like ceremonies and committing them to memory, or will enjoy the constraints of what some might consider as a very old fashioned and hierarchical institution.

### Just how old is freemasonry, and where did it come from?

Born in Edinburgh, Scotland in 1742, William Preston is believed to have moved to London in 1760, at the tender age of eighteen years. It also seems clear that he had, or made, beneficial contacts in the few years that followed, because around three years later, probably in his twenty-first year, he was admitted as a member of a lodge. He was clearly impressed by the conduct of those around him, and the Masonic lore that he encountered, because just ten years later, and after very considerable research and enquiry on his part, he published his first book, *Illustrations of Masonry* in 1772. Two years later he became a member of *Lodge of Antiquity No 1* which had been one of the four lodges that had originally formed the Grand Lodge of London and Westminster. Preston, it seems, then went on to organise and present Masonic lore that was easy for the members to understand, through a process known as *lectures*. Preston's work is still revered today. There are, however, a number of historical connections he makes that have subsequently been shown to be grossly inaccurate by more recent academic endeavour. Such connections involve, amongst others, King Athelstan, St. Alban, and various religious figures from the Old Testament. His work was produced against a background of the religious, academic and social culture of his time.

Likewise, Dr Anderson and the development of his Book of Constitutions, first published in 1723. These were produced against the additional backdrop of around one hundred years of political and religious turmoil, and in some instances, set the basis for material that, probably, Preston was also to use. There are however, some key elements of information in the Constitutions that provide a signpost to Masonic development.

When one is first admitted to freemasonry, and therefore starting on their Masonic journey, the new member is advised several things about the institution, and their position in it. Amongst these are:

- That freemasonry is older than the *Golden Fleece* and *Roman Eagle*.
- That to be admitted as a member of the institution, the applicant must be a *free man*, and asked to confirm that he is.
- That he is being admitted as an *entered apprentice*.
- That he is being admitted to the *secrets and mysteries* of the craft.
- That his admission entitles him to *privileges*.

So, what do all these things mean, and where did they originate? We'll look at them, one at a time, albeit, in different chapters, and not necessarily in a consecutive order. First, we need to establish a starting point, by trying to understand just how old freemasonry actually is.

Modern freemasonry derives from the year 1717 when four lodges based around London, came together and suggested that there should be one organisation that oversaw and regulated their proceedings, and the organisation of lodges. The institution they created in that year was the Grand Lodge of London and Westminster. According to *Coil's Masonic Encyclopaedia* the four lodges comprised of one gentleman's lodge and three that existed for operative masons, and that the *London and Westminster* connection was derived from the area of jurisdiction covered within the livery company trade guild system operating at that time, known as the London Mason's Company. In the records of the *Worshipful Company of Masons – The Masons Company,* based in London, traces its origins back to early records of regulations that governed the trade issued in 1356, followed by a *Grand of Arms* in 1472, and a Royal Charter issued under the seal of Charles II, in 1677. This charter granted the Masons Company control over all masons in the two cities of London and Westminster, and for a distance of seven miles therefrom.[4] There are some people in the organisation who suggest that there was no freemasonry prior to 1717. This is a rather bizarre position to take. After all, four lodges were involved in the creation of the Grand Lodge of London and Westminster, and therefore existed prior to that date. What is more, the organisation has openly stated that there are records of two very prominent men in English history, having been admitted to lodges some fifty years prior to the Grand Lodge of London and Westminster being formed. They were Elias Ashmole who was initiated into a lodge in Warrington, and Sir Robert Moray who was possibly initiated during the Civil War of the 1600s. Following the restoration of the monarchy with the coronation of Charles II in 1660, both men are credited with having been founding members of what we know today as the Royal Society.[5] That both of these men should have been initiated into the institution, and to be acknowledged as having been *freemasons*, then it follows that a system of lodges or gatherings of individuals who had been selected to join together, existed. Records suggest that a freemasons lodge existed in Chichester, Sussex, in 1695. There remains, however, some debate as to what the structure was under which they operated.

The fact that every new member is advised the institution is *older than the Golden Fleece and Roman Eagle* suggests that freemasonry has traceable origins that can be dated to another era.

## The Golden Fleece

When one thinks of the Golden Fleece, it rather suggests the mythological story from ancient Greece, the story of Jason and the Argonauts who sailed off across the seas in search of a ram that had a longhaired fleece of gold. Returning with it would justify Jason's right to be deemed king, and rule over his people. Thus, some earlier writers have concluded that freemasonry started before the rise of the ancient Greek empire. The rise of this empire didn't commence until around the eighth century BCE.

Some historians note that the legend may well have existed long before the Greek empire rose to prominence and interpretations of its meaning are varied. Some believe it may be a reference to a time when sheep and goats were first husbanded in flocks and the fleeces became valuable, and highly sought after trading commodities. Hence, a good flock and careful care of the animals could lead to great riches which in turn could lead to power and influence. Keeping in mind that the story involves water, the sea, another theory is that the story passes on knowledge that by placing a sheep's fleece in the current of a fast-flowing stream, particles of gold could be caught and accumulate in the hairy fibres. In ancient mythologies gold was frequently connected with the sun, so there is yet another theory which connects it with the sun-god. Several other interpretations of the tale exist, but none seem to have any connection with the craft of the mason, other than pointing out the culture of ancient Greece and that many of the geometrical and structural designs that the ancient Greeks built in stone have parallels with those at the time when the Grand Lodge of England was being formed. This was a time when there was considerable interest in the architecture of the ancient world in the two periods known as the Enlightenment and the Renaissance.

The answer actually resides in the statement each new lodge member is told. It refers to the *Order* of the Golden Fleece, and reference to the Roman Eagle, implies that the latter was also an *Order*.

During the era known as the Crusades, many orders of knighthood were created by rulers throughout Europe, in order to ensure a good supply of fighting men on horseback that today we would associate with the term cavalry. When the Christian armies were finally defeated and expelled from the holy lands and territories of Egypt and the eastern Mediterranean, many of the military Orders of knights fell into disuse, or were absorbed into others. In the centuries that followed, several new Orders were established. The Order of the Garter is the oldest of the post-Crusades secular military Orders of Knighthood, whilst the Order of the Golden Fleece is renowned as having been the most wealthy. The Order was founded in 1430, almost one hundred years after the Garter, by Philip the Good, Duke of Burgundy.

The background to the establishment of the Dukedom of Burgundy, and the earlier kingdom of the same name, is a complex tale in its own right, one that extends back to the collapse of the Roman Empire in the fifth century. The territory changed shape and rule several times until in the fourteenth century the king of France established the Dukedom as a title for his son. As a consequence of marriage, the ancestors of Philip the Good acquired a vast area of northern European territory, and titles to go with it. By the time of his death in 1467, Philip III – the Good, had a list of titles, which included:

> *Duke of Burgundy; Count of Artois and Flanders; Count Palatine of Burgundy; Margrave of Namur; Duke of Brabant, Limburg and Lothier [Lotharingia]; Count of Hainault, Holland and Zeeland; Duke of Luxemburg; Count of Charolais; Lord of Friesland; Marquis of the Holy Roman Empire. He was also Premier Peer of France.*

These titles and lands resulted in Philip the Good being extremely wealthy, and a reasonable amount of the wealth was based on trading in wool, the fleece of sheep.

Philip the Good, was married three times. The Golden Fleece was founded to celebrate his marriage to Isabella, daughter of the king of Portugal, which took place in Bruges, on 7th January, 1430. Three days later, on the 10th January 1430, the *Ordre de la Toison d'Or* (Most Illustrious Order of the Golden Fleece), was consecrated. Philip is credited with having had an admiration for the knights of the crusading era, and wished to emulate them.

Bruges was one of the most important ports in northern Europe at that time. Having direct access to the North Sea, it provided the opportunity to ship goods to and from most of the countries that fronted the Baltic Sea, North Sea, Atlantic Ocean and Mediterranean Sea. The Low Countries that formed a major part of Philip's territorial claim, were rich farming lands, ideal for the cultivation of sheep and the by-products of wool and fine lace. Thus, through the income from his vast estates, and the trading through his port, Duke Philip III of Burgundy became one of the wealthiest people in Europe at that time. It is the immense wealth of its founder that has resulted in the Golden Fleece being regarded as the wealthiest of the Orders.

Philip had been a close companion and ally of Henry V, King of England. Philip's port of Bruges traded with ports in England which added to his economic benefit and helped to cement the relationship with Henry. However, Philip was not only friendly towards Henry but he was also had responsibilities and loyalties as the premier peer in France. It was the era when Henry V achieved success over the armies of the King of France, Charles VI, at the Battle of Agincourt in 1415, a battle in which close relatives of Philip, were killed, and as a result, Philip found his loyalties tested by both his alliance with Henry, and his support for the French king. Around one hundred years earlier, Edward III of England had established the Order of the Garter, and Philip was obviously in awe of the success and reputation it enjoyed. Some seven years after the Battle of Agincourt, Philip III was invited to be honoured and elected as a knight of the Garter. Philip requested that the honour be deferred to a later date, clearly to buy time whilst sorting out the conflicts that surrounded him in France as a consequence of Agincourt. However, his request was interpreted as the honour being declined. This action has resulted in Philip being the only person recorded as having been offered membership of the Order of the Garter, and declining it.

There are different opinions as to the reason for the founding of the Golden Fleece, and the origin of the name. Some historians of the past have suggested that Philip III was impressed by the manner, organisation and prestige with which the Garter was associated, and with the realisation that the opportunity to become a knight of the Garter had passed, he set up his own Order as an imitation of it.

Just as a touch of innuendo surrounds the forming of the Garter, based on a similar item of female attire having seemingly fallen from the leg of a Countess and been picked up by Edward III, so there is a further fable, equally based on innuendo, surrounding the Golden Fleece. In it, Philip was apparently visiting his mistress, and entered her chamber without warning, only to find her naked, and brushing her hair, whilst sitting on a stool that was covered by a sheep's fleece. At this sight, Philip decided that the fleece in question was worth a considerable value in gold, and therefore named his Order the Golden Fleece.

Other suggestions are that the name is linked with the Greek mythological tale of Jason and The Argonauts. This mythological tale has many interpretations, one of which is that the Golden Fleece represents the legitimacy of kingship, and that Jason went forth to seek the fleece with a view to restoring legitimacy of his own kingship. Thus, Philip was using the symbolism of the Golden Fleece to establish and reinforce the legitimacy of his own position as Duke of Burgundy and premier peer of the Kingdom of France.

It was common practice in this era for the kings and high-ranking nobles of other countries to be invited to become members of Orders established in other kingdoms. As with the Garter, the number of knights in the Golden Fleece was originally limited to twenty-four, but this stricture on numbers resulted in some of the greatest nobles of Europe, being excluded. With the passing of time, the number increased to over fifty.

Unlike the Garter, whose head has been the sovereign of the country since the time it was established, the Golden Fleece was not, at the time of its foundation, headed by the monarch. Neither was it an Order of the state. It was an honour bestowed by the Dukes of Burgundy and was not connected in any way with the Crown of the French Kings.

Commencing around 1517, there was a move to reform the practices of the Roman Catholic Church from which the Protestant movement began. The Golden Fleece has always been an institution loyal to the Roman Catholic faith.

The Order was adorned with a patron, St Andrew.
A further similarity with the Garter is in the stalls of Saint Saviours Cathedral in the city of Bruges. In the Choir, and above each stall, is a copy of the coats-of-arms of various knights of the Order.
*Left: The insignia of the Golden Fleece presented above the stalls of the knights in the church where the Order was founded in Bruges. That on the far left is the banner of Edward IV, King of England. The A-shaped hanger of that on the right, shows that the holder has died. K. L. Gest*

*Right: The City Library in Bruges, once the Toll house; shows the emblem of the Golden Fleece, a golden chain from which the image of a sheep's fleece is hanging. Duties on the movements of goods would be paid at the Toll House - a form of tax collected by the House of Burgundy. K.L. Gest*

## The Roman Eagle

As noted earlier when it comes to the reference to the *Roman Eagle*, some previous writers, especially from the United States of America, have suggested that it is a reference to the Eagle emblem that Roman Legions carried before them as a symbol of Roman rule and power. With the reference to the Romans again, some suggest, that it points to the magnificent structures that the Romans built in stone, and that the knowledge the masons of that era possessed was the basis of more recent freemasonry. So, if it is not to do with the emblem of the Roman legions, what is it connected to?

There was an Order of the White Eagle, founded in Poland in the year 1325, and an Order of the Black Eagle in Prussia in 1701, but the background to these Orders seem not to fit with the universality that is sought. There is only one *eagle* that had the breadth of time and international acclaim that could fit the bill. That is the two-headed eagle of the Holy Roman Empire.

The Two-headed eagle has associations with the structure of the old Roman Empire, but it was also a sacred symbol that can be traced back to around 2000 BCE. The Holy Roman Empire can be said to have been started around 800 CE, with the crowning of the Emperor Charlemagne, but the two-headed eagle symbol seems to have come to prominence around 1250 CE. The Holy Roman Empire was a major religious and political force in Europe until it was dissolved by Napoleon Bonaparte in 1807.

*An example of the two-headed Eagle of the Holy Roman Empire.*
*K. L. Gest*

Thus, from the above, there is the suggestion that the origins of freemasonry can be traced back to an era earlier than 1250 CE.

# Chapter 5

# UNRELIABLE GUIDANCE

- What are we doing?
- Why are we doing it?
- Where did it come from?

One would think these were quite straightforward questions, and that finding clear-cut answers would not pose too great a difficulty. After all, organised freemasonry has been in existence for nearly 300 years. Although there are hundreds of books and thousands of magazine articles that have been written about freemasonry and published in central Europe, Britain and the USA, as well as other parts of the world, answering those three simple questions is not easy. Yet, therein rests the challenge, because, although many earlier books and articles address issues that are of genuine interest, there are very few that have attempted to answer those seemingly simple three questions at the head of this page.

To make matters worse, some of the information conveyed in those books, was accepted by previous generations as being factual and reliable. In the past, freemasonry attracted a number of men of privileged educational achievement and some with titles. Several produced works on what they regarded as being a backdrop to the evolution of freemasonry, and because of their perceived eminence or titles, what they produced was considered as fact. Some of that material may now be misleading, because the content is based on, what are now, out-of-date concepts that modern research has overshadowed. Then there is a vast array of material that is speculative, at best, and in some instances, absolutely wrong. The difficulty then comes in trying to define what is good and what is unreliable.

To reach a new perspective means approaching the subject from a different viewpoint, but when new approaches to old and trusted ideas are presented, the answers are not always welcome, and subject to challenge and hostility, because indoctrinated ideas and concepts can be deeply entrenched.

Before embarking on the task of finding answers to the questions, it is worth reviewing some of the older information and taking stock of the organisation in a modern context.

## Modern Freemasonry and ancient wisdom

When something is hidden from obvious view, when access to an organisation is limited to but a few individuals who keep their membership away from open scrutiny, and when there appears to be a cloak of secrecy surrounding that organisation, human nature dictates that there will be those in society that will view that organisation, its actions and the people involved with it, with suspicion. That is exactly what has happened to freemasonry at various times in its near three hundred year history.

There have been times when so-called disclosures about Masonic proceedings, and the activities of its members, have been publicised, leading to the organisation being the butt of ridicule, even though such disclosures were, in the main, fictitious. It has been branded a devil-worshipping religion; decried as being anti-religious and blasphemous in its activities, despite the membership attracting men from every rank of all religious denominations. It has been seen as a secret organisation committed to undermining governments around the globe and seeking to develop a new world order. In response to such accusations, politicians, community leaders, military personnel and senior officers in civil administration and defence, were either banned from joining the Order or instructed to declare their membership in prescribed registers. The latter decades of the twentieth century were not immune to these kinds of accusations. Freemasonry was singled out for this treatment whilst other social organisations escaped any such scrutiny. It could be argued that being a member of a power-hungry political party, represented a far bigger threat to national stability and security than membership of an old and established fraternal organisation.

So, what is it about freemasonry that has created these periods of unwarranted hysteria? After all, in many towns and cities across the world where freemasonry exists, the meeting place, the Masonic Hall, is clearly marked, so inhabitants know exactly where the local point of Masonic focus is. In many small towns and communities, Masonic Halls, when they are not being used during the day, provide a community facility for everything from childcare to adult education, and from senior-citizen dance clubs to venues for wedding receptions.

Without doubt it has been the way in which freemasonry has conducted its affairs that has created this veil of distrust. It regards itself as a private organisation and conducts most of its affairs in privacy. This is no different to the way most social organisation conduct their affairs. Yet, whilst with many social organisations, one may merely turn up at a meeting, fill in a membership form, pay a membership fee, and be admitted as an equal participant, freemasonry has always operated on the concept that a person seeking membership must approach an existing member and express an interest in joining. In recent years this procedure has been modified so that a person may be approached and invited to join, but even so, such approaches are only made to individuals that are likely to appreciate the formalities of the Order. Unlike many other social organisations, it has never openly advertised membership recruitment.

Part of a Masonic meeting includes the members having a meal together where toasts expressing national loyalty might be made; there is regalia to buy, and a financial commitment to supporting charitable activity to the benefit of the community in which one lives, is encouraged. So each meeting brings with it a cost in addition to an annual membership fee and it is a price that many in the community may not have the means to support. This is especially true in their younger years when prospective members may have families to provide for, and a home to buy. If that isn't enough, Masonic ceremonies are really a series of small plays acted out before the lodge members, and just like any play, the script and actions must be learnt and committed to memory along with attendance at rehearsals – we want a good performance.

Unlike other social organisations where one could become a member one year and hold an administrative office the next, in freemasonry everyone starts at the same level and becoming an officer takes time, demonstrating one's commitment and integrity along the way. To do all of this requires a commitment of time. The end result is that it attracts men of a more financially stable ability, of middle age, who, perhaps, own their own businesses, are in middle to senior management in a business or institution, and have enjoyed the benefit of a reasonable education.

Although regular freemasonry, especially that which is recognised by and operates under the constitution of the United Grand Lodge of England, is a male-centric domain, a little known fact is that the same procedures are also practiced in separate organisations that exist especially for women. These have become even more significant since equality between the sexes has been a feature of social development. That doesn't mean that the women's lodges are a new innovation; some have roots extending back beyond the era of the suffragette movement.

During the twentieth century, in Britain at least, a common complaint, or statement of jealousy in many instances, was *that the freemasons look after themselves*. This statement is a hangover from the social conditions of the nineteenth century and the first half of the twentieth century. Freemasonry is a fraternal society which means it takes care of those around it. In the 19th century, hospitals were rare, and where they did exist, the treatment was often experimental, harsh, and required the patient to pay a fee. As a result, most people who were sick, tended to be treated at home by family members, who used herbal and family recipes of medicines, some doing more harm than good. If the sick person was the man of the house, the main breadwinner, then there would have been little prospect of money coming into the home whilst the illness prevailed. Often families could not afford the fees necessary to call a doctor.

During this era, a number of mutual fraternal benefit societies were created. For a small weekly investment treated like a savings plan, when there was a need to cover doctor's fees, there was, hopefully, sufficient money in the personal plan to enable the fee to be covered. Some plans also enabled a contribution to funeral arrangements. Such schemes were an early form of private medical insurance. Freemasons had similar schemes that went one stage further. Their charitable monies enabled them to build and operate their own hospitals, retirement homes and schools for their children. They couldn't provide such facilities in every community so they helped provide finance for local hospitals and medical centres, in return for which, they not only received privileged treatment, but also enjoyed the honour of laying the foundation stones for such important buildings. In almost every town in England one can find a foundation stone of a prominent hospital or town hall, or other prominent building, indicating that it was laid with full Masonic Ceremony and hence had probably received some form of Masonic financial support relating to its construction.

So against the social background of Britain in the nineteenth and early twentieth centuries, freemasons did look after themselves, and their families, and did so very well and without being a burden to others. Now, in the twenty-first century, this is perpetuated, but in a different way. Housing conditions have improved, the general health of the populous is better, health services are better organised and available across the developed world. Notwithstanding this, advances in medical care mean that not every hospital can obtain all its needs from central government resources, and, consultants involved in research projects, occasionally need special funding and equipment. Freemasons often pay for such needs through their charity donations. However, unlike many other social organisations who trumpet their charitable works, freemasons seldom seek direct publicity but go about their activities quietly and in an unassuming manner. Such charitable works are not known by the community at large.

The Masonic philosophy today is that by contributing to, and looking after the community in general, they are looking after themselves and their families, because they too are part of the wider community.

In short, freemasonry is a major supporter of charity on a global, national, regional and local level. Most of its activities are unknown by the general community, but facilities provided by freemasons are often there, for the benefit of all.

This commitment to charity brings with it a level of morality, in all its forms. Whilst not interfering with the lives of its members, or preaching, it encourages and reminds members, through its ceremonies, that the practice of a moral and ethical life, avoiding temptations and excesses, leads to a happier and more contented existence.

*Networking* has, through the start of this twenty-first century, been regarded as an essential asset for any young person aspiring to further themselves, within their chosen career, in almost any arena of endeavour. Prior to the change of centuries, such networks already existed, and in some cases had so for many, many years. Freemasonry is arguably one of the oldest such *networks*. The nature of the organisation attracts those individuals that have a sense of duty to society, have a charitable disposition, and a sober outlook on life. By its very nature it will therefore appeal to those individuals that have a natural ability to be leaders, to demonstrate honesty, integrity, loyalty and commitment in all their undertakings. These are just the characteristics one would expect to find in the type of person that undertakes any role of responsibility in public or corporate life.

In the 1950s and 1960s in particular, freemasonry across the world, expanded. New lodges were regularly opened as more and more young men joined. Existing members were spoilt for choice in who they accepted as new members, and in many instances only accepted into membership those that seemed to be of acceptable social standing as they defined it. Lodges with over a hundred members were not uncommon. The members took great pride in their individual lodges and demanded the highest standards of performance from those taking part in Masonic ceremonies. It was a challenge that most new brethren rose to, and made the commitments necessary to render a good account of themselves, by ensuring a good performance. Those that did exceptionally well were applauded by the senior brethren around them, and the performer could glow with pride at the acclaim with which their efforts were rewarded.

Such is the nature of Masonic ceremonies that many young men, who were unacquainted with regularly engaging in public speaking, now found themselves delivering complicated, obtuse and age-old dialogue to a silent audience that hung on their every word and knew the script thoroughly. Within a few years, young men, who perhaps had been rather shy and reserved when they joined the institution, could stand up and issue forth with confidence in a manner that would carry over to their normal working days. Most of these new members would not have had the experience of a private boarding-school education in renowned institutions that observed traditions of dining that had evolved over centuries. There were many that had equally not experienced the traditions of specific codes and formality of dress, dining etiquette, toasts, and general socialising associated with being an officer in one of the military services. Freemasonry provided all of these attributes where such experience might otherwise have never been possible. This enabled confidence to be cultivated which in turn could be expressed in social gatherings or at work.

For all its positive attributes, the considerable expansion of freemasonry also carried a negative consequence. The quest to open new lodges and accommodate the growing membership, resulted in a continuous production line of ceremonies, of learning, rehearsing and delivering them. It seems there was little time in the busy lodge schedule to pass on some of the historical knowledge about the institution, in a structured manner. Members learnt the words and actions of ceremonies without understanding what they were doing or why they were doing them; older members that probably knew some of the answers to the three questions posed earlier, passed on without handing down that knowledge to a younger generation. The result seems to have been that each new generation became increasingly distanced from meaningful knowledge. By the end of the twentieth century there were several people in senior positions in the hierarchy of the institution, who believed there was a danger that some of freemasonry's age-old ceremonies would become empty shells devoid of meaning. When knowledge is lost, it can be a difficult task to rebuild it, and there is always the possibility that some will be lost forever.

### Freemasonry and ancient wisdom

Freemasonry is acknowledged as being probably the oldest fraternal organisation of its type, in the world. Exactly how it came into existence has been the source of much speculation over the past few hundred years. There are those that believe it has a close affinity with the traditions and ceremonies associated with the priesthoods of Ancient Egypt, and that they were handed down to us through the Greek and Roman Empires, rising to prominence again during the period known as the Enlightenment. There are others that believed the ceremonies contained the core esoteric knowledge of the ancient mystery schools, such as that founded by Pythagoras; that it was knowledge that was central to most of the established religions of the world, prior to the arrival of more recent religions such as Christianity and Islam. It has been speculated that it was knowledge accumulated by the Knights Templar in the medieval period and that it is from those Templar roots that modern Freemasonry is derived. Through the eighteenth and early nineteenth centuries, eminent men visited Egypt, saw symbols, building elevations and great treasures from the ancient Egyptian culture and returned to England and wrote about them in Masonic literature, and implied that they were evidence of freemasonry's connection with that culture. Other writers later used that material as reference and quoted it as if it was fact. In the mid-to late-Victorian era of the 1800s, a fascination grew for all things esoteric and yet again, eminent men wrote great treaties purporting to show yet further unquestioned connections with freemasonry.

The ceremonies that are performed in Masonic lodges in the early twenty-first century bear a close resemblance to the ceremonies that were performed over two hundred years ago. The fact remains, that within freemasonry, one finds evidence of *ancient wisdom* of some kind. It is found in symbols that adorn everything from doorsteps to light fittings, from stained glass windows to the jewels that masons proudly wear on their chests. Such *wisdom* is mentioned in the contents of lectures that form part of ceremonies. Most of the symbols were far more prolific in the 18th and 19th centuries than they are today.

This symbolism and *wisdom* seems to be the type of knowledge our ancestors had gathered and understood, perhaps over thousands of years, and played a part in their survival rituals. The accumulation of this knowledge was probably passed down through hundreds of generations in a verbal tradition of story telling in the absence of widespread forms of literacy, and added to by succeeding generations with the progress of time. This *wisdom* encompassed knowledge about celestial mechanics, geometry and its links with the natural world, and the processes that cause the seasons, making food abundant at some times of the year and scarce at others. It was knowledge that was needed for survival. It was knowledge accumulated by and retained in, the priesthoods of ancient civilisations. Just, as in schools today, one can progress in educational attainment by demonstrating various levels of proficiency in understanding over time, so one progressed in the ranks of the priesthoods by demonstrating proficiency and understanding of this *ancient wisdom*.

The close affinity between shapes that can be found in nature and various geometric figures that can be easily replicated using a pair of compasses and a ruler, implied that everything on earth had been originated by design. For there to be a design there needed to be a designer that created these patterns - a creator, the deity. The geometric figures and mathematical constants they contained, together with the symbolism and understanding behind them, became so revered that they were used in the construction and decoration of important buildings, such as temples, where of course, the deity was worshipped.

With the passing of time, this same knowledge was at the centre of what today we know as the *liberal arts* and *sciences* of grammar, rhetoric, arithmetic, music, logic, astronomy and geometry. It was knowledge retained by the

Christian, Judaic and Islamic priesthoods of the medieval period and taught at religious centres of learning, such as at the great cathedral of Chartres, in France. There is evidence that this same knowledge was taught to and by the stonemasons who built the cathedrals, monasteries, churches and castles of the medieval period; the great structures of the Roman era, the magnificent temples of ancient Greece and Egypt. As almost every freemason is told, it was the knowledge that was at the centre of the Master of Arts degree in former times.

The quest to understand *what* the significance is within Masonic ceremonies, depends on *where*, and *how*, freemasonry evolved into what we have today. So, it is necessary to commence the journey by trying to trace the origins and consistency of ceremonies. And it is there that we start the process.

**Organised Freemasonry**
The United Grand Lodge of England (UGLE), the governing body of regular freemasonry throughout the world, acknowledges that despite the effort that has, and still is, being made to understand the origins of this ancient and highly respected institution, we may never know the answer simply because documented evidence to substantiate any theory is unlikely to exist. UGLE traces its origins to the start of the nineteenth century, two hundred years ago. Before that, there was a former organisation known as the Grand Lodge of England that was established in 1717. This was supposedly created by four lodges then existing in London that felt there should be one governing body to oversee their organisation and conduct. London was not the only place that freemasonry existed. It is also clear, and acknowledged within Masonic circles, that some form of freemasonry existed some time prior to the formation of the Grand Lodge of England.

One of the earliest records of a gentleman being made a freemason, who was not a recognised member of a craft or guild associated with the fashioning and carving of stone as a stonemason would do, was Elias Ashmole, who recorded in his diary that he had been made a mason at Warrington in 1646.[6] For this to have happened there must have been a lodge, or some similar organisation, in existence for him to have joined. Another person acknowledged to have been a mason was Sir Robert Moray, who was possibly initiated even earlier than Elias Ashmole, into a lodge based in Scotland in 1641.[7] The English Civil Wars lasted for a ten-year period from 1641 – 1651. Both Ashmole and Moray are recorded as having been on the Royalist side. Moray, it seems, was not only close to the King, Charles I, but after the civil wars and the restoration of the monarchy, he was also a confidant of Charles II. In 1660, Moray may have been a significant influence in the Invisible College, cited as the forerunner of the Royal Society. Moray was a founder member of the Royal Society, along with Elias Ashmole, and was instrumental in the Royal Society receiving official sanction by the granting of a Royal Charter in 1662. It has been suggested that of the twelve original founding members of the Royal Society, eleven of them were freemasons. This implies that at the time of the restoration of the monarchy, several lodges, accepting what became known as *speculative masons*, must have existed.[8]

For the time prior to 1717, it has, for many years, been the view that any lodges that did exist were private clubs of members of the landed gentry. If this was so, then it raises another question; where did they get the idea from? What is also unclear is what the content and structure of the ceremonies of these private lodges would have been, or if indeed, there were any.

This leaves us with another question; where did Masonic ceremonies originate? There are a number of sources from which we might gain a glimpse of ceremonial content. Among them is a range of papers known as the disclosures or exposures; there's Anderson's Constitutions, Preston's - History of Freemasonry; the guilds; the authorised ceremonies - to name but a few. They could all be good places to start. That at least is the theory, but as we will discover, some of the information that had previously been regarded as *factual,* may not be as wholesome as it previously seemed.

## The disclosures and exposures

Clearly, there was something about the persona of freemasonry in the eighteenth century that aroused public interest because from the middle of that century through to recent times, there had been, periodically, several prominent so-called *disclosures* or *exposures* purporting to reveal the secrets of Masonic meetings and the conduct of a lodge and its members. In the eighteenth century these disclosures comprised mostly of pamphlets and booklets that implied first hand knowledge about the craft. In what can only be described as *promotional material* aimed at maximising sales of some of these documents, great play is made of revealing the secrets and the methods of the ceremonies. This suggests that there was a fascination about the workings of a Masonic lodge among the general populace that went beyond mere curiosity. Certainly there are some materials that suggest the writer or informer had a real involvement with the Order, but there are examples of others that were, to say the least, mischievous, and intended to promote ridicule and poke fun at the expense of those involved, or were mischievous and misleading concoctions designed to create the quick turn of a penny for the publisher.

Within just seven years of the formation of the Grand Lodge of England in 1717 such disclosures commenced. One of the oldest appeared in 1724. It was printed for a bookseller by the name of Thomas Payne, who it would seem, conducted his business in Paternoster Row, London. The pamphlet carried the title and sub-text as follows:

> *"The grand mystery of Free-masons discover'd: Wherein are the several questions put to them at their meetings and installations: as also their oath, health, signs, and points, to know each other by. As they were found in the custody of a Free-mason who dyed suddenly. And now publish'd for the information of the publick."*

This pamphlet, it appears, was also reprinted again some time later than the original date. In the promotional leaflet produced to encourage sales of this latter edition, it states that there were only two copies of the original 1724 edition known to exist; one was in the procession of the Grand Master at the time, and the other was deposited in the Bodleian Library, Oxford, England. Those copies still exist. What is noticeable is that some of the language used to describe the outline produced by Thomas Payne has a definite Masonic feel to it, some of which would not be out of place if used today.

Over the next one hundred years, several other *disclosures and exposures* appeared and claimed to provide an authentic insight to Masonic ceremonies. One such document gives the impression that it was written by two freemasons, largely because of the structure of some of the comments. Yet these writers throw the reader off the trail by implying that freemasonry is divided into two groups, the *pedestrians* and the *equestrians,* and go on to describe a bizarre ceremony that involved running around the lodge room with a horse and jumping over benches.

Among other disclosures was a booklet with the title *Three Distinct Knocks* first published in 1760. It is not attributed to any specific individual but publication was just forty years after the founding of the Grand Lodge of England in 1717. *Three Distinct Knocks* was closely followed by a second booklet carrying the title *Jachin and Boaz,* published in 1762. Such was the interest *Jachin and Boaz* created that it was still being printed forty years later, in 1805. The cover merely attributes the writer as a

> *"GENTLEMAN belonging to the Jerusalem Lodge; a frequent visitor at the Queen's Arms, St Paul's Churchyard; the Horn in Fleet Street; Crown and Anchor, Strand, and the Salutation, Newgate Street".*

All of the hostelries mentioned were taverns in London where Lodges met, implying that such material came from one of the members. From then on, and through the nineteenth century, further material was periodically published, aimed at the wider public interest.

The amount of such scurrilous and unfounded material that had been in circulation over the years, greatly concerned the hierarchy of the day, in so far that the impressions the public had of Masonic ceremonies was so distorted that it undermined the credibility of the Order. Such were their concerns that in 1823 the first officially sanctioned text that details the proceedings of Masonic ceremonies was published. Simply known as the *claret edition,* careful scrutiny reveals that the ceremonial texts contained in that edition are extremely close to the texts that are available in the early years of the twenty-first century, two hundred years later – even down to the size and colour of the book they are contained in. So, whilst the ceremonies of the twenty-first century are similar to those of the nineteenth century, neither the *claret edition* or the *disclosures* give any real clues about the origins or meaning of the ceremonies, and in the case of the disclosures, they are mostly misleading.

So, we now turn to what has been seen as the Masonic bible.

### William Preston – Illustrations of Masonry

Preston's *Illustrations of Masonry* was first published in 1772 and for many years was regarded as one of the most important books on Freemasonry. Preston was born in Edinburgh, Scotland in 1742 and in his teenage years, he was apprenticed to a local printer. He moved to London in 1760 and obtained employment with one William Stranhan who, at that time, was the king's printer. Where Preston developed an interest in freemasonry is unknown but he was initiated two/three years later and was soon thereafter elected Master of his lodge. He became very absorbed by what he encountered and subsequently visited many lodges and corresponded with a number other masons, and it was from that effort that he assembled a considerable amount of knowledge about the craft. One must conclude that he found significant variances in the structure of meetings and the content of ceremonies. In consequence he set about the task of trying to bring some consistency to proceedings. Whenever there is a motivation for change, there will always be individuals who oppose it, and Preston's efforts were not entirely welcomed by some of his brethren. He writes:

> *"When I first had the honour to be elected Master of a lodge, I thought it proper to inform myself fully of the general rules of the Society, that I might be able to fulfil my own duty, and officially enforce a due obedience in others. The methods which I adopted with this view, excited in some of superficial knowledge, an absolute dislike of what they considered as innovations; and in other, who were better informed, a jealousy of pre-eminence which the principles of Masonry ought to have checked. Notwithstanding these discouragements,*

*however, I persevered in my intention of supporting the dignity of the Society, and discharging with fidelity the trust reposed in me.*

*"I was encouraged to examine with more attention the contents of our various lectures. The rude and imperfect state in which I found them, the variety of modes established in our lodges, and the difficulties which I encountered in my researches, rather discouraged me first attempt; preserving, however, in the design, I continued the pursuit; and assisted by a few friends, who had carefully preserved what ignorance and degeneracy had rejected as unintelligible and absurd, I diligently sought for, and at length happily acquired, some ancient and venerable landmarks of the Order*

*"I continued my industry till I had prevailed on a sufficient number to join in an attempt to correct the irregularities which had crept into our assemblies, and to exemplify the beauty and utility of the Masonic system."*

A review of the contents of the *Illustrations of Masonry*, reveals a close association with our ceremonies today, and the regular principles set out by Preston. To illustrate the point, the following is the text, quoted to candidates prior to being initiated into a lodge:

*"'A Declaration to be assented to by every Candidate in an adjoining apartment, previous to Initiation.*

*"'Do you seriously declare, upon your honour, before these gentlemen that, unbiased by friends against your own inclination, and uninfluenced by mercenary motives, you freely and voluntarily offer yourself a candidate for the mysteries of Masonry?' - 'I do'.*

*"'Do you seriously declare, upon your honour, before these gentlemen, that you are solely prompted to solicit the privileges of Masonry, by a favourable opinion conceived of the institution, a desire of knowledge, and a sincere wish of being serviceable to your fellow-creatures?' - 'I do."*

Thus we can be confident that the ceremonial aspects of freemasonry, at least in part, have some integrity that extends back to the mid-eighteen century. Large sections of these ceremonies and procedures have not been altered in any significant manner which means that even today the wording of the ceremonies often reflects the *Olde English* language style. As a consequence of this language style, some of the sentence structure can be convoluted and obtuse, to say the least, which in turn can make the process of memorising the text, rather awkward.

Not everything that Preston recorded, however, was as accurate as it was assumed to be. A large section of his *Illustrations of Masonry* was no doubt, printed in good faith, but was later found to be untrue, but not before being misleading to many eminent masons in the decades and centuries following. The section concerned is called:

*"Book 3 - The Principles of Masonry Explained"*

In this section, Preston introduces the text of a letter allegedly written by a Mr Locke to the then Earl of Pembroke. The section reads:

*"Sect 1. - A Letter from the learned Mr. John Locke, to the Right Hon. Thomas Earl of Pembroke, with an old Manuscript on the subject of Free-Masonry.*

*6th May 1696*

*My Lord,*

*I have at length, by the help of Mr. Collins, procured a copy of that MS. in the Bodleian library, which you were so curious to see: and, in obedience to your lordship's commands, I herewith send it to you. Most of the notes annexed to it, are what I made yesterday for the reading of my Lady Masham, who is become so fond of masonry, as to say, that she now more than ever wishes herself a man, that she might be capable of admission into the fraternity.*

*The MS. of which this is a copy, appears to be about 160 years old; yet (as your lordship will observe by the title) it is itself a copy of one yet more ancient by about 100 years: for the original is said to be the hand-writing of K. Henry VI. Where that prince had it, is at present an uncertainty; but it seems to me to be an examination (taken perhaps before the king) of some one of the brotherhood of masons; among whom he entered himself, as it is said, when he came out of his minority, and thenceforth put a stop to a persecution that had been raised against them: But I must not detain your lordship longer by my preface from the thing itself.*

*I know not what effect the sight of this old paper may have upon your lordship; but for my own part I cannot deny, that it has so much raised my curiosity, as to induce me to enter myself into the fraternity, which I am determined to do (if I may be admitted) the next time I go to London, and that will be shortly. I am,*

*My Lord*

*And most humble servant,*

*John Locke "*

The document that Locke purports to refer to is in the form of a question and answer process. Alleging that the document was a copy of one that had originally been written by Henry VI (1421-1471), Locke then alleges that it was copied by the Antiquarian and scholar, John Leland. Leland certainly existed. He was born around 1505 and died in 1552 and had been educated at Cambridge, Oxford and Paris. He lived through the turbulent Tudor years in which Henry VIII sought a divorce from Catherine of Aragon, married Anne Boleyn, set in place the dissolution of the monasteries and the establishment of the Church of England. Leland travelled extensively throughout England, visiting various monastic houses and making use of their libraries. As part of researches he compiled lists of some of the valuable books that he located. As the monasteries were gradually closed, Leland became aware that some of these books were being sent to other countries and thereby lost to England. Noting this, he wrote to Thomas Cromwell pointing out the loss. Thereafter, most of the important libraries were collected and stored in facilities at a number of royal residences.

The following questions and answers give a feel for the Book 3 section. It runs to some twelve such questions.

*"Certayn Questyons, with Answeres to the same, concerning the Mystery of Maçonrye; writtene by the hande of kynge Henrye, the sixthe of the name, and faithfullye copyed by me Johan Leylande, Antiquarius, by the commande of his Highnesse*

*"**Quest.** What mote ytt be? [What mote ytt be?] That is, what may this mystery of masonry be? The answer imports, That it consists in natural, mathematical, and mechanical knowledge. Some part of which (as appears by what follows) the masons pretend to have taught the rest of mankind, and some part they still conceal. ]*

*"**Answ.** Ytt beeth the skylle of nature, the understondynge of the myghte that ys hereynne, and its sondrye werckynges; sonderlyche, the skylle of rectenyngs, of waightes and metynges, and the true manere of façonnynge al thynges for nannes use; headlye, dwellinges,*

*and buyldynges of alle kindes, and all odher thynges that make gudde
to manne.*

*"**Quest.** Where dyd it begynne?*

*"**Answ.** Ytt dyd begynne with the fyrste menne in the este, whych
were before the ffyrste manne of the weste, and comynge westlye, ytt
hathe broughte herwyth alle comfortes to the wylde and comfortlesse."*

This section of Preston's book has been referenced many times since the
original publication. One such prolific supporter of freemasonry who made
a big play of it was the Reverend George Oliver, who was initiated into
St.Peter's *Lodg*e, Lincoln, in 1801, and rose to become Provincial Deputy
Grand Master in 1832. He quoted this item by John Locke in his book *The
Antiquities of Free-Masonry* which was published in 1843. In the footnotes of
the page where this item is mentioned, George Oliver notes:

> *"The whole MS., with annotations by our countryman the learned
> Mr Locke, is published in Preston's 'Illustrations of Masonry;'
> Hutchinson's 'Spirit of Masonry,' and other Masonic works."*

With, what must have seemed like an endorsement of this article, there
then followed a string of other books by prominent authors who all quoted
the same material. For the best part of the next one hundred and twenty-
five years, and thereafter, many enthusiastic masons referred to some of
these works and accepted what was written as absolute fact. The document
is now deemed a fake.

From the privileged position we now enjoy of being able to draw on
more recent historical research undertaken by modern academics, there are
other aspects of Preston's works that have some credibility, whilst others
are subject to question. A couple of examples are as follows. Preston states
in relation to the Roman occupation of Britain:

> *"The wars which afterwards broke out between the conquerors and
> conquered, considerable obstructed the progress of masonry in Britain,
> so that it continued in a very low state till the time of the emperor
> Carausius, by whom it was revived under his own immediate auspices.
> Having shaken off the Roman yoke, he contrived the most effectual
> means to render his person and government acceptable to the people,
> and assuming in the character of a mason, he acquired the love and*

*esteem of the most enlightened part of his subjects. He possessed real merit, encouraged learning and learned men, improved the country in the civil arts, and, in order to establish an empire in Britain, he collected into this dominions the best workmen and artificers from all parts, all of whom, under his auspices, enjoyed peace and tranquillity. Among the first class of his favourites, came the masons; for their tenets he professed the highest veneration, and appointed Albanus, his steward, the principal superintendent of their assemblies. Under his patronage, lodges, and conventions of the fraternity, were regularly formed, and the rites of masonry practiced. To enable the masons to hold a general council to establish their own government, and correct errors among themselves, he granted to them a charter, and commanded Albanus to preside over them in person as Grand Master. This worthy knight proved a zealous friend to the Craft, and afterwards assisted at the initiation of many persons into the mysteries of the Order. To this council, the name of Assembly was afterwards given."*

In this text we are given to understand that the principle character, Carausius, was a highly honourable emperor. The expression *"assuming in the character of a mason"* we could take to mean 'one who was benevolent and charitable', with a care for his fellow man. History now casts doubt on the credentials of this person. The emperor in Rome at this time was Maximiam, and he ordered Carausius to be executed. Carausius had been sent to take command of a small Roman fleet that patrolled the English Channel. At that time there were a number of Frankish raiding parties that sailed down the channel and periodically plundered areas along what today we call the Normandy and Brittany coasts. Carausius was meant to destroy these raiders, but instead, became a raider himself, raiding the raiders, and taking the valuable plunder the Frankish pirates had thought they had secured for themselves. Carausius became quite wealthy as a result, and no doubt shared some of his ill-gotten gains with those on the other vessels under his command, as a way of buying their support, thereby seeming to be benevolent.

When he heard that Maximiam had issued an order for his execution, Carausius crossed the channel in the year 286 CE, and declared himself Emperor of Britain. He clearly had access to high quantities of silver, because he then minted a range of coins (some now in the British Museum) showing his head as emperor. The silver coins are thought to have had great appeal to Britons, and won him great favour, although it is difficult to imagine that this was a *period of peace and tranquillity*. Maximiam sent legions to arrest him, but he could have been saved the trouble because in

293 CE, Carausius was murdered by one of his close associates, Allectus, who promptly declared himself Emperor. In turn, Allectus was hunted down and killed, as were many of his supporters.

No doubt during the reign of Carausius there was building work being undertaken, and some of that work would have had ornate features that demanded the skills of highly qualified stonemasons. This is conjecture, however, and shows no direct connection with freemasonry in the late eighteenth century when Preston was assembling his writings.

Another such misleading observation has to be in respect of St Alban. Preston notes:

> "Some particulars of a man so truly exemplary among masons will certainly merit attention.

> "Albanus was born at Verulam, (now St. Alban's, in Hertfordshire,) of a noble family. In his youth he travelled to Rome, where he served seven years under the Emperor Diocletian. On his return home, by the example and persuasion of Amphibalus of Caer-leon, (now Chester,) who had accompanied him in his travels, he was converted to the Christian faith, and, in the tenth and last persecution of the Christians, was beheaded, A. D. 303.

> "St. Alban was the first who suffered martyrdom for the Christian religion in Britain, of which the Venerable Bede gives the following account. The Roman governor having been informed that St. Alban harboured a Christian in his house, sent a party of soldiers to apprehend Amphibalus. St. Alban immediately put on the habit of his guest and presented himself to the officers. Being carried before a magistrate, he behaved with such a manly freedom, and so powerfully supported the cause of his friend, that he not only incurred the displeasure of the judge, but also brought upon himself the punishment above specified.

> "The old constitutions affirm, that St. Alban was employed by Carausius to environ the city of Verulam with a wall, and to build for him a splendid palace; and that, to reward his diligence in executing those works, the emperor appointed him steward of his household, and chief ruler of the realm. However this may be, from the corroborating testimonies of ancient historians, we are assured that this knight was a celebrated architect, and a real encourager of able workmen; it cannot therefore be supposed, that free-masonry would be neglected under so eminent a patron.

*"On the arrival of the Romans in Britain, arts and sciences began to flourish. According to the progress of civilization, masonry rose into esteem; hence we find that Cæsar, and several of the Roman generals who succeeded him in the government of this island, ranked as patrons and protectors of the Craft. Although at this period the fraternity were employed in erecting walls, forts, bridges, cities, temples, palaces, courts of justice, and other stately works, history is silent respecting their mode of government, and affords no information in regard to the usages and customs prevalent among them. Their lodges and conventions were regularly held, but being open only to the initiated fellows, the legal restraints they were under, prevented the public communication of their private transactions."*

St Alban is acknowledged to have been an early Christian martyr, but quite when he was born and died are very uncertain. Until the late twentieth century, most academics familiar with his story would have recorded him dying around 303 CE, and as such he would have lived in the era of Carasius's reign as Emperor of Britain. However, there is a now a suggestion that he died during the reign of Septimus Severus. Severus became Emperor and was a formidable military strategist. He came to Britain around 200 CE and died at York in 211 CE. Severus also persecuted the Christians of that era. Thus, if St Alban was indeed executed under this emperor he would have lived around one hundred years earlier than previously estimated.

The story of St Alban also fits with other events from the era of Septimus Severus. The legend has it that St Alban was a Christian, and gave sanctuary to a Christian cleric who was evading arrest. St Alban, put on the cleric's cloak, and soon after, was arrested and taken before the local governor. When the governor found out that Alban had attempted to dupe him, he ordered that Alban be taken out and receive the same punishment that the cleric would have received – decapitation. That, the legend has it, is what happened. The origins of this legend seem to stem from Bede's *Ecclesiastical History of the English people* which, if the legend is attributable to the era of Severus, was written some six hundred years after the event. There is absolutely no evidence to suggest that St Alban was in any way connected with any project or the craft of stonemasonry.

It does seem probable that the intricate fashioning of stone as used in major works, and the geometry that was used in setting out structures or constructing the palladium style facades that had become common in Roman and Greek architecture, did arrive in Britain with the arrival of the Roman legions. There are substantial structures fashioned in stone that were erected in Britain thousands of years prior to the Roman arrival, like Stonehenge, and whilst they served their purpose, they lacked the finesse, that the skilled artisan, working with stone, later achieved, and as demonstrated in Roman archaeological sites. In Britain there was a plentiful supply of wood from the forests that adorned the island and the whole of northern Europe, so this became a material that was easily fashioned and hence, widely used. In the area around the Mediterranean, north Africa and places like Egypt, wood suitable for construction was not in such plentiful supply, so, it has been conjectured, for stately buildings and temples, and for its durability, stone became the preferred building material. It is well recorded that in the Roman Republic there existed a range of *collegia* which were trade or business groups, organised in much the same manner as the later guilds. The *collegia* are understood to have existed for centuries prior to the reign of Julius Caesar, who led the first attempt to conquer Britain and include it within the ever-expanding Roman Empire. It was an attempt that failed, and was not attempted again for another 100 years. The fact that the Romans did indeed construct some magnificent structures out of stone during their time in Britain shows that they at least had brought such skills to Britain. No doubt there were indigenous Britons that became similarly skilled and participated in locally established collegia, but that does not mean we can trace the origins of freemasonry in Britain to that time. This is born out by the fact that when the Romans left Britain they seem to have taken their skills with them.

One of the earliest records of the history of Britain was recorded by the Venerable Bede in his work *Historia ecclesiastica gentis Anglorum* (*The Ecclesiastical History of the English People*). Bede was a monk who lived almost his entire life at a monastery near Jarrow (Newcastle) in the northeast of England, one of the most northern outposts of the Roman Empire. Bede (673-735 CE) was born about two hundred years after the Romans left Britain so it is highly probable that some competent sources were available to him. In respect of the skills of the Britons early in the Roman settlement, Bede notes that there were constant attacks by the Picts along the northern borders. Bede writes:

> "...*On account of the attacks of these nations, the Britons sent messengers to Rome with letters piteously praying for succour, and promising perpetual subjection, providing that the impending enemy should be driven away. An armed legion was immediately sent them, which, arriving in the island, and engaging the enemy, slew a great multitude of them, drove the rest out of the territories of their allies, and having in the meanwhile delivered them from their worst distress, advised them to build a wall between the two*

*seas across the island, that it might secure them by keeping off the enemy. So they returned home with great triumph. But the islanders building the wall which they had been told to raise, not of stone, since they had no workmen capable of such a work, but of sods, made it of no use, Nevertheless, they carried it for many miles between the two bays or inlets of the sea of which we have spoken;......Of the work there erected, that, of a rampart of great breadth and height, there are evident remains to be seen at this day...."[9]*

Bede's comment that *there are evident remains to be seen at this day,* was written about two hundred and fifty years after the Roman departure. Now, around one thousand, five hundred years later, parts of that wall can still be seen, particularly near Falkirk. Scotland.  The wall apparently ran between Dumbarton on the River Clyde and Bo'ness on the Forth and is believed to have been built around 142 CE.  It is, today, known as the *Antonine Way,* after Antoninus Pius, who is attributed with organising its construction, and is now listed as a world heritage site. The key element of Bede's comment, though, is that when it came to working with stone, the British inhabitants *"..... had no workmen capable of such a work......"*

*Call Park - A stretch of the Antonine Way near Falkirk.*
*Reproduction by kind permission and assistance of Falkirk Council, Scotland*

Later in Bede's work, however, we find mention of another building project:

> *"But the former enemies, when they perceived that the Roman soldiers had gone, immediately coming by sea, broke into the borders, trampled and overran all places, and like men mowing ripe corn, bore down all before them. Hereupon, messengers were again sent to Rome miserably imploring aid, lest their wretched country should be utterly blotted out, and the name of a Roman province, so long renowned among them, overthrown by the cruelties of foreign races, might become utterly contemptible. A legion was accordingly sent again, and, arriving unexpectedly in autumn, made great slaughter of the enemy, obliging all those who could escape, to flee beyond the sea; whereas before, they were wont yearly to carry off their booty without any opposition. Then the Romans declared to the Britons, that they could not for the future undertake such troublesome expeditions for their sake, and advised them rather to take up arms and make an effort to engage the enemies, who could not prove too powerful for them, unless they themselves were enervated by cowardice. Moreover, thinking that it might be some help to the allies, whom they were forced to abandon, they constructed a strong stonewall from sea to sea, in a straight line between the towns that had been there build for fear of the enemy, where Severus also had formally built a rampart. This famous wall, which is still to be seen, was raised by public and private expense, the Britons also lending their assistance. It is eight feet in breadth, and twelve in height, in a straight line from east to west......"*[10]

The wall Bede is probably referring to, we now know as Hadrian's Wall, that runs from Wallsend (near Newcastle) to Bowness, on the Solway, north of Carlisle. It has to be noted, that there are conflicts in the dates between Bede's writing and that shown by modern academics through archaeology. The Antonine Way and Hadrian's Wall seem to have been built in the early decades of the second century CE. However, if we accept what Bede notes, then it implies that in the early years of Roman occupation in Britain, skills in working with stone did not exist, but some participated in building Hadrian's Wall and would, therefore, have gained some knowledge. That knowledge was likely to have grown as larger and more skilful work was undertaken elsewhere in the country over the next two centuries.

The loss, again, of this knowledge is amplified in another academic work about the London Guilds by P. H. Ditchfield:

> "Whilst there are some authorities that trace the origins of the City
> Companies of London, to the Roman Collegia and Sodalitates, there
> is in this country [England] a fatal gap between the departure of
> the Roman Legions and the coming of the Anglo-Saxon tribes which
> no historical evidence is able to bridge. In France, it is suggested,
> that Roman populations remained in the major cities and that in
> consequence with many of the political and civil organisations
> remained and hence retained a virtual descent into the French trade
> gilds and communes of the Early Middle Ages."[11]

Ditchfield continues:

> "A capitulary [legislation] of Charlemagne decrees the Corporation
> of Bakers shall be maintained in full efficiency in the provinces
> and an edict of 864[CE] mentions the Gild of Goldsmiths...... In
> England we have no such evidence, and for 200 years history is a
> blank, and reluctantly we must abandon any hope of proving that
> the Anglo-Saxon gilds can trace the descent from Roman times."[12]

The reference to Charlemagne is an interesting comment. He was a
Frankish king, who was descended through the dynasties known as the
Merovingians and Carolingians. The Merovingians held sway over most of
France and, what are often referred to as the *Low Countries*, from the time
the Roman Empire finally collapsed in Europe around 450 CE. Merovech,
from which the Merovingians take their name, was a close ally of the
Romans and was a tribal leader of the Franks. It is recorded that in one
of the last major battles fought between the armies from Rome against
the Barbarians, won by the Romans, it included a large contingent of the
Franks led by Merovech. Merovech had a son named Childeric, who in
turn had a son named Clovis, who became a very close ally of the Roman
Empire, then based in Constantinople. With this close association with
Roman culture, it is entirely understandable that systems of administration,
such as that of the collegia, would have survived through the Merovingian
era (c 450 CE – 750 CE). The Carolingian dynasty (c 750 CE – 1100 CE)
of which Charlemagne was perhaps the most influential of leaders, saw
their territorial control grow to cover most of modern Europe, and then
gradually diminish as it was divided into the domains ruled over as kings
by blood related successive offspring. Charlemagne died in 814 CE, but
in 800 CE, and by his contact with the pope in Rome, was crowned as the
first Emperor of the Holy Roman Empire; it was an Empire substantially of
his creation and lasted, at least in name, and with a continuous succession

of Emperors, until it was abolished by Napoleon Bonaparte in 1807, one thousand years later. There is no evidence that Charlemagne came to Britain, though events here may have been influenced by his actions on the continent. Until Charlemagne was crowned Emperor by the pope in Rome, the Catholic Church and the pope were effectively subjects of the Byzantium Roman Empire. So, it is not unreasonable to envisage that the collegia concept continued even under Charlemange. Perhaps Ditchfield's observation about Charlemagne's edict concerning the bakers is evidence of that. And, if there was an organisation for bakers, there may well have been for other crafts and trades.

The main centre of Charlemagne's Empire was in Aachen, in the western fringes of Germany. Aachen has a wonderful cathedral, which, tradition has it, was the place where many subsequent Frankish kings and Emperors of the Holy Roman Empire were crowned. On show in the cathedral is a rudimentary stone chair, referred to as Charlemagne's throne. A part of the original church from Charlemagne's time remains. In the old town square, a tower adjacent to the City Hall is believed to be all that remains of a fortified building used by Charlemagne as a palace. Both of these features are made of stone, but not with elaborately carved detail. So, building with stone was certainly work undertaken by a class of skilled workmen around 800 CE.

Yet again, however, that does not give credence to the idea that freemasonry could in anyway trace its origins back to the Roman collegia system, and the stonemasons that may have been associated with them.

The foregoing extracts and review is by no means complete, but it gives a flavour to the reason why much of the information published in some early Masonic works, and references about history that are used to substantiate a Masonic link back to previous civilisations and cultures, even religious characters, cannot be considered as accurate, or treated with confidence. There is a need to be suspicious of much of the material published about freemasonry, prior to the last century, simply because it draws on works, like that of *Preston's Illustrations of Masonry*, which have been restated over and over again, as if they are fact. The sad thing is that works such as Preston's were close to the formation of the organisation, and therefore should be sources that tell us a lot about how the organisation came into being, the pedigree of those who started it, and the reasons they did so.

Using former Masonic records does not answer those three simple questions that are posed at the start of this chapter.

# Chapter 6

# GUILD AND RELIGION

Much has been made, in the past, that freemasonry traces its roots to the stonemasons who built the great temples of Egypt, Greece and Rome. Some previous writers from the Victorian and early twentieth-century eras have not only perpetuated that line, but suggested a continuous line of descent through the Roman *collegia* system, a series of trade and political groupings that flourished at one time in the later Roman empire. There are other writers that have suggested a link between the guild system in England, and the *collegia*, as a means of establishing a credible connection between freemasonry and ancient civilisations, on the basis of the former Roman invasion and settlement of Britain, nearly two thousand years ago. But as a means of trying to understand what it is we are actually doing in Masonic ceremonies, neither of these approaches is very helpful. The early gilds in England were a different concept to the *collegia*.

There are numerous books and documents that have been published as historical records of the *Livery Companies* and are often written by former masters of a specific company, charting its past. Craft *guilds* of England are not treated so generously, but wrapped up in thesis about the system in general, and by comparison with the livery companies many were poor and perhaps merged with others. Not withstanding that, there are now some more recent excellent works available for reference, produced under the rigour of academic scrutiny but, in relation to freemasonry, add very little. One small book, published around the mid-1800s, entitled *English Gilds* by Toulmin Smith, is more rewarding and gives the following outline of the role of the guilds from mediaeval times:

> *"The early English Gild was an institution of local self-help which, before Poor Laws were invented, took the place, in old times, of the modern friendly or benefit society; but with a higher aim, while it joined all classes together in a care for the needy and for objects of common welfare, it did not neglect the forms and the practice of Religion, Justice and Morality...*

> *"Gilds were associations of those living in the same neighbourhood, and remembering that they have, as neighbours, common obligations...their main characteristic was to set up something higher than personal gain and mere materialism, as the object of men living in towns; and to make the teaching of love to one's neighbour*

*be not coldly accepted as a hollow dogma of morality, but known and felt as a habit of life…*

*"They were the out-come, in another form, of the same spirit of independence and mutual help which also made our Old English fathers join together in the " Frith-borh " or Peace-pledge, the institution which lies at the very root and foundation of modern civil society. The difference between the Gild and the Peace-pledges akin to that which lies between the old words "wed " and "borh " ; as " wed" is that security which is given by a man personally, for himself as an individual, and " borh " the pledge given by a man for others, so a Gild was the association of men together for common objects of private and individual benefit, in which each man gave his "wed " to abide by their internal bye-laws, while a Frith-borh was the banding of men together, within the limits of a boundary, in which each joined in the borh" or pledge for the keeping of the peace, and performance of public duties, by all the others." [13]*

One of the striking features of this explanation about the role and purpose of the guilds, is the very close association it has with both the moral and charitable aspects of freemasonry.

We should keep in mind that during the medieval period, there were men and women who were literally owned by lords, who controlled specific areas of the country. Such underlings were known as *bondmen* meaning they were bound to a lord and undertook work without wages. They are sometimes also referred to as *serfs* and *peasants*. These men may well have farmed an area of land which they rented from a lord, but were expected to provide a certain number of days a year in the service of that lord, without pay, or, in some cases, they were expected to provide a portion of the crops they had grown, as a form of tax, for the use and benefit of the lord. If the land was sold or passed to another by other means, such as being sold or reassigned if the lord had died in battle, for example, the bondmen went

as part of the package. Needless to note, there were bondmen, especially those of younger age, who would resist such tyranny, and seek freedom, by running away. If such a bondman was later caught, then he could be returned to his lord, who would, more often than not, extract some form of punishment, like withdrawing the land available for rent, or increasing the rent substantially. This could be extremely harsh as often such land, and the crops grown, were not just commodities as we might see them today, but the basis of survival. The general guide was that if a bondman could remain free for a period of one year and one day, they would often be granted their *freedom*. As a result, bondmen might join a monastery, or seek sanctuary in a monastic house for that *year and a day* period. He then became a *free man*. Another way of gaining one's freedom was to move to a town that was a considerable distance from their normal home, and seek the right to settle there. Being tied to the land and cultivating it by hand, as was much the custom in those mediaeval times, was tiring work that involved everyone in a family, so there was little opportunity to improve one's lot by trading in other commodities. That became the prerogative of free men who had the resources to become merchants.

Not long after the Norman Conquest, a group of merchants in cities along the northern coast of Europe and the Baltic Sea, sought and gained permission to start merchant guilds. These merchant guilds became known as *Hansa* and together with the cities, in which they were based, founded what became known as the *Hanseatic League,* for mutual trading purposes. It was a trading federation that held considerable sway over the shipment of goods from the twelfth century to the sixteenth. Goods shipped between maritime ports would then be shipped to inland cities and towns. England was not left out:

> "*Hansa societies worked to remove restrictions to trade for their members. For example, the merchants of the Cologne Hansa convinced Henry II of England to free them (1157) from all tolls in London and allow them to trade at fairs throughout England. The 'Queen of the Hansa', Lübeck, where traders were required to trans-ship goods between the North Sea and the Baltic, gained the Imperial privilege of becoming a Free imperial city in 1227, the only such city east of the River Elbe...In 1266, Henry III of England granted the Lübeck and Hamburg Hansa a charter for operations in England, and the Cologne Hansa joined them in 1282 to form the most powerful Hanseatic colony in London.*" [14]

The mention of *Hansa* in reference to bondmen has significance related to their freedom. It was not unusual for a bondman to seek to work on a ship that transported produce between Channel ports, and thereby keep out of the reach of a lord that was seeking him. There are records in many towns, where bondmen from other countries, such as France, came to England and settled for the same reason. The Guild at the northern coastal town of Preston, England, states as part of its constitution:

*"If any nativus [born bondman] dwell anywhere in the same town, and holds any land, and be in the forenamed Gild and Hanse, and pay lot and scot with the Prime burgesses for one year and one day, then he shall not be reclaimed by his lord, but shall remain free in the same town."* [15]

Smith points out that on becoming a member of a gild, the participant undertook an oath associated with ensuring his/her obligations to the responsibilities of the gild. This is yet another connection with Masonic practice.

Smith asserts that the early English Gild system can be traced back to the arrival of the Saxons, following the Roman withdrawal. He draws attention to laws relating to the gilds, that extend as far back as King Ina (AD 688 – 725) through Alfred and Athestane to Henry I. Smith also points out that the gild arrangement of local self-help provided the basis of the term *community*, and traces the origins of that term through Anglo-Saxon times. He then points out that as population grew, so too did the number of gilds. Then as *communities* grew to become towns, so the town gild became an administrative *Council*. Hence the many *Guildhalls* that can be found across England which have/are the place where local councils meet and in the past, were also used as courts for the administering of local justice.

Based on this analogy it is clear that these early Anglo-Saxon gilds were not specifically trade or craft related.

It is this *self-help* practice that set the gilds apart from, and make them different to, the *collegia*. This is a good point at which to draw a line under the idea of the *collegia* as a having a continuous link with freemasonry. As mentioned previously, Ditchfield notes an edict by Charlemagne in respect of the bakers. Although some grouping of trades, in the Frankish kingdoms of Europe, may have existed in the eighth century, they were not *community* gilds, as they are believed to have existed and described by Toulmin Smith. In fact, it seems that gilds were actually forbidden in the Frankish kingdoms. In respect of the eighth century, Toulmin Smith writes:

*"…At the same time we see them forbidden and persecuted everywhere on the continent by ecclesiastical as well as secular authorities. A series of Capitularies of the Emperor Charlemagne and his successors interfered with all kinds of combinations and unions, especially with those which were confirmed by mutual oaths…Gilds, even amongst serfs are met with in Flanders…and the other maritime districts, and their lords were called upon to suppress them, under the threat of being punished themselves…"* [16]

What seems clear from this edict, is that those in power feared gatherings of individuals, by oath or otherwise, where they might conjoin in action to overthrow lords and regional leaders, and ultimately Charlemagne himself – a revolution by the serfs and peasants.

All the above in respect of the early English Gilds relates to a period primarily prior to the Norman Conquest of England. We are today more familiar with the spelling as *guild*. Ditchfield notes:

> *"There is some doubt as to both the meaning and spelling of the word gild/guild. There is a belief that the spelling derives from the Anglo-Saxon era, and that the 'u' crept in the Norman period. The meaning, when spelt gild, is thought to derive from the Anglo-Saxon word 'gylden' meaning "to pay", whilst later theories suggest it meant a society, tributum or sacrificium."*

Noting that the early English gilds were primarily community-based and self-help organisations, it follows that over time, as the population grew, so the number of community-based gilds increased. It seems that around the time of the Norman Conquest, where there were several gilds in close proximity, they merged to create *Corporations*, a local governing body, a concept that continued in England until the mid-nineteenth century. In many of our cities, usually close to the centre, there are roads and thoroughfares named *Corporation Street* noting the area in which the *Corporation*, as the early form of local governance of that area, was based. Over the hundreds of years that some existed, they had not kept pace with local changes; some communities grew and included villages not covered by the Corporation; some communities reduced in size and existed in name only; some disappeared altogether. Although intended as a form of community governance for the benefit of all, as an advance of the *self-help* concept and as a benefit for the community as a whole, the Corporations failed to deliver what was intended of them. For centuries, the one man-one vote ideal did not exist. There was instead a restricted election process whereby only a small selection of the residents in that community, mostly *freemen*, had a vote for the selection of members of the Corporations. As a result, some such Corporations became very much the toy of wealthy landowners and the aristocracy, and were used for political influence rather than good local governance. Over the seven hundred years or more that they existed, some had become quite corrupt, hence they were reformed under the 1835 Municipal Corporations Act.

*"In February 1833 a select committee was appointed to inquire into the state of the Municipal Corporations in England, Wales, and Ireland; and to report if any, and what abuses existed in them, and what measures, in their opinion, it would be most expedient to adopt, with a view to the correction of those abuses…"* [17]

The report that was published by the Select Committee, to Parliament, after reviewing the Corporations of some 285 towns, notes:

- *The corporations were exclusive bodies with no community of interest with the town after which they were named.*

- *The electorate of some corporations was kept as small as possible.*

- *Some corporations merely existed as "political engines", simply to maintain the ascendancy of a particular party.*

- *Members of councils usually served for life and the corporate body was a self-perpetuating entity. Catholics and Dissenters, although no longer barred from being members, were systematically excluded.*

- *Vacancies rarely occurred, and were not filled by well-qualified persons.*

- *Some close corporations operated in almost complete secrecy, sometimes secured by oath. Citizens could not obtain information on the operation of the corporation without initiating expensive legal actions.*

- *The duties of the mayor were, in some places, completely neglected.*

- *Magistrates were appointed by the councils on party lines. They were often incompetent, and did not have the respect of the public.*

- *Juries in many boroughs were exclusively composed of freemen. As the gift of freedom lay with the town council, they were political appointees, and often dispensed justice on a partisan basis.*

- *Policing in the boroughs was often not the responsibility of the corporation but of one or more bodies of commissioners. An extreme example was the City of Bath which had four districts under different authorities and part with no police whatsoever.*

- *Borough funds were "frequently expended in feasting, and in paying the salaries of unimportant officers" rather than the good government of the town. In some towns funds had been expended on public works without adequate supervision, and large avoidable debts had accrued. This often arose from contracts being given to members of the corporation or their friends or relations. Municipal property was also treated as if it were only for the use of the corporation and not the general population.*

The writers of the report concluded:

> *"...the existing Municipal Corporations of England and Wales neither possess nor deserve the confidence or respect of Your Majesty's subjects, and that a thorough reform must be elected, before they can become, what we humbly submit to Your Majesty they ought to be, useful and efficient instruments of local government."* [18]

This is a sad reflection on a once useful medieval concept that was based on self-help and community, but in the end, was debased by the greed of a few aristocrats and landed gentry.

In the Middle Ages, it seems, that as the sophistication of small villages grew, so too did the number and diversity of crafts increase to satisfy the local demand for the various types of produce available. In some crafts there may even have been a surplus of produce that was sold to travelling merchants at markets, thereby offering a wider distribution. With yet a further increase in the size of a community, the number of people involved in any one particular craft might also grow. So, for example, a small village may have had one family that was involved in spinning and weaving, but over the course of, say twenty years, because of its location or some other external event, that village grew into a small town that had some twenty spinners and weavers. Once the community had grown to become a small town, it may have benefited from the establishment of a small brewery, a number of carpenters, candle makers, and so on. These crafts and trades became an important aspect of the economy of that community. Thus, they formed themselves into trade groups to protect their income. As such groups grew in strength and number, and importance in the economy of the town, so they became part of the local community gild. As further time passed, the gilds developed an administration structure of their own, to regulate their particular trade or craft within that community. Needless to note, a town of a certain size might have only had a sufficient population to support four carpenters, and therefore they controlled who would be trained, generation to generation, in such skills, or if the town was expanding, who could come into the town and start a carpentry business. This concept of trade self-management and regulation seems to have been well established by the eleventh century. Equally, needless to note, that if the houses and major civic buildings in a town were constructed mainly from timber, the number of opportunities for masons, would have been somewhat limited. So, the carpenters became the local builders.

So far there has only been mention of the craft guilds, but it seems, there were two other forms of guilds. Toulmin Smith defines these as Religious and Social Guilds, and Merchant Guilds. Before looking for any connections with these guilds, especially the Religious Guilds, it is worth understanding something of the background to religion in Europe during the eighth century.

## Religion in Europe, and Arianism

The Emperor Constantine, also known as Constantine the Great, had been in Britain with his father in the early years of the fourth century. Sometime around 300 CE, Chlorus, Constantine's father, had command over Iberia (Spain), Gaul (France) and Britain. Chlorus died in York in 306 CE. Following his fathers' death, Constantine left Britain with an army, and after several significant battles on his way to Rome, Constantine became the Emperor. From this position of authority, he relocated the centre of administration of the empire, from Rome to the strategic location on the Bosphorus, where today it is often said, that eastern and western cultures meet. Here he built a new city which was named Constantinople (Istanbul). This was an area that had formally been part of the ancient Greek empire. This new capital, and the Roman Empire of the East that developed from it, subsequently become known as Byzantium.

In the years prior to Constantine becoming Emperor, the Roman Empire and its administration had become somewhat fractured and was in need of a unifying identity. The creation of Constantinople was intended to be part of that process. Through both his experiences in Britain and his other earlier postings, Constantine seems to have developed some affinity for the Christian religion and adopted it to be the main religion of the Roman Empire in preference to the pantheon of gods that the Romans then worshipped.

Today, when we think of Christianity, we have one underlying concept of what its dogma represents, yet there are several forms of religious sub-groups that support that main theme; Anglicanism, Catholicism, Baptists, Methodists, and so on. Throughout Europe in the early Middle Ages, the Roman Catholic religion was the only one tolerated, until the rise of Protestantism caused a split. In the early years of Roman Christianity, the unity of the church was threatened by a similar split - Arianism.

In the early years of the fourth century, a dispute broke out between a deacon named Arius, and the Bishop of Alexandria, named Peter. Arius disputed the divinity claimed by, or for, Jesus Christ, as being the Son of God. It wasn't a local debate just involving Alexandria, it was one that involved many bishops from across the Roman Empire to the extent that Arius was at one stage excommunicated and dispatched into exile, only to be reinstated later. The debate surrounding the issue was finally settled at the Council of Nicaea in 325 CE, only in so far that there was an agreed form of dogma that would represent the concept of Christianity as a unified philosophy for the Roman Church. (Nicaea is today in Turkey, and is known by the name Isnik). However, that did not mean that Arianism was crushed into silence. Arius's contentions continued to plague the Roman Church, and although throughout the empire the Christian belief held sway, there were many who had sympathy for the doubts that Arianism underscored. Those who held such beliefs have often been defined as *barbarians* or *pagans,* by the Frankish kingdoms.

Nearly five hundred years after Constantine's creation of Roman Christianity, a king of the Carolingians, Charlemagne, had been extending his territorial control by an almost continuous succession of battles that enlarged his kingdom to cover a land mass that extended from the North sea in the west, to the border of modern Russia, from the Mediterranean Sea in the South, to the Baltic in the north, an area closely resembling what we now know as Europe.

Amongst the many tribal groups that Charlemagne was constantly engaged with in battle, were the Germanic Saxons to the east of the River Rhine. In Charlemagne's terms they held pagan *Arian* beliefs, whereas he was a strong advocate of the Christian message promulgated by the Vatican in Rome. Charlemagne would defeat a tribe and spare their lives if they promised to follow his Christian beliefs. If they refused, they were slaughtered. As a consequence, many converted to Charlemagne's Catholic belief, but as soon as he departed, they returned to their *Arian* ways. Eventually, Charlemagne overcame the problem by ordering the migration of thousands of East Saxons into the Low Countries, and dispersing them far and wide, so that they had to integrate with the rest of his kingdom. This is recorded as one of the biggest forced migrations ever undertaken prior to the twentieth century. It became the basis from which the doctrine of the Roman Church came to be universally established and rigorously defended across Europe.

Charlemagne's strong beliefs and support for the pope resulted in a split from the Roman Byzantium Empire (of the east) based in Constantinople, and that of the west, based in Rome, and led to Charlemagne being crowned King of the Romans by the then pope, and acquiring the title of Emperor in 800 CE. Emperor Charlemagne, died in 814 CE. From this action, the foundations of what has become known as the Holy Roman Empire were formed. Academics now note that this so called empire was neither, Holy, Roman or an Empire. Despite this, and the fact that it was disbanded by Napoleon Bonaparte in 1807, the reference is still maintained.

This background on the development of Christianity in Europe, leads into the existence of the Religious Gilds.

## The Religious and Social Gild

Quite how the *Religious Gilds* came to be formed in the first instance is not known; their origins are lost in the mists of time. It does, however, seem probable that some form of social and formal gathering would have been needed by the clergy to establish a forum for a common means of presenting the doctrine of the church, the way in which ceremonies were to be conducted, furnishings and regalia to be used, the settlement of disputes, and organisation of parades associated with solemn occasions. Such meetings needed to embrace the clergy over a wide geographical area to ensure such commonality, so it would not be surprising that such occasions also became a time for meeting old friends, establishing new acquaintances, accompanied by celebrations, feasts, drinking wines and beers together, and some general revelry.

Some of the earliest records of such gilds are descended from an era about thirty years after Charlemagne's death. In respect of the Religious Gilds, Toulmin Smith notes:

> "In the…statutes of the Gilds at Abbotsbury and Exeter, of the eleventh century…we see the organisation of these Gilds already completely developed. But much earlier, though less detailed, information is afforded by the Capitularies of Archbishop Hinemar of Rheims, of the year 858…the two kinds which must be distinguished among the Religious Gilds. The one exists among laymen; and it alone is called 'Geldonia'. It alone, too, bears already the complete character of the Religious Gilds as it existed during the whole of the Middle Ages. The other kind of Gild exists among the clergy."[19]

In this statute by Archbishop Hinemar, it states that the laymen of the gild must conduct themselves and their meetings with dignity, suggesting that there had been previous occasions when this was not the case, and that their primary purpose is defined thus:

" ...they shall unite for offerings (especially of candles), for mutual assistance, for funeral services for the dead, for alms, and other deeds of piety...Hinemar forbids...feastings and drinking-bouts, because they led to drunkenness, gave occasion for unjust exactions, for sordid merriments, and inane railleries, and ended often even with quarrels, hatred, and manslaughter. If it was the priest of the Gild or any other clergyman who acted against this prohibition, he was to be degraded, but if it was a layman or a woman, he or she was to be excluded until satisfaction was given. If it became necessary to call a meeting of the brothers, as, for instance, for the arrangement of differences which might have arisen among them, they were to assemble after divine service; and after the necessary admonitions, every one who liked was to obtain from the priest a piece of consecrated bread and a goblet of wine; and then he was to go home with the blessing of God...numbers, over all countries under the sway of the Roman-Catholic religion, and they exist even now in such countries. As the Gild Statutes contained in this collection-and they are but waifs and strays of large flocks-show, these brotherhoods existed in considerable numbers in every town; thus there were twelve in Norwich, as many in Lynn, in Bishop's Lynn nine, while abroad, Gallienus counts even eighty in Cologne, about seventy at Lübeck, and Staphorst more than a hundred at Hamburg. But their objects and organisations were so identical everywhere, and remained so essentially unchanged during successive centuries...the Gild-brothers therefore resolved to adopt a regular constitution, to elect aldermen, to begin a Gild-book, &c. Besides for the setting-up of candles, the members united also for special devotions to their patrons; and amongst these Gilds must be named, above all, the fraternities of the Rosary, as those widest spread since the days of St. Dominic. Further, the Gilds got masses said in honour of their patrons, and went in solemn procession to their churches on the days of their feasts. Conventions like that between the fraternity of London Sadlers, and the neighbouring Canons of St. Martin-le-Grand, by which the Sadlers were admitted into brotherhood and partnership of masses, orisons, and other good deeds, with the canons, were common with these religious Gllds. They further obliged their members to engage in devotions and divine services for the souls of their departed brethren, and often, also, to aid pilgrims and pilgrimages, especially to some most revered places, as, for instance, to the Holy Land, to the tombs of the apostles Peter and Paul, or of St. James (of Compostella), ...

*But, as Hinemar pointed out, the [religious observations] included not only devotions and orisons, but also every exercise of Christian charity, and therefore, above all things, mutual assistance of the Gild-brothers in every exigency, especially in old age, in sickness, in cases of impoverishment, if not brought on by their own folly, and of wrongful imprisonment, in losses by fire, water, or shipwreck, aid by loans, provision of work, and, lastly, the burial of the dead. It included, further, the assistance of the poor and sick, and the visitation and comfort of prisoners not belonging to the Gild. And, as in the Middle Ages instruction and education were entirely supplied by the Church, and were considered a religious duty, we find among the objects of religious Gilds also the aid of poor scholars, the maintenance of schools, and the payment of schoolmasters. No Gild pursued all these objects together; in each separate Gild one object or the other predominated, and, besides it, the Gild pursued several others. But often, too, we find Gilds for the fulfilment of quite a concrete and merely local task, as for instance, the Gild of Corpus Christi at York…The case with this York Gild is simply this. In all Roman-Catholic countries the consecrated host is carried every year on the day of Corpus Christi, by the priest of highest rank in the place, in solemn procession, in the towns through the streets, and in the country over the fields. This is one of the greatest feasts of the Roman-Catholic Church. To heighten its solemnity, all the pomp which the Church can command is brought together. With this intention the clergy of York founded a special Gild, of which the sole object was to provide the ceremonies and pomp of this festival. As the solemnities of one of the greatest ecclesiastical feasts were in question, it can easily be understood that those who were at the head of the Gild were priests. Moreover, the reason why the many crafts of York joined so generally in this procession, was neither 'the love of show and pageant which it gratified,' nor was it 'the departure from the narrow spirit of the original ordinances,' but simply that the taking part in this procession was considered as a profession of faith in transubstantiation. I have myself seen at Munich, the King, the Ministers, the whole body of clergy, the University, all the Trades with their banners and emblems, all the Religious Fraternities, the Schools, and even the Army, taking part in a like procession; and that at Vienna is renowned for still greater pomp. As there were Gilds for conducting this procession, so there were also Gilds for the representation of religious plays, which were common in the Middle Ages in all countries, and which are still performed in some places, for instance, every tenth year at Oberammergau in Southern Bavaria. Such were the Gild of the Lord's Prayer at York, and the Gilds of St. Elene, of St. Mary, and of Corpus Christi at Beverley… The performance of secular plays was also the object of some Gilds, for instance, of the Gild at Stamford …"[20]*

*Author's Note: The above text has been copied, word for word, from the original book, as relevant, and deleting references and end notes, etc., that were buried in the text, so as to give a more fluent picture of the structure of this type of gild, than would have resulted from repeating the exact text.*

The following comments also appear in relation to religious gilds. These have been edited to give a flavour of their objectives without the detail:

*"…all objects of common interest for which now-a-days societies and associations provide, - for instance, the various insurance companies, - in the Middle Ages caused all who were interested in them to unite themselves to religious Gilds; the motive and the principles only were other than those of today, namely, Christian charity, instead of profit…*

*"People of all ranks took part in these Religious Gilds…however, people out of a certain class were not to be admitted. The same person might take part in several religious Gilds. The members had often a special livery, as is still normally the case with some fraternities at Rome. These liveries were worn on their ecclesiastical festivals, and probably also at the great feastings and drinking-bouts which were always connected with them. Notwithstanding all the prohibitions against the latter, since the days of Hinemar, they seem to have so pushed themselves into the foreground, that sometimes special references were needed in the Gild statutes, that 'not eating and drinking, but mutual assistance and justice' were the principal objects of the Gild…*

*"The expenses to be defrayed for attaining the objects of the Gild were provided for by the entrance-fee: the contributions, the gifts and the legacies of members. The contributions were sometimes fixed, but sometimes, especially in earlier times, they varied according to the wants of the Gild…*

*"Often the members had, on their entrance, to declare by oath that they would fulfil their obligations…Persons of ill repute were not to be admitted; and members were to be excluded for misconduct.*

*Moreover, the same rules are to be found with regard to proper*
*behaviour and decent dress at the Gild-meetings, as recur in all kinds*
*of Gilds to our day. Disputes among members were to be decided by*
*the Gild. The disclosing of the affairs of the Gild was to be severely*
*punished. In those places in which the Gild had no special hall, its*
*meetings more often held in the Town hall. The fraternities must*
*accordingly have enjoyed high consideration."[21]*

All the above observations in the account of the Religious Gilds, as
outlined by Toulmin Smith, keeping in mind that there is much more detail
not presented here, suggests a very close affinity with the structure and
statutes of freemasonry.

It also seems that all the gilds had a strong affinity with those of a
religious flavour.

Toulmin Smith goes on to point out that the religious gilds were largely
disbanded during the period of the reformation, firstly by Henry VIII, and
then his son Edward VI. With the dualistic aspect of these gilds being clergy
and laymen, many of the latter were also associated with other gilds. With
the dismantling of the Roman Catholic structure, abbeys and monastic
houses, and establishment of the Church of England, the religious gilds
as such, ceased to exist as a major entity in England. The *layman* aspect of
these *religious gilds*, he suggests, continued to operate as Social *Gilds*. He
further suggests that against the background of incredible religious and
social upheaval that resulted from the reformation, and fear of persecution,
meetings may have been in a different form, such as convivial social groups,
in ale houses, and Town Halls, carrying on the charity aspect of the gild as
they had previously done. There is also a suggestion that some of these
gilds were maintained by *gentlemen* with meetings being conducted at their
houses, and as such became *private social fraternities*.

Religious, or social guilds, are also sometimes referred to a fraternities
and confraternities and their roles are perhaps best illustrated by examining
a few for which records still survive.

**Example of Religious or Social Guilds**
The following text is the way in which the Catholic Dictionary describes
the religious guilds.

*"The Church encouraged these associations, but it was the members*
*of the guild who personally administered its affairs, such as alms-*
*giving, assistance to those setting out on pilgrimages, repairing*
*churches, and the establishment of free schools. These religious*

*guilds were comprised of members in all classes of society, rich and
poor, clerical and laical, who were thus joined in brotherhood."*

Nearly every large town and community in England had religious/
social guilds, and the larger towns had many, addressing different groups
within their locality. Cambridge is a good example. The following has been
copied from a volume of books in the City of Cambridge library:

*"The 11th-century guild of thegns was a society of county gentlemen
centred in Cambridge, though worshipping on occasion at Ely; its
purposes were not purely religious, for besides serving as a burial
club, it provided for protection against wrongs and helped in
securing damages. Nothing is known of it except its rules. Nor is
anything known of the fraternity of the Holy Sepulchre of the 12th
century, save that it sought to build a church. By the 13th century,
however…and before their destruction in 1546–7 as many as 31 are
known to have existed. Their objects were devotional and social; they
provided small but adequate pensions for any of their members who
were in need, masses and burial rites for their dead brothers and
sisters…The constitution of the guilds provided for government by a
master, a warden or wardens, an alderman or aldermen, with a small
group of the brethren as his council."*[22]

The article then goes on to describe the activities of some of the guilds,
the one following being s typical example:

*"THE GUILD OF ST. MARY, in the church of St. Mary in the Market
Place, first mentioned 1282–5; its minutes are extant for 1298–1319,
and also its Bede Roll for 1349. Besides many leading townsmen
it had as members the Justice John of Cambridge, its alderman in
1311, Archbishop Walter Reynolds and Richard of Bury, Bishop of
Durham. Women were admitted as members. It probably took an
active part in the rebuilding of the church after the fire of 1290. It is
once referred to as 'the Guild of Merchants of the blessed Virgin of
Cambridge', and it augmented its funds by small-scale trading, but
it cannot be regarded as a Guild Merchant of the chartered type…
In 1352 by royal grant it was allowed to coalesce with the Guild of
Corpus Christi to found a college, and Henry of Lancaster, the cousin
of Edward III, was chosen alderman of the joint guild."*[23]

There is also another interesting mention, this time about pensions for elderly members of a guild. The following is taken from a reference to a guild known as the Fraternity of St. Mary:

> "…*The wives of brethren could be members, but not apparently other women. An allowance of 7d. a week to solitary poor members, or 4d. each if two lived together, was provided for. The annual subscription was 1s. 4d…*"

> [*the currency mentioned is the old pound (£), shilling (s), pence (d)*]

From these examples we can see how these religious/social guilds worked to ensure satisfactory burial, help for one another, and even to the provision of small pensions. These are all the types of functions later provided by mutual assurance and friendly societies of the nineteenth and twentieth century, prior to many of them becoming commercial companies within the financial industry.

There is one such religious guild that is recorded in some detail.

### Guild of St George in Norwich – and the myth of the Snap Dragon

Illustrations of dragons abound in Norwich, Norfolk, carved long ago, by the skilled hands of stonemasons into the fabric of churches, cathedral and public buildings. They are believed to be connected to references of various religious characters who are bound up on mythologies about their confrontation with these fire-breathing serpents. One such character is St George.

The person on whom the character of St George is based is believed to have been a Roman soldier who became a Christian martyr. It is believed he lived around 250 CE. A tomb dedicated to him was apparently in a town called Lydda. This town was originally recorded in the Old Testament as *Lod*, its Hebrew name, but the later influence of the Greeks and Romans resulted in it also being called Lydda[24]. Today it is again known as *Lod* and is a short distance from Tel Aviv. During the Middle Ages, at the time of the religious wars known as the *crusades*, knights from the Christian armies are believed to have rebuilt the tomb, recognising an association between themselves and St George, by virtue of having also been a soldier. The combination of knights, St George, and dragons combined to create the mythology that then settled around this character. At the Synod of Oxford in 1222, St George came to greater prominence by the date of 23rd April being declared a feast day. Thus it was that shortly after the defeat of the Christian armies and their expulsion from the so-called *Holy*

*Land,* that the Guild of St George was founded in Norwich, as a religious guild, in 1385.[25] Its main function was to celebrate the feast of St George, and help its members in time of need. Like all the guilds of that era, *need* was primarily related to helping those members who were sick, perhaps injured and unable to work, aged and unable to care easily for themselves, and ultimately to organising burial rites. In return a small subscription was paid every week into a special guild fund in much the same way that today we would pay a regular amount into a dedicated fund for life and health insurance, pension and even funeral costs. The guild apparently attracted knights, landed gentry and a very high number of the more wealthy merchant citizens of Norwich and the surrounding area, to its membership. Some thirty years after it was inaugurated, it was such a major entity of the town that it received a Royal Charter under King Henry V in 1417. As a result of the influence of the more affluent members of the Guild, it seems that its original fraternal benefit connections became a lesser part of its role, and it became the dominant feature of the local civic administration. As well as attending church services and praying for the souls of their departed members, and feasting, some of the members presented a short play about the mythical life of St George. There was also a great parade in which, it seems, that a wooden hobby horse was created for the enactment of St George, whilst an elaborate costume existed to represent the dragon, from the inside of which the jaws could be made to work in a snapping and snarling contortion as it chased St George around the street. This mechanical jaws ability later led to the dragon being called by the name *snap – snap the dragon.*

With the abolition of the guilds during the time of the religious Reformation, the Guild of St George changed its name to the Company of St George, which seems to have ceased to exist around the time of the English Civil War. Following the restoration of the monarchy in 1660, the procession of the former guild became fused with that of the swearing-in of the new mayor and a subsequent procession through the city, featuring the antics of *snap the dragon.*

The Municipal/Corporation reform act of 1835 changed the structure of civic administration, and *snap* and his antics faded away. However, in the late twentieth century, dragons were again restored to Norwich through an annual *Norwich Dragon Festival.*[26]

The above outline of the religious Guild of St George is an illustration of its founding intentions, its religious connections, support by wealthy aristocratic and merchant families, and the way it changed shape over time with the influence of later political developments and upheaval.

## The Holy Trinity Guild at Sleaford.

The amount of documented evidence to show the existence and character of religious guilds is not high. As a further demonstration of the diversity of these guilds, however, there is one which has an interesting link to freemasonry.

The Rev'd George Oliver lived for many years in Lincolnshire. As a freemason, he was an enthusiastic champion of the fraternity in an era when the Order was periodically viewed with less favour by the community at large. He rose to the rank of Deputy Provincial Grand Master in Lincolnshire, and wrote many books and papers extolling the virtues of the organisation, and its history, as he understood it.

Thus it was that in 1838 he wrote a short paper entitled the *History of the Holy Trinity Guild at Sleaford*.[27] In it he states that the only surviving documents for this guild start from 1477, but that it is believed the guild was founded shortly after the Norman Conquest (1066) and before the reign of King John (1199-1216). It seems that the guild was a charitable institution, and like so many of the religious guilds, provided a funeral fund for burial at the death of one of its members. Oliver notes:

> *"The Saul-Sceat – a payment to be paid to the clergy on death was a very general practice in the 14th century. No respectable person died or was not buried without a handsome present to some branch or other of the ecclesiastical establishment."*

He goes on to state that the affairs of the religious guilds were to *occupy some spare time, lest inhabitants run amuck*. In other words the guild helped absorb energies that might otherwise stray into matters that were not in the interests of members, if they were to preserve their respectability. He also notes that new brethren may have contributed financially to the guild, for some years, prior to being admitted to the privileges of the elder brethren.

Oliver notes that the countryside around Sleaford was marshy fen and bracken, used for the rearing and grazing of sheep. To protect the shepherds in bad weather some shelters were built:

> *"These [sheep] were guarded from the incursions of poachers, by the wretched occupiers of a few huts constructed of mud and lime, thatched with the long tough grass…and distinguished with the appellation of Lodges…The Lodges were of considerable antiquity… Thus the Lodge at Scopwick derives from a grant…Henry II by John Deincourt, Lord of Blankney to the Knights of Temple Bruer. This was a most valuable gift to the Templars…a very necessary appendage to a sheep farm."*

Thus he points out;

> *"Sleaford had not only a weekly market, but fairs four times a year. These fairs, in early times…would be principally attended and supported by Hanseatic League merchants, and those of Flanders and Italy."*

Although he doesn't say so explicitly, Oliver implies that the Holy Trinity Guild may have derived some financial benefit from the fairs that were organised and used for the sale of the sheep's fleeces to the travelling merchants. No doubt it was the elders of the guild that enjoyed most benefit from these arrangements and hence the reason why one was expected to be a contributing member for some years before, perhaps, enjoying a share of the benefits that resulted. The guild was abolished, as they all were, around 1585, but the guild…

> *"…continued to use its funds for the benefit of the poor. From about 1613 the fund was managed by the church wardens."*

This implies that the guild may have continued to operate in a different form to the previous *guild* status, and the funds were sufficient to warrant management by the churchwardens, thirty years after the guild was officially abolished.

*[Author's note: Despite some enquiries made in Lincolnshire, I was unable to discover how long the funds lasted, or if the guild operated in another form.]*

On the subject of the religious guilds in general, Oliver notes that they started slowly, but:

> *"…were later joined by jugglers, minstrels and buffoons. The Church excommunicated those that enjoyed such revelry ….but nobody took any notice, so the Church mimicked these events and entertainments to present religious plays and miracle plays."*

What this illustrates is that despite the Acts passed to close the religious guilds in the reign of Henry VIII, this one seems to have continued to operate, albeit in a different form, throughout the upheavals of religious change during the Tudor period, and for ten years after Elizabeth I had died – well into the reign of James I/VI – the period of the Renaissance.

## Merchant and Craft Guilds

Reference to religious and social fraternity can still be found in literature of the Merchant Taylor's Company, London. It states:

> *"The Gild was originally a religious and social fraternity founded before the beginning of the 14th century by an association of citizens*

*who were Tailors and Linen Armourers. The Linen Armourers, an allied craft to the Tailors, made the padded tunics or gambesons worn under suits of armour. By virtue of various Royal Charters commencing with that of Edward III in 1327, the functions of the Gild were extended and by about the end of the 15th century it controlled the trade. However, as many of its members ceased to be craftsmen and became merchants trading with other parts of the world..."*

From this information it is clear that this Company started life as a Craft Guild, but with the passing of time, gradually changed its shape, and the membership became predominantly Merchant traders - Merchant Guilds, having originally been a *religious and social fraternity*.

Long before the Norman Conquest, materials were being shipped around Europe, and between Britain and the European continent. Some of this was handled by merchants who bought small consignments from local suppliers, and then consolidated such parcels into larger lots that could be sold to other merchants. As a consequence, the money they made put them in a strong position for participation in the community/town gilds and Corporations as *aldermen*. Some of these merchants specialised in particular commodities, such as woollen cloth, whilst other merchants collected wool which they shipped to cloth makers in Flanders. Needless to note, such merchants had networks of connections, and it seems that many of these merchants bonded together, especially after the Hanseatic League obtained permission from Henry II to trade in England, into guilds of their own. Because the merchants dealt with specific types of commodities, it became their role to supervise the producers of those commodities, and, in some cases, the producers of the raw materials. Their importance and power grew, whilst that of the craftsmen remained static and diminished by comparison. As seems to have occurred so often in history, where money and power resided, so too did the influence of the families that were associated with it, such that they became the ruling elite, who in turn became known as the aristocracy.

During the twelfth century, on the continent, the aristocracy grew to be so powerful that they controlled the guilds. The craft guilds were much maligned, for example,

*"...The growth of wealth and of the number of the people necessarily called forth greater division of labour; the full citizens having become rich, only carried on trade, whilst the handicraft was left exclusively to the poor and the unfree. The poor were originally excluded from full citizenship and from the Gild by the want of a property qualification;*

> *and when, in consequence of the development...the poor and the*
> *craftsmen became identical, this led to the ordinance repeated in*
> *Danish, German, and Belgian Gild-statutes, that no one with 'dirty*
> *hands,' or 'with blue nails,' or 'who hawked his wares in the streets,'*
> *should become a member of the Gild, and that craftsmen, before being*
> *admitted, must have forsworn their trade for a year and a day..."*

Britain was not excluded from this form of demarcation, as the text continues:

> *"...of the statutes of Berwick, according to which no butcher, as long*
> *as he carried on his trade, was to deal in wool or hides, except he*
> *were ready to forswear his axe. The facts are that the Gild of Berwick*
> *was a decided Merchant-Gild, and that the members traded chiefly*
> *in wool or hides. Formerly this trade was undoubtedly carried on*
> *with that of the butchers. But after the craftsmen had been excluded*
> *from the Gild, the butchers were forbidden to carry on a trade by Gild*
> *members."[28]*

This was a situation that many of the craft gilds found intolerable and banded together for protection of their trade and rights. (This, of course is no different to the later development of trades unions.) As the merchants grew ever stronger, so the craftsmen became more distanced from them and resentful that they were excluded from the guilds. In the thirteenth century this resulted in civil war in Europe, between the craft guilds and the merchants/ruling families. The merchants, having power and money on their side, made the early gains, with hundreds of craft-guild aldermen being rounded up and burnt at the stake, executed, hunted down and murdered, or sent into exile with their families. With literally nothing to lose, time passed to the benefit of the craft-guilds who gradually gained the upper hand, taking over some of the guilds they had been excluded from. In some places, the craft guilds excluded the merchants from community administration; in others, merchants were only permitted to participate if they joined specific craft guilds and made contributions to the fraternity. In some respects, this was *speculative* or *admitted* membership of the craft guild, by merchants that had no direct affinity for the production of goods provided by the craftsmen.

Although in England, such violence seems to have been averted, the merchants and craftsmen alike, would have been well aware about what was happening in Europe. Laws were passed by both Edward II and Edward III which improved the position of the craftsmen. It wasn't to last. In the reign of Henry VI, the hold over administration of a town by the guilds was diminished, as the *borough* came to the fore in the place of the guild for community management.

However, as will have been realised from all the foregoing observations, through this period of the Middle Ages the gilds / guilds were self regulated without any real or direct influence by the Crown and its Court. During this time the Gilds were styled adulterine or unauthorized, and an enquiry into their objects and conditions in 1179-80 showed that there were no less than nineteen, of which only four were trade Gilds, namely the Goldsmiths', Grocers' or Pepperers', Butchers' and Cloth Workers'.

> *"There was much riot and disturbance in London at this period, and the Gilds as secret societies, were regarded with some ill-favour by the authorities, and as an element of danger. All this was removed by the incorporation of the Sovereign and they became 'nurseries of charity and seminaries of good citizenship'. As they grew in number and became more widespread, not to mention increased wealth as a consequence of the restrictive practices and restrictions on admission to a craft/trade, they became the focus of the exchequer as a means of raising money. Thus, the granting of Charters commenced in the reign of Edward III".[29] [Edward III monarch 1327-1377]*

Just as with the English Gilds of the Anglo-Saxon period where they supported each other as a self-help community, the trade guilds of the post-Norman Conquest era, operated in much the same way.

> *"They were instituted for the purpose of protecting the consumer or employer against incompetency or fraud of the dealer or artisan, and also for securing a maintenance of the skilful artisan preventing him from being undersold in a labour market by an unlimited number of competitors. Each Gild was given a monopoly in its own particular trade. No one could interfere with its members, or start a rival business without becoming a member of the Gild, into which he was formally admitted and had to swear obedience and to preserve the secrets of the trade; to conduct himself orderly with his fellow members, and to observe the ordinances of the Gild. Each Gild had its master or wardens…and apprentices. The Companies acted as domestic tribunals, arbitrating between master and man, and settling disputes, thus diminishing hostile litigation and promoting amity and goodwill."*

Ditchfield adds that the Gilds were also:

> *"…in the nature of benefit societies from which the workman in return for the contributions he had made in health and vigour in the common stock of the Gild might be relieved in sickness or when*

*disabled by age. This was greatly increased by the benevolence of the richer members of the Gild who contributed large funds for charitable purposes, built almshouses for their afflicted folk, erected great schools, and had such confidence in the ruling members of their company that they believed they could not find any better trustees. Hence arose the numerous charitable gifts and foundations which were entrusted to their care. They also possessed the character of modern clubs, in which feasting and social intercourse were regular features of their Gild life."*

What we have seen is that irrespective of the fraternity or brotherhood, every guild, whether it was religious, merchant, or craft, had their ordinances (rules and laws) which, remembering that in the Middle Ages in Europe, religion was dominated by the monotheistic attitudes and doctrines of the Catholic Church, stated the duties the member was expected to perform of a religious, social, charitable and industrial nature. This included attendance at church services, social gatherings for dining and / or general amusement, the charitable activities they needed to perform to support the sick, injured or aged members and families of the Guild, and most especially the working conditions, hours of labour, wages and how apprentices were to be trained in the *mysteries* of the craft or trade.

The major trade guilds, as already mentioned, were the Goldsmiths', Grocers' or Pepperers', Butchers' and Cloth Workers'. There were, of course, many others, and as new ideas and processes were devised, so there were splits, where a small group of brothers from a guild broke away and established a new one more in-keeping with changes, or just because they were in dispute of some kind. Toulmin Smith writes;

*"Sometimes the richer craftsmen withdrew from their poorer brethren into separate Gilds, as, for instance, the Shoemakers from the Cobblers, the Tanners from the Shoemakers; and we frequently hear of disputes among the Craft-Gilds concerning what belonged to their trade."[30]*

There was one such dispute that illustrates this point very well.

Amongst the major Guilds/Companies established in England, and particularly in London, was, and still is, the Grocers' Company. It has a history that extends back to mediaeval times, and may have been the result of several Gilds merging. Amongst these were the Pepperers. The modern Grocers Company traces its origins back to the year 1100, to the Ancient Guild of Pepperers. Pepper is acknowledged as having been one of the earliest spices traded, and this ancient Gild seems to have been in existence trading specifically in such spices. There were other spices also imported and traded by other gilds. The earliest use of the term *grocer* stems from around 1373 when the term used for the fraternity was, Company of Grossers.[31] It is derived from the term *en gros* which can be interpreted as a person who trades in large quantities of produce, a wholesaler and perhaps importer. The range of products sold by the *grocers* was very extensive, ranging from spices, drugs, medicines and potions, to rhubarb, wax and plasters. This vast assortment of produce, much of which was highly prized by the nobility of the times, resulted in the Gild and its members becoming reasonably wealthy.

A Guild / fraternity:

> "...of *Pepperers of Sopers Lane, seems to have existed in the reign of Edward II, and its ordinances state that "it was agreed that no person should belong to the fraternity who was not of the craft, that is to say, a Pepperer of Sopers Lane, or a spicer of the Ward of Cheape or other persons of their mystery wherever they resided".*

Thus, from the earliest time of the formation of the Grocers Company, because of the range of materials and goods they distributed, they also became dispensers of medical remedies, by a group within the grocers who became known as *apothecaries.*

Needless to note, the practice of medicine in the era up to the Tudor period, was hardly based on rigorous science that we now observe, but more the knowledge of observation and alchemy. Thus it was, that in the reign of Henry VIII, a Charter was granted in 1523 for the formation of the College of Physicians. Part of the charter forbade the physicians from dispensing medicines, whilst apothecaries were equally forbidden to undertake a medical examination which would be within the realms of the physician. Following the formation of the College of Physicians, the apothecaries within the Grocers' Company began to feel that they too should have a separate charter. It was in 1540 that the work and knowledge of the apothecary was first recognised as such in an Act of Parliament, as a *mistery*, that is, as having its own skills and knowledge. As such, it became illegal for any person to practice the '*Art, Mystery or Manual Occupation*' of an apothecary, without they had served an apprenticeship of seven years. Thus, the apothecaries commenced a petition for their own Charter. The Grocers could see that if it was granted, they stood to lose control of the dispensing of drugs and remedies, and with it, a slice of their business. Most of the petitioning by the apothecaries was undertaken in the reign of Elizabeth I.

It was usual practice, that when a monarch died, so all Charters and patents were suspended until inspected and ratified by the new sovereign. Thus it was that in the reign of James I, a reign that commenced in 1603, the Charter of the Grocers' Company was reissued, but removed the work of the apothecaries who were noted as a skill in their own right. Needless to note, the Grocers were not particularly happy by this development, and the issue rumbled on until December 1617, with opposition created by the Grocers' and supported by other institutions of the city. There were several enquiries involving the King and the Privy Council before the Charter was finally sealed and issued. Nine days later the relevant oaths were made at the centre of the legal establishment in Grays's Inn, and the first meeting of the new Company was held. Following the issue of the Charter for the apothecaries, in 1624, in the House of Commons. King James said:

> "I myself did devise that corporation and do allow it. The grocers, who complain of it, are but merchants; the mystery of these apothecaries were belonging to apothecaries, wherein the grocers are unskilful; and therefore I think it is fitting they should be a corporation of themselves."[32]

Today, this organisation is known as *The Worshipful Company of Apothecaries* of London.

Guilds, and that they held processions to celebrate various festivals or other events in which the other guilds of a community would participate. One can just imagine the conflict that would periodically arise as to which guilds were the most important and therefore closer to the front of the parade – who was at the tip of the *pecking order* and who would be the *tail end Charlies*. Clearly the Corporation of the City of London faced just such problems, because in 1515 a *Court of Aldermen* was formed to establish precedence, and thereby regulate ceremonial and parade position. It has already been mentioned that control over some of the guilds was in the hands of the wealthy families that grew as a result of their trading activities, and that wealth may dictate one's power, prestige and ability to gain access that will influence political outcomes. Indeed, in literature produced to promote the Guildhall in the City of London, it states:

> "…Guildhall, built between 1411 and 1440, was designed to reflect the importance of London's ruling elite…"[33]

Throughout the world today, there are many organisations, clubs and societies where admission to membership is based on one's wealth and/or social standing. Thus, it was that the *Court of Aldermen* contrived a list of London guilds and Livery Companies, based on *their* perception of the significance of particular companies, in the *pecking order*. In 1515 there were forty-eight such companies of which the first twelve in the order of precedence were, and still are, regarded as the most significant, and the position of those in the lower area, have changed slightly with the passing of time. At the end of the first decade of the twenty-first century, there were one hundred and seven such Companies listed, of which the top fifty of that order were as follows:

**List of Livery Companies, in order of precedence**
1. The Worshipful Company of Mercers
2. The Worshipful Company of Grocers
3. The Worshipful Company of Drapers
4. The Worshipful Company of Fishmongers
5. The Worshipful Company of Goldsmiths
6. The Worshipful Company of Merchant Taylors
   (alternates with the Skinners)
7. The Worshipful Company of Skinners
   (alternates with the Merchant Taylors)
8. The Worshipful Company of Haberdashers
9. The Worshipful Company of Salters
10. The Worshipful Company of Ironmongers
11. The Worshipful Company of Vintners
12. The Worshipful Company of Clothworkers
13. The Worshipful Company of Dyers
14. The Worshipful Company of Brewers
15. The Worshipful Company of Leathersellers
16. The Worshipful Company of Pewterers
17. The Worshipful Company of Barbers
18. The Worshipful Company of Cutlers
19. The Worshipful Company of Bakers
20. The Worshipful Company of Wax Chandlers
21. The Worshipful Company of Tallow Chandlers
22. The Worshipful Company of Armourers and Brasiers
23. The Worshipful Company of Girdlers
24. The Worshipful Company of Butchers
25. The Worshipful Company of Saddlers
26. The Worshipful Company of Carpenters
27. The Worshipful Company of Cordwainers
28. The Worshipful Company of Painter-Stainers
29. The Worshipful Company of Curriers
30. The Worshipful Company of Masons
31. The Worshipful Company of Plumbers
32. The Worshipful Company of Innholders
33. The Worshipful Company of Founders
34. The Worshipful Company of Poulters
35. The Worshipful Company of Cooks
36. The Worshipful Company of Coopers
37. The Worshipful Company of Tylers and Bricklayers

38.  The Worshipful Company of Bowyers
39.  The Worshipful Company of Fletchers
40.  The Worshipful Company of Blacksmiths
41.  The Worshipful Company of Joiners and Ceilers
42.  The Worshipful Company of Weavers
43.  The Worshipful Company of Woolmen
44.  The Worshipful Company of Scriveners
45.  The Worshipful Company of Fruiterers
46.  The Worshipful Company of Plaisterers
47.  The Worshipful Company of Stationers and Newspaper Makers
48.  The Worshipful Company of Broderers
49.  The Worshipful Company of Upholders
50.  The Worshipful Company of Musicians

As the *Worshipful Company of Apothecaries* has been mentioned earlier, their position in the order of precedence is shown as number 58. Number 107 has been allocated to *The Worshipful Company of Tax Advisers*. The position of the Companies at positions 6 and 7 are noted to alternate. This, tradition has it, is because at the *Court of Aldermen* in 1515, there was a dispute about which of these two should be at position 6 and 7. To settle the dispute they agreed to alternate each year, and this is believed to have been the origin of the expression, when a matter is undecided, of *being at sixes and sevens.*

It will be noted that, at the time of writing, the *Worshipful Company of Masons* holds position number 30 in the order of precedence. The fortunes of the Company have varied with the passing of time, and in some older records its position has been lower at number 33. Notwithstanding that, it is governed by a Court of Assistants, which comprises a *Master, who is elected each year* and *Two Wardens.* They are assisted by a number of *Past Masters.* The earliest records of an organisation for the regulation of the craft of stonemasonry, is 1356; in 1472 they received a *Grant of Arms.* The issue of such a grant was a recognition of a single entity regulating the craft, whilst there were still guilds operating in most major towns. The company states that it was not until after the restoration of the monarchy, and the reign of Charles II, that the first Royal Charter was issued in 1677. The era between 1665 and 1677 in London, was one of troubles. In 1665 London had been ravaged by the plague, and then the following year, 1666, it suffered the Great Fire of London. The rebuilding of London after the fire was an enormous challenge, and in consequence, masons and other construction skills from around the country, descended on the city, no doubt looking for easy work that gave them easy money. This led to consistent infringements of the rights of the members of the Masons Guild. To restore the rights of the guild, the Royal Charter was issued and gave the masons control over all stone work in the City of London and Westminster, and within seven miles radius, thereof. Thereafter, the Masons Company was responsible for the building of several prestigious buildings in London, where the primary material, was stone. Amongst these was the rebuilding of the St Paul's Cathedral. The key stonemasons were both *Masters* of the company, working under direction from Sir Christopher Wren.

There is another interesting fact about the Mason's Guild. Richard II (not to be confused with Richard the Lion Heart, Richard I), reigned as King of England from 1367 – 1399. In the few years following 1386, England was threatened with further invasion from France. To gain support for his position, Richard led a tour of the country and held a parliament in Cambridge in 1388:

> "…that it sat thirty-nine days, and that even in that short time it passed ('sixteen good acts'), touching among other things the condition of labourers, and regulating beggars and common nuisances. In this Parliament it was ordered that two Writs should be sent to every Sheriff in England, both commanding him to make public proclamation throughout the shire, the first calling upon 'the Masters and Wardens of all Gilds and Brotherhoods,' to send up to the King's Council in Chancery Returns of all details as to the foundation, statutes, and property of their Gilds; the second calling on the 'Masters and Wardens and Overlookers of all the Mysteries and Crafts,' to send up, in the same way, copies of their charters or letters patent, where they had any. These Writs were sent out on the 1st of November, 1388, the Returns were ordered to be sent in before the 2nd of February next ensuing."[34]

Some forty years earlier, from around 1346-1350, a plague known as the *Black Death* had swept across Europe. Overall the population is believed to have been reduced by a third, but in some towns the reduction was much higher, and in some villages, no one survived. It was at the time the Hanseatic League was at its most productive, with ships transporting goods across Europe, and, no doubt, and unknowingly, some of those ships carried the germ of the plague, and helped it spread. With the population of Europe so drastically reduced, food production became less efficient and the market for many commodities was reduced which undermined the prices for goods and labour. There was rebellion against the old feudal ways and former bondsmen refused to work for surviving lords without pay. The guilds too suffered as the number of craftsmen and merchants was reduced, and entire guild structures and their skills were lost.

It was forty years later that Richard sent out his enquiry, no doubt to gauge how well things were recovering. Just as after the *Great Fire of London* when there had been a number of individuals who sought to relocate to London and take part in the reconstruction, so in the aftermath of the plague, there were people who moved to other towns and then tried to claim skills with the intention of gaining access to specific guilds.

> "*Whilst the statutes before the fourteenth century frequently do not even mention the workmen, after the middle of the fourteenth century it became absolutely necessary to regulate their relations to their masters. Above all things, the provisions for the settlement of disputes between masters and workmen which recur in all countries, are striking, as well as the care that both masters and workmen should fulfil their obligations to each other. The deciding authorities were here always the wardens of the Gild. Masters who withheld from the workmen the wages to which they were entitled were compelled to pay by the Gild Authorities.*"[35]

The *returns* demanded by Richard II duly arrived, and as might be expected from an age when the type and size of paper was not regulated to fit with machines, the responses were in many forms. When it came to the Guild of Masons, they apparently submitted their returns in the form of a rhyme. According to Edward Condor in his *Hole Craft & Fellowship of Masonry, With a Chronicle of the History of the Worshipful Company of Masons of the City of London*,[36] Richard II was sufficiently impressed that he provided a structure for the conduct of feasts at their annual assemblies.

### The end of the guilds

Despite all the wonderful developments that had taken place in and through the guild structure, and the economic advantages that had resulted, two things ultimately led to their downfall.

The first was religion. When Henry VIII wished to divorce his wife and queen, Catherine of Aragon, the Pope, the Roman Catholic Church and the supporters of the Holy Roman Empire, fought against it. There was also a growing Protestant movement across Europe. In the end, Henry VIII solved *his* problem by creating the Church of England, closing the monasteries and priories, and effectively abolishing the practice of the Roman Catholic faith in England.

Needless to note, there were many individuals in the country who had derived power and influence by their support of the Catholic faith and connections with the Vatican in Rome and found this new power base

Roman Empire collapses c450 CE

Merovingian and Carolingian
Dynasties develop c400 – 750 CE

Emperor Charlemagne and
foundations of the Holy Roman
Empire c765 – 814 CE

Saxon Settlement southern England
400 – 500 CE

Gilds commence and recognised by
King Ina c650 CE

Religious Gilds are in operation
in the Catholic Church c800CE

Alfred the Great, King of Wessex
c871–899 CE

Craft Gilds are in place in Europe

Religious Gilds are firmly established
in England. Craft fraternities take
part in processions

Athelstan, defeats Danes and Scots
near York; becomes the first King of
all England c924 – 940 CE

Craft fraternities become the
forerunner of the Guilds and
are part of the Gild system of
local civic administration.
Merchant Guilds develop

Craft fraternities are excluded from
Gilds by Merchant Guilds and then
regain their position

Royal Charters issued by Edward II
& III to regulate Craft fraternities
and other Guilds

Protestantism develops in parts of
Europe as an alternative faith system
to Roman Catholicism

Henry VIII abolishes the Roman
Catholic faith in England. Starts
Church of England. Protestantism
becomes the main religious faith

Edward VI abolishes Craft Gilds

Elizabeth I reforms apprenticeships

contrary to their own interests. Equally, there were other individuals who had been quite happy with the faith they had grown up with, and would have liked it to continue. The guilds represented a series of cells across the country that were not directly controlled by government and hence they became a place that those close to Henry VIII feared could be centres that could instigate rebellion against the King and his new order. By abolishing the guilds of all kinds, especially the religious guilds, that risk was reduced. Hence the guild structure that had existed for several hundred years was abolished. This abolition was further underlined by his son, Edward VI, when he became king. The only guilds that were excluded were the major guilds in the City of London, who changed their structure to being *Livery Companies.*

Through various associations, it was in the reign of James I/VI that the structure gradually reinvented itself, was forced to decline again during the Civil War, but rose again with the restoration of the monarchy, through Charles II.

The second major event surrounded the latter part of the industrial revolution and into the twentieth century. The guilds had formulated the process that dictated who could join a trade and how many individuals could operate in a given area; what pay they should receive and the type of work to be undertaken. This resulted in, what today, we would call, *restrictive trade practices.* It reduced competition and inflated the cost of goods and services. Also, the industrial revolution saw the development of many new trades and crafts, like pattern makers, who made wooden moulds that were used in casting metals, sheet metal workers, foundry workers, and so on. These kinds of trades, and the way in which the craftsmen were taught, albeit under an apprenticeship scheme, saw trade unionism develop as an alternative to the guild structure. But this too caused its own problems, especially through *restrictive working practices* and control over the numbers of people joining an industry.

The old trade and craft guild system withered and died.

When it comes to *religious guilds* we see a different process. Many of them joined together, created *Friendly Societies* which provided the same charitable and financial support process as the religious guilds had done. From these, grew the mutual insurance companies that offered a much broader range of protection than that relating to the individual crafts and trades. Today, many of those Friendly Societies and mutual insurance services, have been merged and become major international financial corporations.

The foregoing information about the guilds, their probable origin, structure and purpose, is intended to give a mere outline of them. Studying them in greater depth gives an interesting picture of various phases of

English history, because they are so linked with the ebb and flow, pain and joy, that accompanied the passing of the centuries.

It will be noted, that the early gild system was one of mutual self-help in a community, and bonding together for mutual support and protection. If freemasonry did indeed originate through the stonemasons craft, or association with it, then the origin in England had to be by another route by which the structure and content that we now know, developed, and it must have had a purpose. For the possible origins of that route, we need to look at other potential influences.

The following chart shows a pictorial representation of events that influenced the development of the various Guilds.

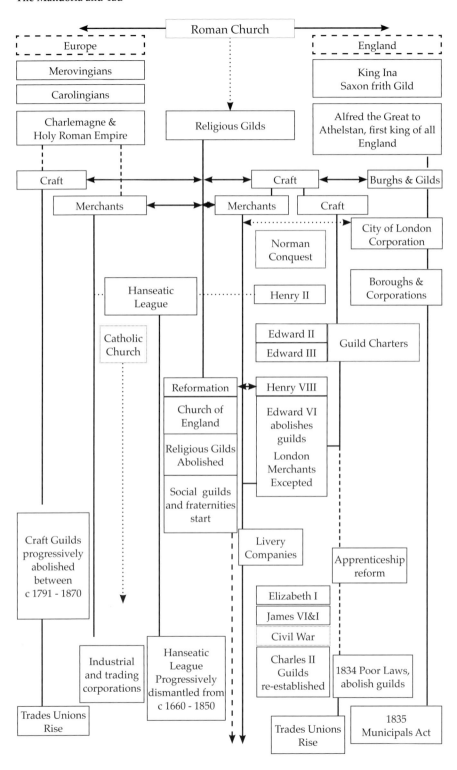

# Chapter 7

# LEGENDS, EUCLID'S REDISCOVERY

When Anderson wrote his *Constitutions,* it is widely held that he used and referred to a number of old manuscripts as references for some of the statements made. This is particularly the case with the section on the *Charges.* Chief amongst these reference documents was one known as the *Regius Manuscript (MSS).* This document is in poetic form and is dated as being from circa 1390. This would have placed it as being written during the reign of King Richard II.

It was recognised as a Masonic document, by a Mr James Orchard Halliwell-Philips, and for this reason it is also sometimes referred to as the *Halliwell Manuscript.* A facsimile copy of the document and other information is available in the library of Freemasons Hall, London. The widely held view is that it is probably the oldest document yet to have survived which is a record of the craft of masonry. Records suggest that the existence of the document was well known for many years, but it was Halliwell who recognised its value in trying to establish a link between freemasonry and the craft of the stonemasons. It also enables one to understand a connection with the Masonic legend of *Maymus Grecus,* who is credited in some earlier Masonic works, with introducing the geometry of the Greek mathematicians and philosophers to Europe in the reign of Frankish king, Charles the second/Charles Martel. However, in order to put the legend into a proper perspective, we should first look at a couple of other background aspects of history, that affect freemasonry.

**Dates in freemasonry**

In Anderson's Constitutions, there is reference to *"History, Laws, Charges, Orders, Regulations, and Usages of the Right Worshipful fraternity of Accepted Free Masons: collected from their general Records, and their faithful Traditions of many ages…"* on the opening page. There is a *Dedication* preface at the start of the book to *His Grace the Duke of Montagu,* in the name of J.T Desaguliers, Deputy Grand-Master. In the dedication, Desaguliers makes the following comment:

> *"I need not tell your Grace what pains our learned AUTHOR [Anderson] has taken in compiling and digesting this book from old Records, and how accurately he has compar'd and made everything*

> *agreeable to History and Chronology, so as to render these New*
> *Constitutions a just and exact account of Masonry from the*
> *Beginning of the World to your Grace's mastership..."*

The first edition of the Constitutions was published in 1723, just six years after the foundations of the Grand Lodge of England were formed. Needless to note, our understanding and knowledge of the world has changed dramatically in the past one hundred years of the twentieth century, so Anderson's Constitutions are a reflection of the perceived knowledge at that earlier time. A simple example of this is on the opening page of the Constitutions which not only shows the publication year, 1723, but also shows another year and states:

*"In the year of Masonry – 5723".*

This implies that Masonry had a history 4,000 years older than the chronological calendar year, or that Masonry started in the year 4,000 BCE – a date that is a nice round number. So where did this start date originate? The answer is linked to religion, and in particular, to biblical chronology.

It is believed that the early Books of the Old Testament were originally written down in their current form around 500 BCE – 600 BCE, by unknown scribes. The widely held view is that prior to that time they were an accumulation of stories that formed part of a verbal tradition which provided a means of conveying information from one generation to the next.

Throughout the Old Testament there are numerous references to people and their life-spans, to events and their places in the order of occurrence, and, to intervals of time between major events. This has led to a number of attempts being made to precisely identify the dates, based on our current calendar structure, as to when certain biblical events occurred, or when characters supposedly lived.

Our current calendar dating system owns much to one *Dionysius Exiguus*, a monk who is credited with its creation circa 527 CE[37], in the Common Era (sometimes also referred to as in the Christian Era). Using various methods of calculation he had fixed the date for the year in which the Christ was born as being 25th March some 753 years from the foundation of Rome, a strange number to say the least. This gave us year 1 AD/ 1 CE and hence noted it as the first of Christ's era. It forms the basis of the calendar system that had been adopted by most of the governments of the world by the end of the twentieth century.

It is, however, the calculations of another prominent member of the clergy who is responsible for the Masonic calendar start date. His name was James Ussher, who added together all the time intervals in the bible and came to the conclusion that the date of creation, as stated in the opening verses of the Book of Genesis, was 23rd October 4004 BCE. James Ussher (1581-1656) was a respected man of his time. He was Archbishop of Armagh, Primate of All Ireland and Vice Chancellor of Trinity College, Dublin. Indeed, his resulting perspective on biblical chronology was so highly regarded that, to quote the Encyclopaedia of Religion:

> *"…it was included in an authorised version of the Bible printed in 1701, and thus came to be regarded with almost as much unquestioning reverence as the bible itself…"*[38]

From this, and the reverence Ussher's chronology enjoyed, it was applied to some aspects of Masonic ceremonies where dates and a chronology for the Order are based on Ussher's scheme. With the sum total of the accumulated knowledge that we have at our disposal today, Ussher's idea is patently ludicrous. Yet, based on the knowledge and perceptions of the world as seen through the eyes of such eminent people who lived in the very different world and culture of 300 years ago, together with their interpretation of the religious faith to which they had committed their very being, then such conclusions were a source of encouragement and enlightenment which would have influenced the establishment for several generations that were to follow.

Ussher's dating system seems to have influenced Anderson and the early publication of his Constitutions, and has been reflected in Masonic events ever since.

This dating system shows how a simple and seemingly innocuous reference that is considered as factual and sustainable at a point in time, can become less so with the passing of yet more time, and the accumulation of other validating information. In the case of Ussher's chronology, it was perhaps overtaken by the combined influence of Charles Darwin's theory of evolution and the discovery and close examination of fossilised vegetation, crustaceans and animal remains that took place during the nineteenth century and undermined the entire concept of the creation theory.

**Regius, Cooke and Dowland Manuscripts.**
As mentioned earlier, one of the oldest surviving records of the Craft of Masonry is the seldom-visited old document referred to as the Regius Manuscript.

James Orchard Halliwell-Philips was an acclaimed scholar who had been educated at Cambridge University. He wrote and published a significant volume of works and is described as having a special interest in the plays of Shakespeare and the origins and use of children's poems and nursery rhymes. It was probably his interest in both these fields, composed in poetic form, that drew his attention to the Regius manuscript.

The manuscript is believed to date from around the year 1390, and is generally regarded as the oldest surviving document yet found and available that is related to the craft of masonry, though various other writers have suggested that it may be a copy of, or influenced by, a much older document. The original document is retained in the British Library, but a facsimile is available in the library at Freemasons Hall, London.

The text of the *Regius* is in old English, and Halliwell is credited with translating it into more modern language. The first and last verses, together with Halliwell's translation are shown in the following table as examples of the original text and Halliwell's version:

| | | |
|---|---|---|
| 1. | Whose wol bothe wel rede and loke, | Whoever will both well read and look |
| 2. | He may fynde wryte yn olde boke | He may find written in old book |
| 3. | Of grete lordys and eke ladyysse, | Of great lords and also ladies, |
| 4. | That hade mony chyldryn y-fere, y-wisse; | That had many children together, |
| 5. | And hade no rentys to fynde hem wyth, | And had no income to keep them with, |
| 6. | Nowther yn towne, ny felde, ny fryth: | Neither in town nor field nor frith; (enclosed wood) |
| 7. | A cownsel togeder they cowthe hem take; | A council together they could them take, |
| 8. | To ordeyne for these chyldryn sake, | To ordain for these children's sake, |
| 9. | How they my[g]th best lede here lyfe | How they might best lead their life |
| 10. | Withoute gret desese, care and stryfe; | Without great disease, care, and strife; |
| 11. | And most for the multytude that was comynge | And most for the multitude that was coming |
| 12. | Of here chyldryn after here [g]yndynge. | Of their children after their ending |
| 13. | (They) sende thenne after grete clerkys, | They send them after great clerks, |
| 14. | To techyn hem thenne gode werkys; | To teach them then good works; |
| 775. | When thou metyst a worthy mon, | When thou meetest a worthy man, |
| 776. | Cappe and hod thou holle not on; | Cap and hood thou hold not on; |
| 777. | Yn churche, yn chepyns, or yn the gate, | In church, in market, or in the gate, |
| 778. | Do hym revera(n)s after hys state. | Do him reverence after his state. |
| 779. | [G]ef thou gost with a worthyor mon | If thou goest with a worthier man |
| 780. | Then thyselven thou art won, | Then thyself thou art one, |
| 781. | Let thy forther schulder sewe hys backe, | Let thy foremost shoulder follow his back, |
| 782. | For that ys norter withoute lacke; | For that is nurture without lack; |
| 783. | When he doth speke, holte the stylle, | When he doth speak, hold thee still, |
| 784. | When he hath don, sey for thy wylle; | When he hath done, say for thy will, |
| 785. | Yn thy speche that thou be felle, | In thy speech that thou be felle, (discreet) |
| 786. | And what thou sayst avyse the welle; | And what thou sayest consider thee well; |
| 787. | But byref thou not hym hys tale, | But deprive thou not him his tale, |
| 788. | Nowther at the wyn, ny at the ale. | Neither at the wine nor at the ale. |
| 789. | Cryst then of hys hye grace, | Christ then of his high grace, |
| 790. | [G]eve [g]ow bothe wytte and space, | Save you both wit and space, |
| 791. | Wel thys boke to conne and rede, | Well this book to know and read, |
| 792. | Heven to have for [g]owre mede. | Heaven to have for your mede. (reward) |
| 793. | Amen! amen! so mot hyt be! | Amen! Amen! so mote it be! |
| 794. | Say we so all per charyté. | So say we all for charity. |

From this, one can see that the original document is very long, extending to nearly 800 lines. However, thanks to Halliwell's efforts in translation we can pick out several specific verses. A few are shown below, but the text is edited to highlight the context. In the above translation, there is clear connection with some of the wording used with Masonic customs, today.

*And pray we them, for our Lord's sake.*
*To our children some work to make,*
*That they might get their living thereby,*
*Both well and honestly full securely.*
*In that time, through good geometry,*
*This honest craft of good masonry*
*Was ordained and made in this manner,*
*Counterfeited of these clerks together;*
*At these lord's prayers they counterfeited*
*geometry,*
*And gave it the name of masonry,*
*For the most honest craft of all.*
*These lords' children thereto did fall,*
*To learn of him the craft of geometry,*
*The which he made full curiously;*

*Through fathers' prayers and mothers' also,*
*This honest craft he put them to.*
*He learned best, and was of honesty,*
*And passed his fellows in curiosity,*
*If in that craft he did him pass,*
*He should have more worship than the lasse, (less)*
*This great clerk's name was Euclid,*
*His name it spread full wonder wide.*
*Yet this great clerk ordained he*
*To him that was higher in this degree,*
*That he should teach the simplest of wit*
*In that honest craft to be parfytte; (perfect)*
*And so each one shall teach the other,*
*And love together as sister and brother.*

*Furthermore yet that ordained he,*
*Master called so should he be;*
*So that he were most worshipped,*

*Then should he be so called;*
*But masons should never one another call,*
*Within the craft amongst them all,*
*Neither subject nor servant, my dear brother,*
*Though he be not so perfect as is another;*
*Each shall call other fellows by cuthe, (friendship)*
*Because they come of ladies' birth.*
*On this manner, through good wit of geometry,*
*Began first the craft of masonry;*
*The clerk Euclid on this wise it found,*
*This craft of geometry in Egypt land.*

*4 In Egypt he taught it full wide,*
*In divers lands on every side;*
*Many years afterwards, I understand,*
*Ere that the craft came into this land.*

*Fifteen articles they there sought*
*And fifteen points there they wrought,*

**The first article** *of this geometry;-*
*The master mason must be full securely*
*Both steadfast, trusty and true,*
*It shall him never then rue;*
*And pay thy fellows after the cost,*
*As victuals goeth then, well thou woste; (knowest)*
*And pay them truly, upon thy fay, (faith)*
*What they deserven may; (may deserve)*
*And to their hire take no more,*
*But what that they may serve for;*
*And spare neither for love nor drede (dread)*

**The second article** *of good masonry,*
*As you must it here hear specially,*
*That every master, that is a mason,*
*Must be at the general congregation,*
*So that he it reasonably be told*
*Where that the assembly shall be holde; (held)*

*And to that assembly he must needs gon, (go)*
*Unless he have a reasonable skwasacyon, (excuse)*

*Or unless he be disobedient to that craft*
*Or with falsehood is over-raft, (overtaken)*
*Or else sickness hath him so strong,*
*That he may not come them among;*
*That is an excuse good and able,*
*To that assembly without fable.*

***The third article*** *forsooth it is,*
*That the master takes to no 'prentice,*
*Unless he have good assurance to dwell*
*Seven years with him, as I you tell,*
*His craft to learn, that is profitable;*

*Within less he may not be able*
*To lords' profit, nor to his own*
*As you may know by good reason.*

***The fourth article*** *this must be,*
*That the master him well besee,*
*That he no bondman 'prentice make,*
*Nor for no covetousness do him take;*
*For the lord that he is bound to,*
*May fetch the 'prentice wheresoever he go.*
*If in the lodge he were ty-take, (taken)*
*Much disease it might there make,*
*And such case it might befal,*
*That it might grieve some or all.*

*For all the masons that be there*
*Will stand together all y-fere. (together)*
*If such one in that craft should dwell,*
*Of divers diseases you might tell;*
*For more ease then, and of honesty,*
*Take a 'prentice of higher degree.*
*By old time written I find*
*That the 'prentice should be of gentle kind;*
*And so sometime, great lords' blood*
*Took this geometry that is full good*

*Grammar is the first science I know,*
*Dialect the second, so I have I bliss,*

*Rhetoric the third without nay, (doubt)*
*Music is the fourth, as I you say,*
*Astronomy is the fifth, by my snout,*
*Arithmetic the sixth, without doubt,*
*Geometry the seventh maketh an end,*
*For he is both meek and hende, (courteous)*
*Grammar forsooth is the root,*
*Whoever will learn on the book;*
*But art passeth in his degree,*
*As the fruit doth the root of the tree;*

*Rhetoric measureth with ornate speech among,*
*And music it is a sweet song;*
*Astronomy numbereth, my dear brother,*
*Arithmetic sheweth one thing that is another,*
*Geometry the seventh science it is,*
*That can separate falsehood from truth, I know.*
*These be the sciences seven,*
*Who useth them well he may have heaven.*
*Now dear children by your wit*
*Pride and covetousness that you leave it,*
*And taketh heed to good discretion,*
*And to good nurture, wheresoever you come.*
*Now I pray you take good heed,*

From these few edited verses, supposedly written in 1390, one can see some essence of modern freemasonry. The writer is pointing out the hope that children will follow the craft of masonry as a way to earn their living through obtaining an honourable skill; the role of the apprentice; who are fit and proper persons to become mason's apprentices; the period the apprentice is to be in training; the responsibility of the master who is training the apprentice; the relationship between the master and the craftsmen; and so on. What is also referred to throughout, is that the craft of masonry is related to geometry - that masonry *is* geometry - in particular the writer refers to Euclid. There is a reference to attendance at meetings and the circumstances under which the mason, thus summoned, may be excused from attending. And amongst it all, is reference to what we now refer to as the *Seven Liberal Arts*.

There is another document referred to as the Matthew Cooke Manuscript, which is supposedly dated at around the year 1450. This also picks up on the geometric theme and suggests that the subjects related to in the *liberal arts* can only exist because of geometry. A translation of the original document in the library of Freemason's Hall states:

*"How and in what manner that this worthy science of geometry began, I will tell you, as I said before. Ye shall understand that there be 7 liberal sciences, by the which 7 all sciences and crafts, in the world, were first found, and in especiall for he is causer of all, that is to say the science of geometry of all other that be, the which 7 sciences are called thus. As for the first, that is called [the] fundament of science, his name is grammar, he teacheth a man rightfully to speak and to write truly. The second is rhetoric, and he teacheth a man to speak formaly and fair. The third is dialecticus, and that science teacheth a man to discern the truth from the false, and commonly it is called art or sophistry. The fourth is called arithmetic, the teacheth a man the craft of numbers, for to reckon and to make account of all things. The fifth [is] geometry, the which teacheth a man all the metron, and measures, and ponderacion, of weights of all mans craft. The 6th is music, that teacheth a man the craft of song, in notes of voice and organ, and trumpet, and harp, and of all others pertaining to them. The 7th is astronomy, that teacheth man the course of the sun, and of the moon, and of other stars and planets of heaven.*

*Our intent is principally to treat of [the] first foundation of the worthy science of geometry, and we were the founders thereof, as I said before. There are 7 liberal sciences, that is to say, 7 sciences, or crafts, that are free in them selves, the which 7 live only by geometry. And geometry is as much to say as the measure of the earth,*

*"Et sic dicitur a geo ge quin R ter a latin et metron quod est mensura. Una Geometria in mensura terra vel terrarum," that is to say in English, that gemetria is, I said, of geo that is in gru, earth, and metron, that is to say measure, and thus is this name of Gemetria comounded and is said [to be] the measure of the earth.*

*Marvel ye not that I said, that all sciences live all only, by the science of geometry, for there is none [of them] artificial. No handicraft that is wrought by mans hand but it is wrought by geometry, and a notable cause, for if a man work with his hands he worketh with some manner [of] tool, and there is none instrument, of material things, in this world but it come[s] of the kind of earth, and to earth it will turn again, and there is none instrument, that is to say a tool to work with, but it hath some proportion, more or less. And proportion is measure, the tool, or the instrument, is earth. And*

*geometry is said [to be] the measure of [the] earth, Wherefore, I may
say that men live all by geometry, for all men here in this world live
by the labour of their hands…"*

Yet again there is the reference to the seven liberal arts.

There is one more manuscript to note. It is the Dowland, so called after a
Mr James Dowland who published it in a magazine called *The Gentleman*
in 1815, and is one of several of the *old charges* that are believed to have
existed, and referenced, especially by William Preston. Dowland claimed
that the manuscript was dated from around 1550 and had been written on
rolled-up parchment. The trouble is that the original went missing shortly
after publication and no other copies have been found since. This has raised
doubts as to both the integrity of the translation, and if it ever existed.
Despite these doubts it carries considerable credibility among a range of
Masonic writers, primarily for one reason – the mention of a character
named Maymus Grecus who is credited with introducing the geometry
of the Greek mathematicians and philosophers to Europe in the reign of
Charles II / Charles Martel.

## The Legend of Maymus Grecus and Charles Martel

In compiling his *Constitutions,* Dr Anderson is credited with having
accessed a range of *old charges.* In his text, Anderson makes reference to
Charles Martel (Martell), as is also the case with the *Cooke* manuscript, but
there is no mention by Anderson of *Maymus Grecus.* The *Cooke* manuscript
is considered to be at least 100 years older than the claim that is made
for the Dowland. This invites the question, *'why did Anderson feel that the
reference to Charles Martel had credibility, that a reference to Maymus Grecus did
not?'* There has been much head-scratching and speculation in the past by
Masonic researchers, about this omission. Opinions suggest that it is the
result of a translation error. The reality may be very simple.

## Charles Martel

Charles Martel (around 700 CE) was a Frankish king who lived towards the
end of the Merovingian dynasty, and was the grandfather of the renowned
later Carolingian king, Charles, better known as Charlemagne.One of the
feats that Martel is famous for is winning the *Battle of Tours* in 721 CE.

During the period of the Roman Empire, Iberia (Spain and Portugal) was
a territory controlled from Rome, but with the collapse of Rome around 450
CE, a power vacuum developed in the Iberian peninsula. Notwithstanding
that, the territory had been predominantly Christian, following from the
edict of Constantine and the Council of Nicaea in 325 CE that made it the

religion of the Roman Empire. Following the creation of Islam in the early seventh century, and its rapid expansion by conquest, most of Iberia became a Muslim territory. By the year of the *Battle of Tours* armies of Muslims had crossed the Pyrenees, had been raiding towns in what today is southwest Europe, and seemed intent on capturing the land area that we know today as France. Charles Martel and his army inflicted a massive defeat on the Muslim invaders and pushed them back over the mountains, where they settled for around a further 600 years and developed some of the great cities in Spain, such as those we know as Cordoba and Granada.

When the Regius and Cooke manuscripts were originally written, they may have been so by monks on behalf of operative masons. The monks were from the religious community, and as such, may well have been taught that Charles Martel had saved the Christian faith from being overrun by the heathen Moors. He was therefore regarded with some reverence, and was mentioned to give substance and credibility to stonemasons' guilds for which the documents had been written. There is also the possibility that there was some confusion between two kings named Charles, the warrior Charles – Martel, and his grandson and warrior, Charles - Charlemagne.

During the reign of Charlemagne, there was a split in the residual Roman Empire between that based in Rome, and that which had been created by Constantine, based in Constantinople. The area that Constantinople was established in had previously been part of the old Greek empire and was called Byzantium. Despite the collapse of the Roman Empire around 450 CE Frankish kings, like Clovis through to Charlemagne, had close links with Byzantium, and visited it as if it was their duty as the administrative and cultural centre of the residual Roman Empire that they respected and supported. The city of Rome was in some disarray at the time of Charlemagne. Most of the land in Italy was no longer controlled by Byzantium. Byzantine influence in Frankia, and over the Roman Church, had diminished. Thus, in the reign of Charlemagne there was a clear split between Rome and Constantinople, and *The West* was established.

Byzantium was adorned by some magnificent buildings, reflecting the architectural styles of earlier Roman imperialism which in turn were based on some of the geometric concepts that defined proportion and form that the ancient Greeks and Egyptians had previously developed. In Frankia, and most of the old western empire, the knowledge of the earlier Greek philosophers and mathematicians like Euclid, was virtually unknown.

Charlemagne had established the base of his vast kingdom in a town that is today in modern Germany – the town of Aachen, also referred to as Aix-la-Chapelle. Even in the earlier days of the Roman Empire, it had been a spar town where people bathed in the warm waters that Mother Nature bubbled up from the depths of the earth. Charlemagne built a palace there, and it is believed that he brought a highly skilled mason from Byzantium to Aachen to oversee the construction. This man may well have been the Maymus Grecus, referred to in the Dowlands manuscript, a Byzantine Greek brought to Aachen to oversee the building of Charlemagne's palace. If this is so, then the parallels of this with the Masonic story of the building of Solomon's Temple, are stark. Here we have the Emperor in Constantinople (Hiram king of Tyre) sending a skilled craftsman (Hiram Abif) to another land and king, Charlemagne in Frankia (Solomon in Jerusalem).

*[Author's Note: This information about the Charlemagne Aachen palace, was explained to me by an architect I met, in that town, when I made a visit there to view the cathedral for a previous book, Chivalry. It seemed a minor comment at the time, but as I researched this book, the comment came back to me. I have since noted the architect's observation in several works on architecture, especially in relation to the Rhenish and Romanesque developments. At the time of writing there were also a number of websites containing the same data. In my view, it is a subject that requires more research by someone with an interest.]*

### Rediscovering Euclid.

Having looked at a few of the early manuscripts (Regius, Cooke and Dowland) that are linked to the *Old Charges* that may have a connection with modern freemasonry through the Anderson Constitutions, and noted that there are references to geometry, it raises yet another question – *Why did the writers of those manuscripts consider this aspect of mathematics, to be of such merit, that it should be mentioned? – and Euclid in particular?*

This was an era when religion was the driving force in the management of everyone's lives, throughout the west. It would have seem logical that if man could measure the earth by the use of geometry, and that all things that were made by the hands of men could be related to geometry, then if God had designed heaven and earth, then he too was a practitioner of the same geometry. Therefore if one mastered geometry and built temples for his worship in the form of abbeys, cathedrals, churches, monastic centres, and anything else to serve and hopefully satisfy the deity, then one would be working within the same parameters that the deity had himself used; he would be pleased and the designers and the constructors would be ever closer to understanding *His* ways. Geometry and God were therefore one and the same.

There needed to be something that had driven geometry to achieve this position of eminence, such that it is recorded in a manuscript supposedly compiled in the year 1390.

The *Dark Ages* refers to a period of around 700 years, in the era between the fall of the Roman Empire in Europe and the twelfth century. Progress in the development of the west came virtually to a halt. Religion dominated and permeated every aspect of life; the feudal system that developed in the same era created a hierarchy of social structuring making movement between the social layers very difficult; war between rulers and aspiring rulers was almost constant; free thinking and scientific exploration of new ideas was a taboo subject.

In an area south of the Mediterranean, something else was happening. Arabs moved north and effectively gained control over much of North Africa. Around 610 CE, the religion of Islam was created and with it a dogma that encouraged its followers to pray at specific times of day. To get those times exactly right each day required an understanding of astronomy/astrology, and an arithmetic knowledge to make the observations that enabled those specific times for prayer to be noted, especially against the changes of the seasons.

Periodically in the development of man, there have been times when a series of separate events have combined, and the result has been a significant step-change in our understanding. Thus, around 200 years after the creation of Islam, the stage was set for just such a step-change.

Islam had expanded and its influence stretched throughout Arabia, across most of the ancient world that had been established in North Africa, the Middle East and Iberia. It controlled most of the ancient centres of learning, of Babylon, Carthage and Egypt, and was in contact with the ancient centres of knowledge that existed in North India and the religion of the Hindu's. In the hope of finding a peaceful coalescence with Islamic territories on their borders, the rulers of Byzantium acquainted the Islamic scholars with the knowledge of the ancient Greeks. Around the years 810 – 840 CE an Islamic study centre was created in Baghdad. Islamic scholars made great use of all the ancient knowledge they had gained access to and translated all these works into Arabic. The fusion of Arabic characters, advanced algebra studied by the Hindus and the knowledge from ancient Greece and Egypt, provided a springboard for the development of the Islamic world and culture. At that time they were able to make enormous advances in many walks of life, by comparison with the west. Islamic scholars developed a thorough knowledge of spherical geometry; they built on the astronomical thesis of Ptolemy the Great; Muhammad al-Battani developed some trigonometrical ratios which we still use today, and he recorded tables of astronomical data that 500 years later Copernicus used in his own deductions to show that the sun was the centre of the universe, not the Earth. The result was that the Islamic world held a position of academic superiority for at least the next seven hundred years.

One of the items translated into Arabic in Baghdad, was the work of Euclid, including *Euclid's Elements.*

The period from around 1100 – 1250 CE was dominated by the religious wars known as the Crusades. Thousands of knights, soldiers and even kings went into battle in the Holy Land in a belief that they would find favour in heaven. Their time in the Middle East brought them into contact with Islamic scholars and they rediscovered the knowledge that had become so much a part of Islamic education and study. It is believed that the Knights Templar captured Islamic builders and shipped them back to Europe and learnt their geometric design processes.

Just as Baghdad had been a centre for the accumulation and translation of knowledge, so, over a period of around thirty years commencing in 1120 CE, in Rome, that same knowledge was accumulated and translated from Arabic into Latin. Euclid was rediscovered in *the west.*

It is believed that the rediscovery of Euclid's Elements, the range of geometric theorems evolved by Islamic scholars, and the capture of Islamic builders by the Knights Templar, provided the basis for one of the great building revolutions that swept Europe from the mid-twelfth century – the French/Gothic style, so much associated with the building of the great cathedrals of the Middle Ages.

Euclid was rediscovered in *the west* about 150 years prior to the setting down of the stonemasons' *old charges,* known as the Regius manuscript, which features the importance of geometry, and Euclid. The Regius manuscript was set down at a time when the great building revolution of the thirteenth and fourteenth centuries was at its height.

The following table shows the major events in approximate chronological order, and eras when the great philosophers lived.

## Table of main cultures, events and people in history

*Note: This table is not intended to show the exact dates when events occurred, but to give a good approximation in the context of the whole.*

| Era -Circa | Event or person | Sumer-Akkad | Egyptian | Greek | Roman | Minoan | Frankish | Arab-Islamic |
|---|---|---|---|---|---|---|---|---|
| 5000 BCE | Foundations of Sumer in Euphrates and Tigris basin | | | | | | | |
| 3500 BCE | Foundations of Ancient Egypt | | | | | | | |
| 3000 BCE | Sumerians have developed a form of writing; understand circle and divide it into 360 degrees; arithmetic based on the numbers 10, 6, 60; basis of time. | | | | | | | |
| 2650 BCE | The first pyramid built by Egyptians | | | | | | | |
| 2550 BCE | Pyramids of Giza built. Show alignment to the cardinal points; understanding of triangle geometry; knowledge of astronomy and sun, moon movement | | | | | | | |
| 2000 BCE | Development of Minoan culture on Crete. | | | | | | | |
| 1600 BCE | Thera (Santorini) volcanic eruption and plagues in Egypt | | | | | | | |
| 1450 BCE | Israelite Exodus from Egypt - Moses | | | | | | | |
| 1000 BCE | Era of Biblical Saul and David | | | | | | | |
| 950 BCE | Solomon's Temple built. Precessional era of Aries. | | | | | | | |
| 850 BCE | Early foundations of Greek culture | | | | | | | |
| 750 BCE | Early foundations of Roman culture | | | | | | | |
| 600 BCE | Early books of Jewish Torah written | | | | | | | |
| 575 BCE | Pythagoras born. Went on develop triangle geometry learning from Egyptians. | | | | | | | |
| 550 BCE | Solomon's Temple destroyed by Babylonian invading army | | | | | | | |
| 450 BCE | Socrates born. Greek philosopher | | | | | | | |
| 425 BCE | Plato, mathematician, philosopher, student of Socrates; Platonic theory; Platonic solids. Big influence on later Christianity. | | | | | | | |
| 380 BCE | Aristotle born. Student of Plato | | | | | | | |

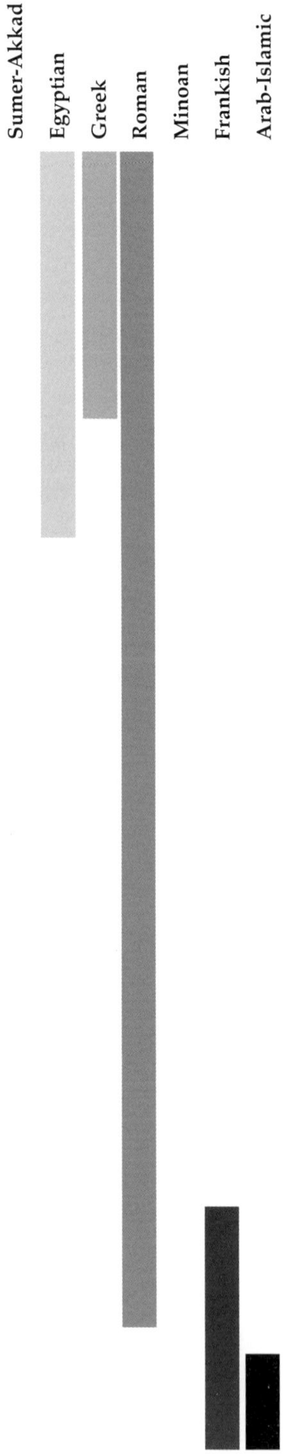
Sumer-Akkad
Egyptian
Greek
Roman
Minoan
Frankish
Arab-Islamic

| | |
|---|---|
| 350 BCE | Alexander the Great |
| 300 BCE | Euclid born. Called the 'Father of Geometry'; developed Euclid's Elements still referenced in geometry. |
| 285 BCE | Archimedes born |
| 225 BCE | Eratosthenes measured the circumference of the world, to great accuracy, using a shadow |
| 145 BCE | Rome absorbs Greece |
| 55 BCE | Julius Caesar makes attempt to invade Britain. Conquest fails. |
| 45 BCE | Julius Caesar, Cleopatra, Mark Anthony. |
| 1 CE | Probable start of precessional era of Pisces. |
| 43 CE | Romans invade and settle in Britain – Emperor Claudius. Roman Britain starts. |
| 70 CE | Jewish uprising against Roman rule |
| 140 CE | Ptolomy lived in Alexandria; studied and wrote about Astronomy, the Earth at the centre of the Universe. |
| 320 CE | Emperor Constantine (the Great) founds Constantinople as the new centre of Roman rule on original Greek territory known as Byzantium. Now Istanbul. |
| 325 CE | Constantine adopts the Christian religion as the main religion of Rome. Formalised at the Council of Nicaea (modern Iznik in Turkey). Nicene Creed developed. |
| 400 CE | Synod agrees which books will be included in Holy Bible, and which left out. |
| 405 CE | Jerome (saint) translates the bible from Hebrew and Greek. Now known as the Vulgate version. |
| 450 CE | Collapse of Roman Empire in the west. Loss of the knowledge of the Greek philosophers. |
| 460 CE | Merovingian (Frankish) dynasty commences with Merovech. |
| 610 CE | The religion of Islam founded. |
| 637 CE | Islamic armies invade and capture Jerusalem. |

| | Sumer-Akkad | Egyptian | Greek | Roman | Minoan | Frankish | Arab-Islamic |
|---|---|---|---|---|---|---|---|

**750 CE** — Carolingian dynasty replaces the Merovingians. (Frankish Empire), starts with Pepin the Short

**768 CE** — Charlemagne becomes King of the Franks; expands kingdom through almost constantly being at war.

**800 CE** — Charlemagne crowned Emperor of the Romans; Holy Roman Empire commenced. Roman rule from Constantinople ceased. The West founded.

**830 CE** — Greek and Hindu mathematical and philosophical texts translated by Islamic scholars in Baghdad, into Arabic.

**875 CE** — Islamic scholar and astronomer, Muhammed al-Battani, developed advanced astronomical understanding; calculated the exact time of one solar year (365 days, 5 hours, 46 minutes, 24 seconds). Credited with developing some mathematical ratios used in trigonometry.

**1097 CE** — Pope Urban II urged the Crusades to recapture Jerusalem as a city important to Christianity.

**1099 CE** — Christian armies capture Jerusalem. Despite subsequent battles, the crusaders are exposed to the advanced ideas that have developed in the Arabic culture, and by Islamic scholars.

**1100 CE** — Works by Greek Philosophers, mathematicians, astronomers, including geometry, translated from Arabic to Latin, commenced. Completed c1125.

**1124 CE** — The first known pointed arch used in building in the western world, later to be known as gothic, was constructed at an abbey in Morienval, north France.

**1137 CE** — Abbot Suger redevelops the western end of St Denis cathedral (the royal church of the Merovingian dynasty) drawing on new features such as the pointed arch.

**1291 CE** — Muslim armies capture Acre and bring the era of the crusades to an end.

## The Ancient of Days – William Blake.
*(Whitworth Art Gallery, Manchester)*
*As reproduced in Freemasons' Guide and Compendium*
*By Bernard E. Jones PAGDC Member of Quator Coronati Lodge*

## St Bernard and Abbot Suger

The *Catholic Encyclopaedia* notes that Bernard was from a high family of the nobility of Burgundy, his parents being Tescelin, lord of Fontaines, and Aleth of Montbard. His mother died when he was in his early twenties and shortly after, in 1113, he, his brothers, his sister and his father all took holy orders. Bernard joined the relatively new Order of Cistercians at a monastery in Citeaux, not far from Dijon, France. Several other young men from Burgundy are recorded as having joined at the same time.

Monastic life in that era dictated that advancement required not only one to demonstrate one's obvious religious devotion, but also to receive the approbation of ones fellow monks, especially the Abbot. Bernard was obviously singled out at an early stage in his career, because just two years after joining the monastery at Citeaux, he was sent, with twelve other monks, to form a new abbey at Clairvaux. Bernard would thereafter be associated with that monastery, St Bernard of Clairvaux.

The area of land given for the monastery at Clairvaux was donated by the Count of Champagne who had been encouraged to do this by one of his vassals, Hughes de Payns. Two years later, an exhausted Bernard made his way to a small town which is, today, just on the Italian side of the border between France and Italy, in a mountainous region just north of the Mediterranean coast. That town is called Seborga. According to records in that town, a group of knights met with Bernard, and were referred to as *Bernard knights*. According to the Seborga information, at the time he was joining the monastery at Citeaux, Bernard had sent two other men, Gondemar and Rossal, to Seborga, *"...in order to protect the Great Secret..."*. Bernard arrived in Seborga four years after he had dispatched Gondemar and Rossal on their mission. It must have been a very big secret. In all there were nine knights that met at Seborga, including Count Hughes de Champagne, he who had given land for the monastic settlement at Clairvaux; Hughes de Payns, who had encouraged the donation of the Clairvaux land; and Andre de Montbar, a possible relative of Bernard's mother. This group of nine knights were ordained as *'the Poor Militia of Christ'*, later to be known as The Poor Soldiers of Christ and the Temple of Solomon – *the Knights Templar*. This group of knights then travelled on to Jerusalem and did not return until 1127, where they were met again in Seborga, by Bernard, who then set about composing the *rule* (constitutions) of the Knights Templar. In the following year 1128, he attended the *Council of Troyes* where the Templars were formally acknowledged and granted the protection of the Pope. From then on, their growth, wealth, power and influence, was astonishing. As another writer notes:

> *"They [the original nine knights] had gone west with nothing and came back with a Papal Rule, money, objects, landed wealth and no less than 300 recruited noblemen..."*[39]

All this was taking place within the first few years of the translation of the ancient texts, including those of Euclid, from Arabic into Latin, in Rome.

At this time, the most significant and influential monastic community in France was Cluny Abbey. They thought themselves to be the premier monastic community and superior to the Cistercian Order to which Bernard had been admitted. Bernard wrote two documents that the monks of Cluny took to be a slight against them and the fervour of their devotions. This resulted in a malicious campaign against Bernard who was accused of being a *troublesome monk* who *meddled in affairs that were nothing to do with him*[40]. This led to Bernard issuing what became known as his *apology*, which not only took the heat out of the matter but also won him many friends in the Church. One of those friends was a former Cluny monk, the Abbot of St Denis, a man named *Suger*.

Suger is believed to have been born around 1080 and entered the monastic orders when he was around twenty years of age. He had previously been at the school attached to St Denis, and had as a fellow student, the future King of France, Louis VI. Suger and Louis remained firm friends, with Suger being held in such high esteem that when Louis went off to the second crusade, Suger was appointed as *regent of the country,* effectively ruling in the absence of the king. At around the age of thirty-five, in 1118, he was asked to take up a post in Rome. This was around the time when the translation of the ancient texts was at its height; the first nine knights who were to form the Knights Templar were setting out for Jerusalem, having been met in Seborga by the Abbot of Clairvaux, Bernard. On his return from Rome, Suger was appointed Abbot of St Denis in 1122. The Order of the Knights Templar was officially formed a few years later in 1128.

Suger, by this time, clearly had the text of Euclid's Elements at his disposal. In 1125 the construction of an ambulatory at the monastery in Morienval, not far north of the monastery at St Denis, was commenced, the first to use the pointed arch design and ribbed vaulting which we now refer to as being associated with the *gothic* style, although it was originally known as the *French style.* In 1130, Suger began redeveloping the cathedral of St Denis, in the *French/gothic* style, with work on the west end of the building.

In that same year, a schism had occurred at the heart of the church; it had appointed two popes, Innocent II and Anacletus II. The latter initially gained the upper hand and forced Innocent II into exile in France. The king of France called a meeting of bishops and such was the esteem with which Bernard was then held, that he was not only asked to attend the meeting, but also to act as judge to decide which of the two popes should receive favour. Bernard sided with Innocent II, an act that ensured that Bernard would rise to the pinnacles of esteem amongst the Church power brokers. Bernard travelled extensively with Innocent II, including a visit to St Denis, where the pope could see first hand the new work and design concept that Suger was constructing. From there they went on to Clairvaux, the monastery founded by Bernard on lands donated by the leading members of the Knights Templar. When Innocent II arrived at Clairvaux, the Catholic Encyclopaedia states that *"...his reception was of a simple and purely religious character..."*[41]

The diagram, opposite, shows the interfaces that may have existed between the various elements that led to the rediscovery of Euclid's

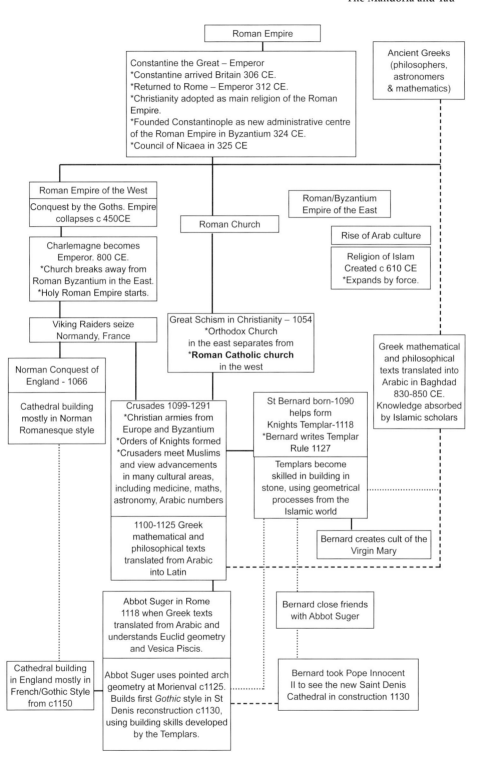

Roman Empire

Constantine the Great – Emperor
*Constantine arrived Britain 306 CE.
*Returned to Rome – Emperor 312 CE.
*Christianity adopted as main religion of the Roman Empire.
*Founded Constantinople as new administrative centre of the Roman Empire in Byzantium 324 CE.
*Council of Nicaea in 325 CE

Ancient Greeks (philosophers, astronomers & mathematics)

Roman Empire of the West
Conquest by the Goths. Empire collapses c 450CE

Roman/Byzantium Empire of the East

Roman Church

Rise of Arab culture

Religion of Islam Created c 610 CE
*Expands by force.

Charlemagne becomes Emperor. 800 CE.
*Church breaks away from Roman Byzantium in the East.
*Holy Roman Empire starts.

Viking Raiders seize Normandy, France

Great Schism in Christianity – 1054
*Orthodox Church in the east separates from
**Roman Catholic church** in the west

Greek mathematical and philosophical texts translated into Arabic in Baghdad 830-850 CE. Knowledge absorbed by Islamic scholars

Norman Conquest of England - 1066

Cathedral building mostly in Norman Romanesque style

Crusades 1099-1291
*Christian armies from Europe and Byzantium
*Orders of Knights formed
*Crusaders meet Muslims and view advancements in many cultural areas, including medicine, maths, astronomy, Arabic numbers

St Bernard born-1090 helps form
Knights Templar-1118
*Bernard writes Templar Rule 1127

Templars become skilled in building in stone, using geometrical processes from the Islamic world

1100-1125 Greek mathematical and philosophical texts translated from Arabic into Latin

Bernard creates cult of the Virgin Mary

Abbot Suger in Rome 1118 when Greek texts translated from Arabic and understands Euclid geometry and Vesica Piscis.

Bernard close friends with Abbot Suger

Cathedral building in England mostly in French/Gothic Style from c1150

Abbot Suger uses pointed arch geometry at Morienval c1125. Builds first *Gothic* style in St Denis reconstruction c1130, using building skills developed by the Templars.

Bernard took Pope Innocent II to see the new Saint Denis Cathedral in construction 1130

Elements, and the philosophies of the ancient world, through to the development of gothic architecture and the first major implementation by Suger at the cathedral of St Denis, just to the north of Paris.

In his lifetime, Bernard also achieved another astonishing feat. He is credited with encouraging the cult of the Virgin Mary. Although Mary, as mother of Jesus, had always been an integral part of the Christian story, it is widely held that for the first one thousand years of the existence of Christianity, Mary was an adjunct to the doctrine. Mary's rise to prominence is credited to the Cistercian Order founded at Citeaux, the monastery that Bernard was admitted to. The Cistercians adopted Mary as a patron saint, after which, Bernard began preaching more about her and her virtues, the result of which was the rapid ascension of Mary as a character within the Catholic dogma.

Bernard's part in the promotion of Mary is underlined by a statue that sits on the Charles Bridge in Prague. Around the time of Bernard's life, Prague was a major centre and residence for the Holy Roman Emperors, including Charles IV, who lived at the same time as Bernard, was crowned King of Burgundy (Bernard's family were nobles of Burgundy), King of the Romans and Holy Roman Emperor. In view of the eminence that Bernard had reached, and the interface he would have had with many of the ruling elite of the time, it is highly likely that the future King of Burgundy was known to him. The Charles Bridge, which for hundreds of years was the only one across the river Vltava, and connected the Castle with the old town of Prague, was commenced in 1157, shortly after Bernard died.

Bernard died in 1153.

According to the *Catholic Encyclopedia* in his lifetime he was responsible for the:

> "...founding of one hundred and sixty-three monasteries across Europe; at his death they number three hundred and forty three. He was the first Cistercian monk placed on the calendar of saints and was canonised by Alexander III, 18 January 1174. Pope Pius VIII bestowed on him the title of Doctor of the Church. The Cistercians honour him as only the founders of orders are honoured, because of the wonderful and widespread activity which he gave to the Order of Citeaux."[42]

The above image is of St Bernard in praise of the Virgin Mary, a sculpture on the Charles Bridge in Prague, Czech Republic. *K. L. Gest*

*Author's Note:*
*Reference is made above and in the following pages to the Gothic style of architecture. Until around the 17th century, it seems that the pointed arch and other characteristics that typify this design style was known as the French style. The early days of the Roman Christian Church were set against the background of the decline in the Roman Empire, and the attacks on it by the forces of the Goths and Visigoths resulted in them being characterised as Barbarians and Pagans, and as such to be treated with contempt, offering little to recommend them. Thus the term gothic came into use as a disparaging terminology to discredit some of the styles of architecture that had evolved in the previous centuries.*

# Chapter 8

# THE BUILDERS IN STONE

We have already noted that the early English gilds were founded in Saxon times, and became a feature of Anglo-Saxon life as a facility of community self-help and charity, for protection and security. In that process we also noted that such gilds are traceable as far back as King Ina (AD 688 – 725), who, incidentally, is believed to have been a founder of Glastonbury Abbey. The legend of King Ina is that he was from Somerton in Somerset, and ruled as King of Wessex prior to King Alfred. Ina was in the southwest of England at a time when something else was happening in the northeast.

### St Benedict Biscop
Just outside Newcastle on the River Tyne is the modern town of Jarrow. Today it is an area dominated by heavy industry, but around two hundred and fifty years after the Romans left Britain, it was the site of a monastery dedicated to St Paul. Not far away was a second monastery at Monkwearmouth (now part of Sunderland), named after St. Peter. According to tradition, around the year 680 CE, a small boy was entered by his family to the care of the monastery. He grew to pass into history known as St. Bede – the Venerable Bede (c 673 – 735 CE).

There is some suggestion that Bede was a son of noble birth, and being entrusted to the monastery was probably for the purposes of gaining an education, not necessarily with the final objective of a life in the clergy. Yet, he later took Orders and remained a monk at Wearmouth and Jarrow for the rest of his life and probably travelled no further than about 70 miles from the monastery. Despite that, he clearly amassed a great deal of information and knowledge from a variety of sources, as during his lifetime he wrote some 60 books, most of which still survive. Not only was he a great scholar such that he has been credited with the title of being the Father of English History, but he was clearly a great thinker and observer, and, what today we would call, a scientist. Bede discovered the relationship between the phases of the moon and the movement of the tides, and it was he that developed the *Anno Domini (AD)* calendar dating system; he developed an understanding of why the length of the days vary with the seasons because of the movement and influence derived from the spherical nature of the Earth, and much more. His tomb is in Durham Cathedral.

When Bede entered the monastic life, his first Abbot was a man named Benedict Biscop, who, tradition has it, was also descended from a noble family. Further tradition has it, that Biscop may have served the King of Northumbria, King Oswig. For reasons that are unclear, Biscop, when in his mid-twenties, decided to visit Rome in company with a friend named Wilfrid (later St. Wilfrid) who was also from a noble family. Wilfrid had attended the Synod of Whitby in 664 CE, at which the Celtic Christian community agreed to accept the dogma espoused by Rome, thereby creating a uniform dogma of the Christian faith in England. Wilfrid also backed the Catholic way of calculating the date of Easter. This process was agreed at the Council of Nicaea in 325 CE. Easter is not set to a specific calendar date, but is a reflection of the movement of the earth and moon around the sun, and is deemed to be the first Sunday after the first full moon following the Spring Equinox in the northern Hemisphere, Autumn Equinox in the Southern Hemisphere.

Biscop was clearly impressed by what he saw and experienced in Rome, because it wasn't long after his return to England that he set off again, not only visiting Rome, but also spending time at other locations en route. By the time he returned to the northeast of England he was around forty years of age. In the meantime King Oswig had died and his son, EcgFrith had assumed the throne. In 674 CE, EcgFrith granted Biscop some land at Wearmouth on which to build a monastery. Influenced undoubtably by what he saw in Rome and on his journeys, Biscop decided to build the monastery of stone.

Just to the north of the sprawling urban mass of modern-day Paris, is the cathedral of St Denis. The foundations of the cathedral are built on the remains of a church that was built in the Merovingian era, and still holds tombs of important people from that dynasty (c 400 – 750 CE). If Biscop took that route to Rome, it is difficult to imagine that he would not have visited that church and its associated monastery.

Having secured the land, Biscop went back to Francia (this was the area we now know as France and the Low Countries) and brought back masons who could build in the Romanesque style; glaziers to make windows out of glass, the first such windows ever used in Britain, and, according to the Catholic Encyclopaedia, were viewed as being quite a novelty. Hence, this became the first known ecclesiastical building constructed from stone in England.

Bede would have been around 10 years of age when construction of the church was undertaken, and there has, in the past, been some speculation that he may have assisted with the work, as no doubt all the monks did. Thirteen hundred years later, St Peter's church in Wearmouth, still stands, and is in regular use.

The main point in drawing attention to Benedict Biscop is that it is quite clear from his actions, that by bringing masons across to north-east England from Francia (France), in the late seventh century, it suggested that such skills were not known, or were very rare, in England at that time. Plus, there is the additional feature about the glass windows – a great novelty.

### More stone masonry developments

The Wearmouth monastic community was not the only one in the area. Some fifty miles north, one comes to the island of Lindisfarne. A Celtic Christian community had been founded there by Aidan (later known as St Aidan) a few decades prior to the foundations of the Wearmouth monastery. Clearly at its founding it is unlikely to have been built of stone, the island did not have it in sufficient abundance. What is more, Biscop had to import the skills for his own development which is recorded as being *the first in stone*. Perhaps influenced by Biscop's achievements, the monastery on Lindisfarne followed. A visit there, shows there were two types of prominent architecture, Romanesque and French styles. The French style did not commence until long after the Norman Conquest, and the widespread use of Romanesque in such buildings did not emerge until around the ninth century. So Lindisfarne and Wearmouth were clearly originally built in other materials. We get some idea of what this may have consisted of from Bamburgh Castle, just a short distance from both monasteries. It seems that around 550 CE the outer fortifications were reinforced using timber stakes in the form of a stockade, whilst the buildings within the stockade were also fashioned from timber.[43]

One of the oldest churches in England, is stated to be St. Martin's, in Canterbury. Tradition has it that when Augustine (Austin the monk) first came to England in 597 CE, the church was already standing on the site and was being used as the personal chapel of Queen Bertha of Kent. Bertha was a princess from within the Frankish community, across the English Channel, so it is not inconceivable that builders had come from there to erect that church for her. King Ethelbert is believed to have given this church to Augustine as the base from which he developed his missionary enterprise in England. The church, as we see it today, has clearly been through many phases of modification. Notwithstanding that, it contains many Roman made bricks with an out shell mainly of flint. This, though, is not fashioned stone. Nearby, however, are the ruins of St Augustine's Abbey. Whilst Augustine is believed to have laid the foundations of the Abbey, it was built in the Romanesque style suggesting it was built in that way some time after Augustine had departed from the country.

The second oldest cathedral in Britain is that at Rochester, Kent. It traces its foundations to the year 604 CE, just six years after Augustine arrived. The main part of what we see today was built after the Norman Conquest, by Bishop Gundulf, who also built the Tower of London. The earlier section of the cathedral is in the Romanesque style, predating 1066 CE. As the Romanesque style was not prominent until around the eighth century, it is unlikely that intricate stone-craft would have been used in the earlier work.

*The interior of Rochester Cathedral clearly showing the point at which new building work was undertaken, and the architectural style changed from Romanesque to French style/gothic. K.L. Gest*

In the village of Sompting, West Sussex, there stands a church which was built in the eighth century. It uses flint for the exterior walls, a construction material that was natural and widely used in this area. More significantly, it has the only remaining Rhenish tower in England. At one stage it was an asset of the Knights Templar but when they were disbanded, it reverted to the Order of St John, and retains a connection with that Order today. Yet again, it is a structure that does not use quarried stone.

*Sompting Church with its eighth century Rhenish tower. K.L. Gest*

Canterbury Cathedral was rebuilt after the Norman Conquest by the French Archbishop *Lefranc*e in 1070-1077, replacing the former Saxon edifice that stood on that site. Three hundred years later in 1377, the *Lefranc* nave of the structure was demolished and replaced by the existing structure, which also incorporated the French/gothic style.

Peterborough Cathedral had been destroyed by Viking invaders in 870, and was rebuilt in 1069. It was then destroyed by fire in 1116 and was rebuilt again over a forty-year period commencing in 1118.

In the same time period, York Minster was destroyed by fire in 1069 and was rebuilt by Thomas of Bayeux, who had been appointed as Archbishop, between 1080 and 1100. It was again damaged by fire, after which over the next three hundred years it was enlarged and modified several times.

What this suggests is that there were stonemasons or people who could cut and fashion stone between say 700 – 1000 CE, but what is not clear is whether they were Anglo-Saxon locals, or in the main, from places like France, brought over to do a job. Neither can we ignore the possibility/probability that the structures were mostly monastic or ecclesiastical buildings, or that they may have been substantially built by the monks themselves, rather than specialist hired-in knowledge.

From around 1000 – 1350, was the era when most of the great cathedrals of Europe were built or extended. Several subsequently suffered fire damage having been struck by lightning, and, from around 1150, in rebuilding them, such work was gradually undertaken in the French/gothic style, as its advantages came to be understood.

### The Knights Templar – the builder warriors

The period of religious wars in the Middle East, known as the *Crusades,* commenced in 1097, and Jerusalem was captured by Christian forces in 1099. Shortly afterwards, the monks who had maintained the Holy Sepulchre became known as *The Knights of the Holy Sepulchre,* an Order of Augustine monks that lasted for some two hundred years before being integrated with the Knights Hospitaller (Order of St John). Around this time, a small group of French Knights arrived in Jerusalem, and within a few years had grown into a strong and wealthy organisation that we know as the Knights Templar. Their origins are traced to 1118 and they received their *rule* in 1128 at the Council of Troyes. Defined as warrior-monks, they not only participated in military actions in the Holy land, but they were builders of many churches, castles, bridges, fortified houses, and barns. The massive structures they produced, and the intricacy of some of the stone carving to be found in their structures across Europe, is a demonstration of the skill, knowledge and organisation that the stonemasons involved had achieved.

In Cambridge, just across the street from one of the major colleges of Cambridge University, is a small round church. For many years this has been referred to as having been built by the Templars, largely because it is similar to other such churches, like the Temple Church in London, which a positively identified with them. Some individuals claim this little church was built by the Knights Templar around the year 1130. Others claim it was built by the *fraternity of the Holy Sepulchre* around the year 1101. The *Knights of the Holy Sepulchre* certainly existed in Jerusalem in 1101 but there is some doubt that they existed in Britain at that time. Irrespective of the date and the fraternity that built it, it is a fascinating building constructed of stone, including eight very strong circular columns inside, set on a circle about half the diameter of that of the outer walls. The space created forms a nave and ambulatory. The usual description of the design is that it replicates the concept of the Holy Sepulchre in Jerusalem. It is estimated that at one time there were about fifty round Templar churches in England, all built within the first one hundred years of the founding of the Order. Today just four such churches remain. To build around fifty such structures demands an incredible commitment to a concept and the provision of skilled men and materials to achieve the end result.

There is little knowledge about the individuals who built the round church in Cambridge, or where they came from, but keeping in mind that the construction was just a few decades after the Norman Conquest, it suggests that maybe the skills were imported from France. The Knights Templar organisation was started by knights from France, which remained the principal country in which its operations were based for most of the twelfth and thirteenth centuries.

The small round church in Cambridge was built at about the time that the great revolution in building with stone, the pointed arch of the French/gothic style, was devised, and it is not inconceivable that the Knights Templar were involved with its development.

The Templars were particularly prominent during the later half of the twelfth century and through the whole of the thirteenth century. They built an incredible array of castles, fortified Manor houses and preceptories, across Europe and the Middle East. Fighting Knights were usually based in the Holy Land but those that were too old to play a part in such events, and those that were just not capable of being part of their front-line army, were involved in the administration of the Order. The Order had a high demand for horses to transport people and goods, as well as for fighting. Many horses were killed in the battles to secure the Holy Land. There was also a need to supply food and money, which may have been obtained from their farming activities. They were extremely efficient in their farming methods, as outlined in the earlier observations in the chapter about the religious guild known as the Holy Trinity at Sleaford, and the connection to Temple Bruer. They built massive barns for the storage of harvested produce, which were either fully completed in stone or half stone half-timber. Examples of their skill, and the thought that went into the building of such storage facilities, can be still be seen in two wonderful barns that have survived the passage of time, and were built at Temple Cressing in the county of Essex.

There are also records that show that the Knights Templar played a considerable role in financing the building or alteration/extension to existing large abbey churches that, as a result, became cathedrals.

One of the other influences in the twelfth and thirteenth centuries was the growth in religious Orders and Orders of knighthood dedicated to supporting the religious wars that were taking place in the Holy land; the Order of St John being just one to mention, in addition to the Knights Templar. They all sought their own fortified premises and monastic housings. And they were invariably built with stone.

## The builder masons

Throughout the era of the Knights Templar, demands for the skills of the masons would have been enormous. Demands for the associated crafts, such as carpenters, would also have been high. Nearly all the major cathedrals in Britain and continental Europe, were built in this same period, projects that lasted up to 100 years each, that's the equivalent of five generations, using a time span of twenty years as a definition of a generation in that era. Thus, it is reasonable to assume, that around such areas where there were large and long-term projects, communities would have been reasonably stable, with sons following fathers into the various trades.

Once there was a high installed base of properties built in stone, there would, with the passing of time, have been the need for maintenance as foundations and walls settled. As monasteries grew, plans made in one era may have been outgrown in another, designs were found not to work in practice despite having been carefully conceived many years earlier, so the result would be a need for modification and and/or extension. These would in the main be smaller projects of shorter duration.

This suggests a high level of new build activity of the type in which stonemasons would have been very involved, in the era of approx 1100–1350 CE, a period of some two hundred years. Much of this new work would have involved the introduction of the French/gothic style of arch construction. It was also an era when kings of England were still of Norman origin, and lived for the most part, in northern France, and hence there would still have been considerable French/Norman influence in the building process.

The Knights Templar were substantially based there as well. So it seems a reasonable leap of faith, supported in some cases by cathedral records at least, to find that the primary master mason in a building project was from France. In addition, most of the Archbishops and Bishops in Britain also still had strong French connections. It was the monastic communities, and taxes they imposed, that resulted in the money being provided to meet such construction costs. Hence we find such individuals as Bishop Gundulf of Rochester, or William de Wykeham, Bishop of Winchester, being named as *builders* whereas they were the financiers, and in today's language, probably the project directors who conceived or authorised a plan and oversaw the progress. It would probably have fallen to the master mason on the site, to take project management responsibility for ensuring the flow of materials, the number of craftsmen needed and the skill levels required, the quality of the work that was produced, the scheduling of which part of the works had priority over others, and of course, payment of the workers. It would have been the bishops and the master masons that understood the Euclidian geometry that was needed and used in the development of the French/gothic style.

Around 1350 the country was ravaged by a plague known as the Black Death. Monasteries, priories and abbeys, monks and nuns, bishops, master masons, carpenters, merchants, anyone, was at risk of infection. The population of Europe was substantially reduced; in some areas everyone died, in others half died; few communities escaped some measure of affliction. Against this background, after about 1360 the volume of new build work would have inevitably declined and the available work was likely to have been more associated with maintenance and repair. Such work does not usually require a great deal of knowledge of geometry. Work would not have been so easily come by for the stonemasons, and as such, a high proportion of them became more itinerant as they searched for work. This state of affairs would likely have lasted for about one hundred years.

There is one other factor to consider. In an area where there was a big project requiring lots of craftsmen, a local guild probably existed to regulate the works. The hours of daylight would have been precious for doing the physical work and so guild/community meetings or gatherings would take place at the end of the day, emergencies excepting, when they may have been earlier.

As the fourteenth century came to an end, we entered yet another new era. The power of the Church based in Rome was challenged by a new movement we call Protestantism. Out of that came a period when new build work almost ceases. Henry VIII broke with the Church in Rome, established himself as the head of the Church of England, distanced himself, and the country, from the influence of the pope; the monasteries, priories and associated abbeys were closed. Now the skills of the stonemason were employed in the demolition of the work their forebears and brethren of earlier generations had erected.

## The influence of ancient Greece and Rome returns

Following the collapse of the Roman Empire in the west, Europe descended into a period of almost endless conflicts between various families and factions within families, all seeking to be kings and rulers. Britain was attacked by the Danes, Angles and Vikings in the east, and in the south, the Saxons claimed their area of the country. Through this period, the knowledge of the ancient architectural processes that had been the enlightened domains of the ancient Greeks and Romans was lost.

In the latter stages of the era we define as BCE – Before the Common Era - a Roman architect by the name of Marcus Vitruvius, produced a series of works that outlined processes and methodologies that were useful in the design and proportion of what today we consider to be a classical style. These works are known as the *Ten Books of Architecture*. Vitruvius was also a great engineer and devised several instruments used for surveying, and as aids in construction. For around five hundred years from 700-1200 CE, important buildings using stone were, in the main, constructed to a style known as Romanesque, with some Rhenish style as well, especially in Europe. The result was heavy and dark interiors.

In Italy, at a time that coincided with the reign of Henry V, the works of Vitruvius came to light again. A man by the name of *Gian Francesco Poggio Bracciolini* is credited with having found a copy of Vitruvius's work in the year 1414. Biographies of his life state that from an early age he studied Latin and Greek in Rome and became proficient at copying manuscripts, noting that at that time the printing press had still to make its mark. He came to the notice of prominent Florentines, and, at the age of twenty-one years was admitted to the *Arte dei giudici e notai* - Notaries guild. He was soon absorbed into the world of the Catholic Church, working for cardinals and bishops and the papal offices, although he never became a member of the ecclesiastical establishment by taking holy orders. Through this connection with the Church, he had access to the libraries of many of the oldest and more famous monasteries, and it was in such libraries that he found copies of ancient Greek philosophical documents, and the works of Vitruvius. A copy of Vitruvius's work was apparently published in Rome in 1486, but it was around one hundred years after its rediscovery before copies in other languages became available; the first English translation is quoted to have been in 1543.

A year after Vitruvius was first published in Rome, Leonardo da Vinci is believed to have made a study of it. It was in that year that he produced his famous drawing of Vitruvian Man, based on the text of Vitruvius's work and the subject of proportion together with connections to the natural world.

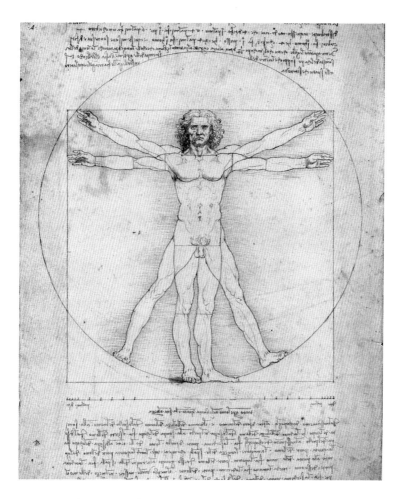

Vetruvian Man by Leonardo da Vinci

A text relating to the proportions reads:

*"For the human body is so designed by nature that the face, from the chin to the top of the forehead and the lowest roots of the hair, is a tenth part of the whole height; the open hand from the wrist to the tip of the middle finger is just the same; the head from the chin to the crown is an eighth, and with the neck and shoulder from the top of*

*the breast to the lowest roots of the hair is a sixth; from the middle of the breast to the summit of the crown is a fourth. If we take the height of the face itself, the distance from the bottom of the chin to the under side of the nostrils is one third of it; the nose from the under side of the nostrils to a line between the eyebrows is the same; from there to the lowest roots of the hair is also a third, comprising the forehead. The length of the foot is one sixth of the height of the body; of the forearm, one fourth; and the breadth of the breast is also one fourth. The other members, too, have their own symmetrical proportions, and it was by employing them that the famous painters and sculptors of antiquity attained to great and endless renown. Similarly, in the members of a temple there ought to be the greatest harmony in the symmetrical relations of the different parts to the general magnitude of the whole. Then again, in the human body the central point is naturally the navel. For if a man be placed flat on his back, with his hands and feet extended, and a pair of compasses centred at his navel, the fingers and toes of his two hands and feet will touch the circumference of a circle described therefrom. And just as the human body yields a circular outline, so too a square figure may be found from it. For if we measure the distance from the soles of the feet to the top of the head, and then apply that measure to the outstretched arms, the breadth will be found to be the same as the height, as in the case of plane surfaces which are perfectly square."[44]*

The images of both the square and circle in Vitruvian man have different centres, but the point at which they touch in the region of the outstretched hands, is very close to the geometric position for the development of the *golden ratio* or *divine proportion* considered as the perfection of proportion, and produced geometrically using a square and circle in a slightly different way. (This will be shown later in the book).

### The Renaissance

The Renaissance is often quoted as having commenced towards the end of the fourteenth century, the era in which the *Regius Manuscript* is believed to have been written, and extended to the seventeenth century. The years of the religious wars known as the *Crusades* had come to an end. A number of the philosophical works of the Greeks had been translated from Arabic into Latin and were, no doubt, being picked up and studied throughout Europe, especially in the ecclesiastical world and the early universities that had developed across Europe. This would have included the universities at Oxford and Cambridge, and the schools that were still attached to major cathedrals. The works of Vitruvius had been rediscovered and with it a renewed interest in the architectural features developed by Greece and Rome

The renaissance is broadly a two hundred year period in which a number of influences emerged that brought about an interest in the philosophies and works of ancient Greece and Rome. The point is made, however, by various writers, that it was an interest that was kindled and studied by a relatively small elite that had the time, wealth and education to devote to appreciation of what was unfolding. For the majority of the citizens of the western world, life was still hard, uncertain and had changed little in hundreds of years. It was for them still the Dark Ages. It was an era of religious turmoil with the advance of the Protestants; kings who still promoted wars in an effort to secure territory and power, and expected ill pressed citizens to fight in such wars.

It was also an era in which, those who had the resources, laid the foundations for a period of profound change that followed. In our story, it involves two more men – Andrea Palladio in Italy and Inigo Jones in England.

Palladio (1508 – 1580) is described as being an Italian Renaissance architect whose main works were built in northern Italy. He was, apparently greatly influenced by Vitruvius, a study of the liberal arts, and classic buildings that he found in ruins in Rome. Through his designs he has come to be regarded as the most influential individual in Western European architecture of the renaissance period, and thereafter, through a series of studies that were published entitled *The Four Books of Architecture*.

Inigo Jones (1573 – 1652) is often described as the first and greatest of the English architects that promoted the Renaissance-style. He did not come from a privileged background. He went to Italy and there he was influenced by the designs of Palladio, as well as those of the classical era. On return to England he was clearly identified as having talent, and may well have made influential connections on his journey, because he was first employed in designing stage settings and theatrical style costumes at the court of James I/James VI a few years after the death of Queen Elizabeth I. By the age of forty, he had made such a name for himself that he was appointed as Surveyor-General of the Kings Works.

Although he undertook several smaller development projects, his first major work was to design and build the *Queen's House* in Greenwich, for which he received the design commission in 1616. Built in a classical style, it incorporates a wonderful spiral staircase, cantilevered from the walls, and reflecting the spiral of the golden ratio, a feature of what today is called *sacred geometry*. A visitor document at the *Queen's House* notes that when viewed in our modern times of high-rise glass and steel buildings, the design may seem plain, but when it was built *it was regarded as sensational*.

The Banqueting House in Whitehall, London was the next project that, in

1619, Inigo Jones was commissioned to design on behalf of James I, following a fire that had destroyed the previous venue. It was from this building that, in January 1649, Charles I stepped onto the scaffold for his execution. Inigo Jones' design also contains an interesting feature that is not immediately obvious to the casual observer – a feature that will be passed over by many a visitor, even when they read it in literature. It is that the main hall is based on the dimensions of the *double cube,* being 110 ft long x 55 feet x 55 feet.[45] This room also features a wonderful ceiling painted by Reubens, *an allegory,* regarded by historians as one of Reuben's finest works.

Inigo Jones' introduction of the classical style of architecture to England, its acclaim, and his elevation to the position of Surveyor-General, resulted in design commissions being awarded by a number of aristocrats and wealthy landowners. In the first edition of *Anderson's Constitution of Free- masons,* he lists thirty-six such buildings undertaken in the renaissance style, of which thirteen were by Inigo Jones. Many of the buildings listed by Anderson are, today, regarded as national treasures.[46]

*An original 1723 edition of Anderson's Constitutions. K.L. Gest*

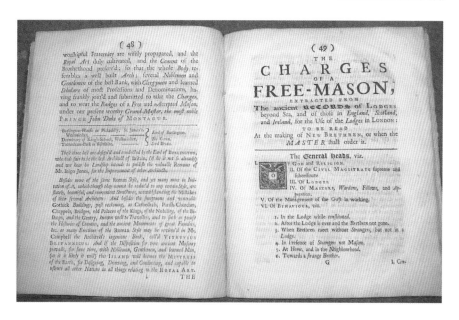

*Pages showing the start of the section dealing with the charges, and part of a list of 36 buildings undertaken in the Renaissance classical style, starting with the Queen's House, Greenwich. K.L. Gest*

tain'd

*It were endless to recount and describe the many curious Roman Buildings in Great-Britain alone, erected since the Revival of Roman Masonry; of which a few may be here mention'd, besides those already spoken of, viz.*

| | | |
|---|---|---|
| The QUEEN's House at Greenwich, | —— | Belonging to the Crown. |
| The great Gallery in Somerset-Gardens, | —— | The Crown. |
| Gunnersbury-House near Brentford, Middlesex, | | { Possess'd by the Duke of { Queensbury. |
| Lindsay-House in Lincoln's-Inn-Fields, | —— | Duke of Ancaster. |
| York-Stairs at the Thames in York-Buildings. | | |
| St. Paul's-Church in Covent-Garden, with its glorious Portico. | | |
| The Building and Piazza of Covent-Garden, | — | Duke of Bedford. |
| Wilton-Castle in Wiltshire, | —— | — Earl of Pembroke. |
| Castle-Ashby in Northamptonshire, | —— | — Earl of Strafford. |
| Stoke-Park in ditto, | —— —— | —— |
| Wing-House in Bedfordshire, | —— | Arundel Esq: |
| Chevening-House in Kent, | —— | Hon. Wm. Stanhope Esq; |
| Ambrose-Bury in Wiltshire, | —— | Earl Stanhope. |
| | | Lord Carleton. |

*All design'd by the incomparable INIGO JONES, and most of them conducted by him, or by his Son-in-Law Mr. Web, according to Mr. Jones's Designs.*

*Besides many more conducted by other Architects, influenc'd by the same happy Genius; such as,*

Bow-Church Steeple in Cheapside, —— —— ....

*An enlarged view of the part of the page that starts the list of Renaissance buildings. K.L.Gest*

## Wonderful buildings

Inigo Jones lived through most of the English Civil War that deposed Charles I. It was a period when almost no major new construction work was commissioned. The restoration of the monarchy with Charles II in 1660, ushered in the era known as the *enlightenment*. Initially work for stonemasons would have been repairing damage caused by the war, although some former castles and fortifications were destroyed beyond recovery. Then came the plague of 1665 followed by the Great Fire of London in 1666. The reconstruction of London brought new opportunities for skilled masons. In his Constitutions, Dr Anderson comments:

> "...the City of London erected the famous Monument, where the Great Fire began, all of solid stone, 202 foot high from the ground, a pillar of the Dorick Order, 15 foot diameter...and is the highest column we know upon the Earth..."

The building of this column would have involved the London Company of Masons, and was started in 1671 and completed in 1677. Anderson makes other observations:

> "In this time also [Charles II] the Society of Merchant Venturers rebuilt the Royal Exchange of London ...all of stone, after the Roman style, the finest structure of that use in Europe..."

The Royal Exchange had been originally built in the reign of Elizabeth I as a centre for commerce in London, in effect a place where merchants met to do business. The replacement mentioned by Anderson was destroyed in a separate fire in 1838 and replaced by the existing building which retains much of the character of the previous Exchange.

*Image – the Royal Exchange London – in the classical style. K.L. Gest*

Following the revolution of 1688 when William of Orange was invited to take the throne of England, the hospitals at Greenwich and Chelsea were completed, as was the palace at Hampton Court. Anderson adds:

> *"…the bright example of that glorious prince, (who some reckoned a Free-Mason) did influence the nobility, the gentry, the wealthy and the Learned of Great Britain, to affect much the Augustan stile."*
> *[Renaissance architecture]*

All of this leads up to the period just prior to when four lodges, based in London, supposedly met and formed the basis of the Grand Lodges of England in 1717.

Where did these Lodges come from?

# Chapter 9

## LODGES PRIOR TO 1717

For many years, the official line taken by the United Grand Lodge of England (UGLE) had been that freemasonry did not exist prior to 1717, and that it had been created as a gentleman's club. In the latter years of the twentieth century, this opinion was challenged by several eminent and popular writers, who highlighted one significant fact. Masonic literature has long claimed that Elias Ashmole was made a Free-Mason some sixty years prior the Grand Lodge of England being formed, and that Grand Lodge existed one hundred years prior to the formation of UGLE. In an informative and promotional video/film made in the mid 1980s under the authority of the UGLE, it notes that Sir Robert Moray was made a Mason during the English Civil War, possibly at Newcastle. Sir Robert Moray and Elias Ashmole were later founding members of the Royal Society. Furthermore, Ashmole and Moray were Free Masons during the period when Inigo Jones was Surveyor-General and renaissance architecture, introduced to England by him, was just beginning to flourish.

In his book, *The Invisible College*, the well-known writer and Freemason, Dr Robert Lomas, traces the life of Sir Robert Moray and questions the Newcastle Masonic connection. He also points out that when the Royal Society was founded in November 1660, of the twelve founding members, eleven were Freemasons.

### The early Free Masons – Elias Ashmole

Elias Ashmole was born in Lichfield in May 1617. Ashmole's family were well connected. His father was a saddler. A relative of his mother was Sir James Pagit, who was a Baron of the Exchequer of Pleas – a high legal office akin to being a Judge, whose role it was to ensure a system of fairness and justice in cases brought before it. When he was around sixteen years of age, Ashmole moved to London and lived with the Pagits. His father died the following year. Through this connection to James Pagit, Ashmole was able to set himself up as a solicitor in London in 1638, at the age of twenty-one years, and apparently developed a successful practice. He married Eleanor Mainwaring, also in 1638. She was the daughter of Peter Mainwaring, a minor aristocrat and landowner who was settled a few miles from Congleton, Cheshire. Eleanor, sadly died three years later during pregnancy.

The year after Ashmole's wife died, saw the start of the English Civil War

(1642-1651). Ashmole sided with the royalist forces of Charles I. It seems that for the first few years the war passed him by, but caught up with him in 1644. He received a post as a Kings Commissioner in his hometown of Lichfield, but was moved to Oxford when his knowledge of the law and his connections within the legal establishment were realised. Whilst in Oxford he took time to study mathematics and physics and developed a personal interest in astronomy. 1645 found him in Worcester where, in addition to other duties he was given the rank of Captain in the royalist infantry. It seems his time studying mathematics at Oxford was well spent, because he was posted to an artillery battery and didn't have to face the horrors of having to fight directly in the field of battle. In mid-1646, Worcester surrendered to the Parliamentarian forces. Ashmole had obviously equipped himself well in the eyes of the royalists, and was rewarded accordingly when Charles II was restored to the throne some twenty years later. After the surrender of Worcester, Ashmole returned to Lichfield, only to find that his mother had died the previous year. From there he travelled on to his father-in-law's property in Cheshire. It was during the visit to his father-in-law that he became a Free-Mason. The following is an extract from his diary:

> "4.H.30.'PM. I was made a Free Mason at Warrington in Lancashire, with Coll: Henry Mainwaring of Karnicham in Cheshire. The names of those that were then of the Lodge; Mr Rich Penket Warden, Mr James Collier, Mr Rich:Sankey, Henry Littler, John Ellam, Rich: Ellam and Hugh Brewer."[47]

All of those present appear to have been landowning *gentlemen*. Henry Littler is described as being a *Yeoman*, and one definition of a Yeoman is that of being a *free-man* with a small landed estate.

Karnicham is probably a reference to the modern village of Kermincham near Congleton, Cheshire which in turn is around 30 miles from Warrington, and 35-40 miles from Chester. Records in Cheshire show that there was a family of *nobility and gentlemen* that had lived in the area for several generations. Sir Ralph Mainwaring has traceable ancestors back to 1400. He had fifteen children of whom two were named Henry and Piers. Sir Ralph died in 1557 and was possibly the grandfather of both Henry and Peter. Certain names tended to remain in families at that time, so it would not have been unreasonable for Piers to have become Peter. Furthermore, the family were landowners of estates between Congleton and Warrington. If this connection is accurate, then Elias Ashmole had enhanced his prospects through both his mother's connection with nobility and Sir James Pagit, and his wife's connection through the Mainwarings. Indeed, he added further to his prospects by marrying a widow some years older than himself, Lady Mary Mainwaring, in 1649. There is much speculation that she was connected to the family into which he had previously married. Although, it is reported, that this was not a happy marriage, for Ashmole it worked out well, bringing certain estates and additional connections with nobility, from which incomes he was able to comfortably pursue his academic interests. Included in such studies was the natural world and the philosophy of Sir Francis Bacon, which led to a connection with the *Invisible College* that later became the foundation of the Royal Society.

Notwithstanding any of his connections, there is no mention that Ashmole was admitted into a *lodge,* only that he was made a Free-Mason. Many writers from previous generations have taken the leap of faith to suggest that if he was a Free Mason, then he must have been a member of a lodge, and used the word *lodge* to connect back to the operative masons. The word *lodge* has several meanings. One is that it was a temporary structure with a reed roof, that provided a shelter under which the craftsmen could work in rain or shine whilst undertaking elaborate carving. Other definitions include a hut or cabin, or a meeting place. Ashmole makes no reference to the word *lodge*. His visit to Warrington would certainly have been to a *meeting place,* and that may well have been within the home of one of the landed gentlemen, that served as that meeting place.

The diary entry by Ashmole and the research by Dr Robert Lomas show that there was a flourishing organisation(s) of some kind that was in place well before 1717, and by virtue that Ashmole was made a Free Mason in Warrington, and Sir Robert Moray elsewhere, suggests that such organisation(s) was not limited to London.

Nothing more is known of Ashmole's connection as a Free-Mason until 1682. The gap of some thirty-five years in which there is no apparent further comment about freemasonry in his diaries, has been a great source of speculation about his interest during that lengthy period. However, during that intervening period the English Civil War had continued for a further five years; Charles I had been captured, tried and executed; Oliver Cromwell had died; Charles II had been restored to the monarchy; the Royal Society had been formed. These events, momentous in their own way, were then overshadowed by a series of disasters. There had been the plague in 1665; the Great Fire of London of 1666, and, in 1667 the Dutch navy had sailed up the River Medway in Kent and destroyed a number of naval vessels, moored at Chatham dockyard, including three capital prestigious ships that were the pride of the English navy in what has since been defined as the worst defeat in the Royal Navy's history. They were very unsettled years and the subject of changed allegiances.

Then, on two days, March 10 and 11, 1682, Ashmole notes in his diary:

*10. About 5H.PM. I rec'd a Summons to appear at a Lodge to be held the next day, at Masons Hall, London.*

*11. Accordingly I went & about Noone were admitted to the Fellowship of Free Masons, Sr William Wilson Knight, Capt. Rich: Borthwick, Mr Will Woodman, Mr Wm Grey, Mr Samuell Taylour and Mr William Wise. I was the Senior Fellow among them (it being 35 yeares since I was admitted). There were beside myselfe the fellows after named. Mr Tho: Wise [Master] of the Masons Company this presentyeare. Mr Thomas Shorthose, Mr Thomas Shadbolt, Wainsford Esq., Mr Nich: Young, Mr John Shorthose, Mr William Hamon, Mr John Thompson & Mr Will: Stanton. We all dined at the halfe Moone Taverne in Cheapside, at a Noble Dinner prepared at the charge of the New-accepted Masons.*[48]

The fact that Ashmole makes the point that he was the *senior fellow among them (it being 35 yeares since I was admitted)* suggests that there was some unity between what he was admitted to in Warrington and the gathering at Masons Hall.

In his *Freemason's Guide and Compendium*, Bernard E. Jones notes that if we take Ashmole's diary notes at face value, then of those present, the first six men mentioned were being admitted as new members. Of these, four were members of the London Company of Masons, but perhaps more important is that two were not, although they were obviously at whatever ceremony or process was involved at Masons Hall. The London Company of Masons was further represented by the Master for that year, Mr Thomas Wise, and two Wardens of the Company, John Shorthose and William Stanton. Of the sixteen men at the meeting, including Ashmole, just two were not members of the Company (three including Ashmole), leaving fourteen that were Free-Masons by the time they went to dinner. Bernard Jones also notes that of those who were associated with the London Company of Masons:

*"…Three were free of the Company; Seven were on the livery of the Company; four were on the Court of Assistants of the Company; all but two of them were, had been, or would be Wardens; and six of them had been, were, or would be, Masters. …Nich (Rich) Young, John Shorthose and William Hamon were well-known contractors, whose names will be found in the records of the building of the present St Paul's Cathedral, and Hamon, in addition, was known to be the chief importer of stone into London at that period."*

## More early Free Masons – Randle Holmes & Dr Plot

Various Masonic works suggest that another early freemason, who was not in the operative craft, was Randle Holmes. There were four generations of the same family, all with the same names. The one that is of interest to this quest is the third generation who was born in 1627 and died in 1699.

The successive generations of the family were associated with the *College of Arms*, the organisation that regulates coats of arms used by the aristocracy, corporations and institutions of state. Needless to note, the development of a *coat of arms* requires fees to be paid. At the age of thirty-one, Holmes became a steward of the Stationer's Company in Chester and was an alderman (senior councillor), also in Chester, some three years later. His father had supported the royalists during the civil war, having been the Sheriff, Mayor and alderman in Chester. All his positions of authority were lost when Chester surrendered to the Parliamentarians. Two years after the restoration of the monarchy with the enthronement of Charles II, Randle Holmes (the third) was granted a *sinecure*. This was/is a form of patronage which enables the awarding of a salary without the need to do any work for it.

According to the work by Bernard E. Jones he *was made a freemason at a Lodge in Chester about 1665*. Jones also notes that in documents produced by Randle Holmes and held at the British Museum, is one prepared in 1673 in which he lists twenty-seven individuals in which Holmes, own name appears as number fourteen. Jones then states:

> "There can hardly be a doubt that this was a list of the members of the Lodge at Chester about 1665..."

Here again we have a question mark over the use of the word *lodge*. According to Jones, of the twenty-seven persons named, six were operative masons and fifteen were associated with other trades connected with the processes of building. This leaves six people, including Holmes, that had no direct connection with the building trade.

A few years later, in 1688, the year of the so-called *Glorious Revolution*, Randle produced a book entitle the *Academie of Armory*. Bernard Jones cites a comment he wrote in it:

> "I cannot but honour the Fellowship of the Masons because of its antiquity; and the more as being [myself] a member of that society called Freemasons."[49]

Another early reference to Free Masons is by Dr Robert Plot (1640-1696), an eminent man of his time who held several important positions including being Secretary of the Royal Society and the first Keeper of the Ashmolean Museum in Oxford. In a book entitled *The Natural History of Staffordshire* published in 1686, he comments on the customs of the county and notes:

*"...whereof they have one, of admitting men into the Society of Free-Masons...I find the custom spread more or less all over the nation; for here I found persons of the most eminent quality, that did not distain to be of this fellowship..."[50]*

Dr Plot goes on, as Bernard Jones notes, that there are a number of other aspects attributed to freemasonry. In consequence there has been much further speculation by other writers, that the type of information noted by Dr Plot is included in the original Constitutions prepared by Dr Anderson, and later quoted again by William Preston.

Bernard E. Jones' work, *Freemason's Guide and Compendium*, is to say the least, impressive for the number of miscellaneous facts it contains. He draws on observations by other eminent men of the seventeenth century, who were not freemasons, but makes observations about other societies and fraternities of men. There is a very loose use of the term *lodge* when building arguments around reference to pre-eighteenth century connections, even though the word *lodge* may not have been mentioned. He also draws attention to, for example, the Alnwick Lodge, Northumberland, but he goes on to note that this was an operative lodge where the members were working stonemasons, and that the first *speculative lodge* to use that same name was not founded until 1779.

From all the comment surrounding Elias Ashmole, there is a tendency to suggest that there was a direct connection between the London Company of Masons and Free-Masons at that time, and that it can be used to substantiate a continuous connection with the stonemasons craft, back through the medieval period, and perhaps, forward, such that forty years later, Dr Anderson is referring to the *old charges* of the operative stonemasons to cement the historical link as a means of giving credibility for the newly formed Grand Lodge. The meeting with the London Company of Masons was in 1682, which raises a question about gatherings at other locations around the country prior to that date.

What if incorrect assumptions have been made in the past? We will then be faced with trying to establish just what freemasonry really was at that time.

### Scottish Freemasonry

In Scotland there was a very different structure. The Act of Union between England and Scotland did not become effective until 1707, and Westminster became the centre of parliament for Great Britain. Until then, Scotland was an entirely separate country; it had its own monarchical system and crown jewels and system of governance.

Scotland also had its own system for the management of operative masons.

In an earlier section it is mentioned that as far as the London Company of Masons was concerned, the first Charter was issued in 1356 in the reign of Edward III, and that a *Grant of Arms* did not take place until over a hundred years later in 1472 during the reign of Edward IV. A Charter and Grant of Arms would have been an endorsement for a single entity, whereas there were stonemason's guilds in operation in most major towns.

Shortly after the *Grant of Arms,* we find that the Masons and Wrights in Edinburgh were incorporated as a body in 1475. There are also records of other lodges in major towns in Scotland. All of them, however, are noted as being *operative masons* not speculative or accepted.

One hundred years later, there were efforts to regulate the work of the Scottish masons when, in December 1583, James VI (later also James I in England) appointed William Shawe as *Master of Works* in Scotland, responsible for the building and maintenance of castles, palaces and other works that might be agreed with the king.

This was an era when the renaissance was gathering pace; Vitruvius' design concepts were being further developed by Palladio in Italy; Mary Queen of Scots (mother of James VI) had been married to the king of France and spent a considerable amount of time in the Loire Valley, where Leonardo da Vinci, who had created the classical image of Vitruvius man, had not only lived, but was buried at Amboise, in a tomb dedicated to a French king. There had been the reformation in England; monastic centres had been closed and the buildings that had held them had been substantially dismantled, in many cases by stonemasons; the guilds that had governed the crafts had been abolished. Prior to all of this the stonemasons and the ecclesiastical establishment, the nobility and royalty, had dictated the designs of castles, palaces, abbeys and major public works. Now there was a shift of power towards the professional architect who created designs which the stonemasons merely implemented – designs by men like Palladio and Inigo Jones.

Against such a background William Shawe introduced the Shawe Statutes of 1598 and 1599. Those of 1598 he called a convention of master masons and used the occasion to organise a regional structure where several operative lodges were effectively controlled by one *senior* lodge that had a supervisory role over the others, so that, for example, in the west of Scotland, Kilwinning lodge looked after the other lodges in that part of the country. There was a hierarchy in each lodge which comprised masters, wardens and deacons. Master masons in each lodge had to elect a warden each year, and that warden was charged with regularly communicating with the warden of the supervisory lodge. A master mason could not take on more than three apprentices during his working life – this was probably to regulate the number of skilled craftsmen entering the craft and thereby retaining a constant flow of work and pay; the period of an apprenticeship was seven years and when completed, the time-served apprentice would not be admitted as a full member of the craft for a further seven years – *seven years and upwards* - no doubt so that the individual had the opportunity to demonstrate proficiency and gain experience from different types of work. A register of those entering the trade as apprentices, their interim period as *journeymen* and their full admission to the craft was maintained. The supervisory lodge had to ensure not only the quality of the work undertaken, but that the masons doing so had the means to finish it, in other words, not take on projects they could not possibly complete. There were a number of other requirements including the conduct of the proceedings of lodge meetings, responsibilities of masons to attend, and penalties to apply for absence. All this was apparently agreed by the master masons attending the convention.[51]

There is a general consensus that the Statutes of the following year 1599, were to overcome problems and conflicts that were encountered when implementing the structure agreed the previous year.

The Shawe Statutes and the convention of master masons that took place in Edinburgh are matters relating to the operative craft of stonemasonry and has no obvious connection with accepted or speculative freemasonry.

What we can see from this, however, is a desire and means of implementing a national organisation that provided communications and management between Shawe as the *Master of Works,* and the individual operative lodges, and it provided a system of accountability and a structure that was common throughout the country. This was all in place for nearly one hundred years before Elias Ashmole met with others in Masons Hall, London in 1682.

Four years after the second convention of master masons, Elizabeth I of England died, and James VI of Scotland also became James I King of England. Shawe died three years after the second convention and one year prior to the Scottish king ascending to the throne of England.

A few years after James I took up the throne of England, Inigo Jones was implementing some of his early designs on behalf of this king.

## Thesis - the evolution of Speculative Freemasonry.

*Author's note: Irrespective of the thousands of pages and millions of words devoted to the subject by eminent men of their times, and for around 200 years, there is no clear idea as to how speculative freemasonry came into existence, or what its object has been. The following is a summary of the conclusions I have reached after nearly 20 years of visiting sites and document archives at various places around the world, enquiring, reading and ploughing through official records.*

## My findings suggest that:

1. There is no direct link between freemasonry and the masons/ stone carvers of ancient Egypt, Greece or Rome, although the many remains of temples and other structures indicate a highly developed sense of skill, geometric and esoteric knowledge.

2. Every new member of freemasonry is told that the institution is older than the *Golden Fleece* (founded in 1430) *and the Roman Eagle* (traceable to 1250). This places the origins of freemasonry to earlier than 1250. The most logical era prior to that is around 1120-1150 CE when the works of the classical philosophers of ancient Greece and Rome was translated from Arabic to Latin. This included the works of Euclid (geometry) which were then used as a basis for the development of the French/gothic style of architecture and the pointed arch, which were used extensively in cathedrals, ecclesiastical and state buildings for the next few hundred years. This does not mean that freemasonry started at that time, or was in any way active at that time, only that the traceable roots, and a strand of knowledge available in freemasonry, derive from that era.

3. A second strand of knowledge available in freemasonry derives its origins from the rediscovery of the works of Vitruvius and the development of the *Renaissance*, especially in the period from the *Reformation* through to the period following the Great Fire of London (a period extending through 1500 – 1675).

4 There is probably no direct link between freemasonry and the guilds that regulated the crafts in the middle ages in England, simply because there is no evidence that any such link existed.

5. That the real development of the stonemason's craft in Europe developed in Frankia in the eighth century with the evolution of the Rhenish/Romanesque style. It is possible that this was started by stonemasons imported from the Roman Byzantium Empire based in Constantinople. The Romanesque style is a relatively simple form of construction, the bulk of which relies on squared blocks of stone mounted one on the other, relatively simple carving, and round columns that are easily produced from square blocks. The style produces a bulky structure which restricts light to the interior of

buildings by having relatively small windows, though this would have been a bonus in winter when the requirement was more related to keeping the cold draughts out, and the production of glass for windows was reasonably expensive.

6.     References to characters such as King Athelstan, St Alban, St Swithins, plus Roman activity in Britain, and many more instances besides, as quoted by Anderson, Preston and other early Masonic writers, have no connection with freemasonry.

7.     That in England stonecutters grew in ability from around 900 CE, but prior to that, and for more artistic skills associated with carving or sculpting stone, masons were brought to England from the continent. Those skills and basic knowledge about the alignment of buildings with celestial events, gradually transferred to English masons so that by around 1050 CE, English stonemasons were equal to their continental brethren in building in the Romanesque style. Many highly respected cathedrals started as wooden structures in the sixth and seventh centuries, were then demolished around the eighth and ninth century and gradually grew into stone structures in the Romanesque style in the tenth and eleventh centuries. This often involved a need to transport the stone over quite long distances - Glastonbury Abbey and Ely Cathedral being examples. Westminster Abbey is, perhaps an example of a development of the Romanesque style, from around 1000 CE.

8.     The Norman Conquest of 1066 CE put back the development of English stonemasonry crafts with an influx of masons again from the continent, mainly no doubt, for linguistic reasons. Several major developments were undertaken such at Glastonbury, Rochester and the Tower of London. A lot of stone was shipped from France to England for building purposes.

9.     The real development of the stonemasons' craft in England commenced around the year 1150 CE, shortly after the rediscovery of Euclid's geometric understanding and translation in Rome, and the subsequent development of the French/gothic style. The first people likely to appreciate this geometric knowledge would have been individuals within the ecclesiastic community, as Abbot Suger had been, mainly because they were among that group of people that could read and write; even amongst the aristocracy there were many that did not

have that skill. That knowledge transferred to the stonemasons and in particular, that group of craftsmen that we refer to as master masons. It was this knowledge that set them apart from the ordinary stonecutter / hewer. Guilds for the regulation of the craft were firmly established.

10. In the period commencing 1100 CE, there was the development of the *Religious Guild* associated with the stonemason's craft, as a means of providing support to aged brethren and their families when they were no longer able to work, were sick, or had been involved in an accident that prevented them from working in both the short and longer terms; provided funeral rites and possibly a small pension for widows; assisted dependent children to be apprenticed to obtain a skill from which they could earn their living and way in life.

11. The period from around 1200 – 1400 was a golden era of the Middle Ages for stonemasonry in general, with extensive work on abbey churches that turned them into cathedrals. There were castles, monastic buildings, fortified manor houses, storerooms for agricultural produce and some bridges. In this period sculpture skills improved. Having acquired the geometric knowledge that was in the translations of Euclid, the stonemasons became a rather select group of craftsmen – they had knowledge that few others had and understood, and were in a position to deploy it. Thus the status of the Master Mason grew.

12. The nobility and ecclesiastic community were still the main commissioners of major works, but the wealth of the merchants was also on the rise. They helped fund public works. The connection of a *religious guild* with stonemasons, and the latter's new status, resulted in members of other crafts associated with the building process, joining. Prosperous merchants and towns people also joined. The *religious guild* became more of a friendly society and what today we regard as *mutual insurance* societies. Being *religious guilds* at a time when religion still permeated almost every function of life, some of the elemental tools and working practices adopted by the stonemasons became metaphors for the way one conducted one's life. For example: Imagine a column being built in an abbey church ready to provide a roof support. A stonemason is observed dropping a long length of cord from the top of the pillar to the ground, with a pointed iron or bronze weight at the ground end. He is asked by a merchant what he is doing. The stonemason replies that he is checking that the pillar is upright because if it was not and was leaning in any direction, it

would become a weakness in the structure, and would not be able to support the weight of the roof as it was supposed to do. With time it would collapse. The roof might fall and if there were people of all stations of life in the church, some might be killed, some maimed; there would be no discrimination between nobility and peasant. So, getting the pillar *upright* was absolutely important to the long-term integrity of the structure. The merchant then interprets that as a code for living one's life. If he is upright in all his undertakings, a pillar in society, then his business structure might remain sound. But, if he is not upright in all his undertakings then things might go wrong, his business might fall leaving him and his family destitute and vulnerable to the vague whims of life. With the passing of time more such metaphors for life were translated from the process of building, to the moral code of the religious guild. And, the guild provided a social outlet at times of festivals. It was still also a time when the religion of Rome still held sway over events in England.

13. The *religious guilds* grew in stature but they had no significant role to play in town affairs or commerce, and as such were not treated in the same way that a stonemasons or weavers guild might. Then in the reign of Henry VIII and Edward VI, and the period of the Reformation, these religious guilds were abolished as being potential harbingers of the old religious ways, and hence a threat. Any properties or other such assets became the property of the crown. Yet, there was still a need for charitable activity in society that these guilds satisfied, and they still had money. They changed their name to become *fraternities*. This distanced them from the religious guild concept of the past. In the same era, the craft guilds were also abolished. Ironically their skills and trade were still needed. How could palaces and castles, the fortified manor houses of the nobility, be repaired and extended without them? Hence they continued for a while as loose associations of men in various trades. The *fraternities* that had previously been religious guilds associated with the building crafts, of which the premier group were the stonemasons, now needed to distance themselves from the craft guild structure as well, so they defined their fraternities as *free – masons,* that is, free from an association with the craft. Yet, they continued to use the metaphors of the masons as a code of conduct in life and with the passing of time this fraternal culture became known as *speculative masonry.*

14. Through the period of the Reformation we have religion as a key component of distrust and upheaval in society. People are rounded

up and burnt at the stake for uttering the wrong things; others are hanged or imprisoned. Religion moved from Catholicism under Henry VIII to Protestantism in the same reign. The boy king, Edward VI retained the Protestant change. He was followed by Mary, a devout catholic, who purged many that were Protestants. Then came Elizabeth I, who showed tolerance but leaned towards the Protestant cause. Outside of England, the pope and the nobility of the Holy Roman Empire plotted to reintroduce Catholicism by force. There were plots to assassinate the Queen, and an armada of heavily fortified ships and men set sail to conquer England, but failed. Against this background of uncertainty, the fraternal societies of free-masons kept a low profile.

15.    The arrival of James I did not bring too much change, initially. The nobility, aristocracy and wealthy merchants, all sometimes one and the same, were the main landowners, in some cases, having acquired extensive property holdings that had previously been under the control of monasteries. Noble families retained connections with each other; they didn't always agree with one another, but they had one thing in common – they derived their patronage from the monarchy. Nobles may have had large families but only one could inherit the titles. Daughters were married to the sons of other nobles and the sons that would not inherit titles were helped to acquire land. People didn't travel extensively at that time, transport was hardly any different from the era of the Roman invasion of Britain one thousand five hundred years earlier, it was still ride on a horse or, ride in a cart pulled by a horse or take shanks' pony – walk. The fraternal societies of free-masons became regional groups that still adopted the metaphorical context of the religious guilds, but became more a means of providing charitable support amongst each other. Regular meetings as such, were not needed. However, families might get together periodically, the meaning behind some of the terminology, handed down through the centuries, would be explained, new members of the family through marriage would be formally made *members of the fraternal society of free-masons*. If the society had common links with other aristocratic families, so there might be social gatherings between them. These fraternities have later been referred to as *gentlemen's lodges*.

16.    In the case of Elias Ashmole, he had married into a family with aristocratic heritage, the Mainwarings, and his mother had

connections with nobility as well. His in-laws may well have been landowners who managed their estates, but had no other outward skills. Thus, by admitting Ashmole when he visited a family seat at Warrington, they were admitting a family member, one who had proved himself loyal to the monarchy from which they all derived their patronage and position in society, and they had access to one who was a lawyer and could help them look after their affairs. It is highly probable that they introduced him to another member who had also married into the family and was now a widow, Lady Mary Mainwaring, who needed someone to take interest in her affairs, and rewarded Ashmole by providing the opportunity to become a landowner in his own right, through marriage. Further connection with the Mainwarings in Cheshire may have been for business and social purposes that involved looking after the affairs of the fraternity, but no formal meetings as such were necessary, hence the gap of thirty-five years in his diaries.

17. In the latter years of the reign of Elizabeth I, the merchants who had hitherto achieved great dynastic wealth through trading with and through the Hanseatic League, now spread their wings towards the Americas. Slavery was big business. Sir Francis Drake and Sir Walter Raleigh had both ventured to areas of the globe not previously the subject of merchant exploitation and returned with spices and products that were valuable and changed our way of life. Against this background, Elizabeth I granted a Royal Charter to a new enterprise on the eve of 1601 - the *Company of Merchants of London Trading into the East Indies*. This was the forerunner of the East India Company that established trading centres across the Far East in the eighteenth century. Trading entities such as this needed capital, and some of that capital came from the landed gentry and merchants of the times. It is in just such companies as this that Elias Ashmole may well have made investments on behalf of his in-laws and the fraternity.

18. Meanwhile, Inigo Jones had introduced the architectural concepts developed by Palladio, into England. They had developed considerable interest, especially when it became known that they were based on the same geometric ideas of ancient Rome and the father of architecture, Vitruvius. With the endorsement by the Royal Court and the building of the *Queen's House* at Greenwich and the Banqueting House in Whitehall, many of the prosperous members of the aristocracy, landed gentry and merchants, wanted to be seen

to be associated with the regal endorsement of the style. They sought out Inigo Jones to develop and implement designs for them, away from the hitherto need for castles and fortified houses that were old, draughty and expensive to maintain. Furthermore, by 1682, many castles and fortified houses had been destroyed during the civil war, so new houses were needed.

19.   After the Civil War, when Charles II had been restored to the throne, the plague and the great fire of London in 1666 had been extinguished; the period of the enlightenment had begun. Construction work involving impressive public buildings was taking place. Much it was in stone, and in the classical style. The only trades that had the authority to deliver such works were those that were associated with the London Company of Masons. New enterprises, such as that of the *Company of Merchant Adventurers of London* that was incorporated by a Royal Charter dating back to 1407 - and may have been founded even earlier through the *Fraternity of St Thomas*, a religious guild that had existed in Canterbury - built an impressive meeting place known as the Royal Exchange. Its architecture was based on the classical style. Needless to note, as merchants, they footed the bill, and no doubt wanted an overview of the design and how it would be implemented. The same would have probably been true for other major works. Hence a separate organisation, attached to the London Company of Masons developed. It was not controlled by the London Company, but had close associations with them. Many of the merchants already had connections with fraternities such as the *fraternity of free-masons* whose ethos was based on the metaphorical interpretation of the stonemasons' craft and their geometric knowledge. Some wanted more direct involvement in where and how their money, invested in the Royal Exchange, was spent. They were *accepted* as honorary members of the London Company. Likewise, members of the London Company were also accepted as members of the *fraternity*. The stonemasons referred to the places where they worked, where they met and stored tools, etc, as the *masons lodge*, so gradually the places where the fraternities met to discuss investments and building progress became known as *lodges*.

20.   In the forty years after the restoration numerous works were started and completed in the classical style, and they were outside of London as well as within it. This enabled the development of more gentlemen's lodges, especially in areas close to where major construction was taking place. Such as Oxford. The result was

widely distributed groups, descended from the religious guilds, using the metaphorical association with the craft of the earlier stonemasons, largely organised as gentlemen's *fraternal societies,* that had connections with major building projects in the classical style. Several such groups realised that with the merchants banding together to create livery and trading companies, they too should bring about a single entity to orchestrate and guide their affairs. Hence the events that led to the formation of the Grand Lodge of England from 1717.

21. The period from 1700-1714 saw the Wars of the Spanish Succession. Most of Europe was still under the influence of the Holy Roman Emperor, a position that had descended from the Frankish kings and Charlemagne in particular, the House of Burgundy, and the Habsburgs. Charles II was the last king of Spain of the Habsburg line and when he died he left no sons to inherit the title. The Spanish title was extremely wealthy as a result of the gold and mineral wealth that Spain had withdrawn from South America. The French crown was now in line to inherit, but this provoked immense concern that the French King would ultimately control vast territorial areas of Europe, the Americas - north and south, as well as French and Spanish territories elsewhere. The wars were an attempt to stop that happening. The alliance, of which Britain was a part, succeeded. One of the spoils of that war went to a group of merchants based in London who formed the *South Sea Company* in 1711. This company, again financed by wealthy merchants and landowners, was granted sole trading rights with Spain's territorial areas in South America, in return for which, the company bought the debts that the English government had accrued in financing their part of the wars. Thus by 1717, three major privately-financed trading companies were operating in different parts of the world.

- The East India Company
- South Sea Company
- The Governor and Company of Adventurers of England trading into Hudson's Bay, which had been formed by Royal Charter in 1670 – the forerunner of the Hudson's Bay Company.

22. As a consequence, immense wealth and trade was associated with England through this period and the merchants who were benefactors built prestigious houses for themselves, usually in the

classical style. These companies also provide foundations for the development of freemasonry in other regions of the world through the trading connections they established and the British subjects that went abroad and fostered that trade.

23. The descendents of the old aristocratic families and the new wealthy merchants, influenced by the style of architecture then being built, travelled through Europe, visiting the classical centres of France, Italy, and Greece. They returned with a range of items that are now regarded as classical works of art of high value. Their education was based on the subjects of the *Liberal Arts and Sciences* that had been the basis of education in the cathedral schools since the medieval period. To this was added the Greek language and a thorough grounding in Latin. Along with this came the mythology, stories and history of classical ancient Greece. It was the era for the study of the *classics* that still influence our lives today.

24. By the end of the eighteenth century, eminent men who had had a *classical* education were now confronted with a new fascination, that of ancient Egypt, that had started to unfold its mysterious temples and pyramids along the Nile. The combined effect of the Egyptian and Classical mystical cultures that these eminent men encountered, led to the introduction of certain esoteric devices into the fraternities. Many have been rejected with time, but nevertheless, have, in some instances been cited as further evidence of the origins of the mysteries of freemasonry.

From the fore-going, it is possible that the term *speculative freemasonry* derives from religious guild/fraternities that may have evolved in the Middle Ages; *accepted* masons were those that joined lodges associated with the London Company of Masons, or other regional equivalents directly associated with building in stone.

There have been several writers in the past, with Masonic connections, that have been clergymen or otherwise attached to the church. They have noted that ceremonies performed in lodges have a religious feel to them and that they believe this has come from the operative masons of the middle ages working in close proximity to monastic communities and other ecclesiastical establishments, where they witnessed similar ceremonial practices. It has been a tenuous link, but plausible. If, however, freemasonry descended from the *religious guilds,* the religious context would be obvious. Furthermore, the *religious guilds* were established primarily for charitable reasons. They were the forerunner of the mutual benefit societies that provided small pensions, help for the aged and infirm, and so on. This is exactly the role freemasonry has provided over the past few centuries, and still does.

*Author's Note: I acknowledge that much of the above theory is a speculative history of freemasonry on my part. Like so many areas of what has become the traditional teaching, finding substantiating evidence to support crucial junctions in the theory has proven impossible. It just does not exist, has been lost in the mist of time, or may never have been created. But those crucial junctions are surrounded by documented events that provide circumstantial evidence that something similar was happening, and could easily have been translated into masonry.*

I have no doubt that on publication of this theory, I will receive my fair share of negative comment, especially from those in the established echelons of freemasonry that have grown to accept the *traditional* perspective. However, in my defence I would point out that I have tried to look and chart freemasonry by looking more closely at events that were going on outside of the organisation, or that may have influenced it, rather than merely following a path that others have previously trodden. If I had walked down the same path that others before me had walked, I would only see what they saw; by taking a different path, one gets to view things from a different angle, and what may have looked familiar from the other path, now changes shape. I accept that the theory presented above, does not fit easily with conventional ideas that have been established over time.

Maybe this theory will influence a young freemason somewhere to pick up the challenge and go and *seek for that which is lost.*

Around 450 BCE a Greek philosopher by the name of Anaxagoras, studied the heavens and came to the conclusion that the moon was a rock about the size of one of the small Greek islands. This idea did not meet with the approval of the Greek hierarchy. Anaxagoras was ridiculed, accused of presenting irreligious ideas, and sent into exile. I am not in the same league as Anaxagoras, but I can't help wondering what those who evaluated Anaxagoras' theory would make of the moon with the knowledge we have today.

# Chapter 10

# SECTION REVIEW

*Author's Note: In the previous section, I have tried to set out various aspects of the development of historical background material that may have influenced subsequent developments, which, in their own way, may have set in process a series of circumstances that created the conditions in which modern freemasonry could have been formed.*

*I have used, wherever possible, the latest tools and most recent research wherever possible, but I must also add that some of that recent research also draws on documents, like that by Toulmin Smith, which were produced over one hundred years ago.*

*By looking at what was happening in the wider world, other than merely taking the works of Anderson and Preston at face value, we get an insight to life and events of long ago. We also see a number of threads that provide a possible link that will enable us to answer the question about How? freemasonry began.*

**Summary of the observations that can be drawn:**

1.  Bede's observations indicate that there was no knowledge amongst the Celtic English in the early years of Roman occupation, about how to build with stone. This seems to be verified by the fact that Roman Legions were sent to help protect the northern borders from incursions by invaders. They provided the design for defences and supervised the construction. (c 100 – 150 CE)

2.  The more elaborate buildings the Romans constructed in Britain, to be used as temples, palaces and centres of administration, were most likely built by masons who were brought from elsewhere in the Roman Empire, and who were familiar with the construction techniques and designs of that time. (c 100 – 450 CE)

3.  It is highly probable that when the Romans departed, the skills of working with stone went with them, because around 250 years later, Benedict Biscop was again importing those skills to build the monastery and St Peter's church at Wearmouth (c 674- 685 CE), noted as being the oldest stone church in England.

4. In roughly the same time frame of Biscop's building project, we find that there are records and references to gilds in the reign of King Ina, the Anglo-Saxon king of Wessex in the south west of England.(c 688 – 725 CE).

5. The early gilds, it seems, were not of the later craft and merchant variety, but rather tribal-based communities, where the gild provided a focus for self-help, protection, care of the elderly, and assisting those in the community who were in need. They were an early form of local council and charity, all in one. (c 650? – 1000? CE)

6. As communities grew into small towns, so a few of the gilds became *Corporations*, a more sophisticated form of local administration, but one that ended amid the stigma of corruption and political manipulation. (c 1000 – 1835 CE).

7. As crafts grew into a trading opportunity that satisfied a local and wider market potential, so they bonded together within their own craft and were recognised as such within the gilds. (c 1000 – 1300 CE)

8. An earlier form of gild was associated with the Roman Catholic Church, especially on the European continent. There were two elements: one was associated with the clergy and the regulation of religious parades, ceremonies and plays, and one that provided a social and charitable benefit. With the passing of time, craft and merchant gilds participated in the parades and ceremonies, and assisted in the provision of a range of service functions. These clerical and social gilds became known as Religious Guilds. (c 700 – 1550 CE).

9. With the English Reformation of the sixteenth century in the reign of Henry VIII, the Roman Catholic Church was effectively abolished and the Protestant Church of England took its place. Monasteries, priories and abbeys were dismantled. It seems that the Religious Guilds that may have existed at that time were also disbanded, but the religious nature of them and some ceremonies were retained by groups who have later been styled as social guilds and fraternities. It is probable that these guilds met in social surroundings, or the homes of prominent individuals, gentlemen of wealth such as merchants and the landed gentry. (c 1550 – 1700 CE).

10. The growth of trade in the products of the craft gilds resulted in a new merchants group emerging. As with the crafts, the merchants also bonded together and created guilds of their own. As their networks increased, especially outside of England, so some became part of the Hanseatic League, which created yet further guilds. Not making anything in particular, but trading in the goods and produce made by others, they became very wealthy, excluded the craftsmen from the guilds, and began to dictate what activities certain crafts could undertak. This led to resentment and violence in Europe but eventually led to the crafts gaining the upper hand and being restored to guild participation. Such was the concern and upheaval surrounding the craft-merchant conflict that in the reigns of Edward II and Edward III, various forms of regulation were introduced along with charters. (c 1070 – 1380 CE)

11. Prior to the Norman Conquest in 1066, great churches such as Westminster Abbey, had been built. Edward the Confessor's Abbey, was dedicated in 1065, but the Abbey as we now see it, was not commenced until 1245, well into the French/gothic period.

12. Churches, like the *Round Church* in Cambridge, show that there was a skill available in the late eleventh and early twelfth centuries, in fashioning stone to a high standard of finish and with intricate detail. What is unclear is how much of this skill was imported and how much was indigenous.

13. The earliest record of an organisation, specifically to regulate the craft of stonemasonry, is from the year 1356 during the reign of Edward III. (A few years before this date, Edward III had rounded up as many masons as he could find, under extremely severe penalty, to undertake work on Windsor Castle.)[52] By virtue that an authorised organisation existed in 1356 to regulate the industry, it seems logical that the craft, in English hands, existed well before that time, say 1200 – 1300 CE. To suggest any links with indigenous skills in the craft of stonemasonry, of any great capability, prior to that time, seems tenuous.

14. Any links between any form of stonemason fraternity in Britain, and the *collegia* systems of ancient Rome, seem very unlikely.

It seems from this review that the only positive connection there is that establishes the craft of stonemasonry as a purely English Guild, is the year 1356 when a Charter was issued, and extending back to around 1200, when Norman influence of language and customs may have been fully assimilated. Again, this would fit with the claim that freemasonry is older than *the Golden Fleece and Roman Eagle,* assuming that the Roman Eagle referred to is the two-headed eagle of the Holy Roman Empire.

Religious gilds are known to exist prior to 1356, and are traceable, even on the continent, in the Frankish empire, to the era of Charlemagne around 800 CE. We have noted that certain of the *Livery Companies of London* can trace their roots back to the religious guilds. We have also noted, through the *snap Dragon* guild in Norwich, how it changed its shape with the different religious and political changes that occurred, such that it became associated with the local administrative council for Norwich. This suggests that many other such guilds may have changed their shape and continued to operate long after they were officially disbanded.

Euclid's geometric theorems were rediscovered and translated into Latin in Rome, coincidentally with the religious war adventures known as the Crusades, St Bernard's rise to fame; the formation of the Knights Templar, and the subsequent development of the pointed arch architectural style known today as *Gothic* and first implemented to a major advantage by Abbot Suger, at St Denis cathedral, France.

Not long after the *Gothic* style was in full development, we note the rediscovery of the works of Vitruvius, and the development of the renaissance, along with the introduction of the classical style of architecture into England, by Inigo Jones.

What has not been established is any proof that freemasonry can trace its history or connection to the craft of the stonemason, up to the time the guilds were disbanded during the period of the reformation. Yet, there is a very strong connection with the role of the religious guilds. Could it be, that is the path down which freemasonry descended?

## Section 2

## Chapter 11

<u>ORIGINS OF OFFICES</u>

To understand what it is we are doing, we need to examine how the ceremonies we now participate in, arrived in their current form. The immediate difficulty one encounters is that freemasons have long pledged themselves to keep such matters a secret, so there are no ancient illuminated manuscripts that help. The process of writing down the ceremonies only commenced in the nineteenth century. All we have available to us are the words of our current ceremonies, the details recorded in ritual books from of the last century, an interesting source from the mid-eighteenth century known as *the disclosures* which have been mentioned in the previous section, and the charges recorded in Anderson's Constitutions. It is from Andersons' writings that we gain a glimpse of the proceedings in 1723, just six years after the formation of the Grand Lodge of England in 1717, and one hundred years prior to the merger of the two strands of Masonry that existed until 1813 when the antients and moderns merged together as one organisation that ultimately became the United Grand Lodge of England (UGLE). To understand what we are doing we must look outside of freemasonry, and at the ceremonial content.

As stated earlier, most members of lodges learn words and actions to ceremonies (and some pride themselves on being extremely proficient ritualists), but they have no idea what it is they are actually explaining, the meaning by the words they are using, or what they are re-enacting when they are performing various actions.

The official description of freemasonry is that it is a *peculiar system of morality, veiled in allegory and illustrated by symbols*. An allegory is a veneer or way of illustrating something that is hidden from obvious view, but if you know how to interpret the allegory, then what is beneath the veneer – the veil – is revealed. What you see is not necessarily what you get.

Allegories are extremely common in art. You may look at a painting that illustrates a scene that could be conveying an image typical of ancient Greece, only to find out that it is an allegory for the love between a king, in the 1600s, and his queen.

When we look at Masonic ceremonies, they are so obtuse that they must have come from somewhere. In view of the close association with the process of building in stone, then the logical conclusion is that they are a memory of events associated with that building method, a process much broader than merely cutting and shaping the stone into regular sized blocks, and some with elaborate patterns. The stonemasons of one thousand years ago may not have been the sole custodians of all the knowledge that was needed. If, as we are led to believe, that in the Middle Ages, very few people outside the ecclesiastic communities could read and write, then other disciplines may well have been involved or used to convey information or knowledge. In the process this may have introduced a broader spectrum of knowledge, other than could merely be written down. Eventually that knowledge could later form part of the stonemason's skills, but no written evidence of it would exist.

Some of these knowledge elements are, or may be, reflected in the duties associated with offices within a regular lodge.

**The Master:**
Tradition tells us that once in every year, master masons would elect one of their number to preside over them for the following year. This is most likely a reflection of a process that has been taken from the Guild/Livery Company structure where, especially in the latter instance, the Master and Wardens are elected once each year. However, in the Middle Ages, when guilds also provided the means of local community governance, it would have been impractical to have had every mason attend such a meeting, along with every member of every other craft guild that was also entitled to be represented, not to mention the addition of merchants and other traders. A small town would have needed a substantial building to hold them all. Thus, one suitably qualified individual would be elected by members of a guild, to represent their views in local *council* meetings, or liaison with the client. They would also have been responsible for ensuring that the traditions of the craft were upheld, such as the number of apprentices that were entering the trade, and that they were properly trained by their individual masters.

Until after the Norman Conquest, when a massive programme of building castles and fortified manor houses took place, there would have been very little demand for ordinary residences to have been built with stone, not least because of the cost involved. It required the later development of the merchants to create the financial resources for that to happen. Instead people built their homes with materials that were available locally. What is more, if you didn't build your own place, then you didn't have one. Thus, in the southeast of England one finds many older style of properties built with flint, because the chalky ground yields an abundance of this material. Even the first chapel given to St Augustine by the Queen of Kent in the sixth century, had walls substantially made using flint. Around central England and East Anglia, flint and stone are hard to find it is relatively flat country with areas of clay soil. Here, a construction method akin to the adobe structure evolved, of puddling clay (treading soft clay with ones feet) and mixing in straw and horse hair, then making blocks that would dry in the sun. Such houses were quick to build, strong, provided excellent insulation from adverse weather, were extremely warm, fire resistant and easy to modify or enlarge. A thin skin of the clay-mix over the outer walls helped stop the worst of the rain from eroding the walls, and again was easy to maintain. In other parts of the country, where wood from forests was plentiful, so timber became the main building material.

In the Middle Ages, the majority of works undertaken in stone were associated with monastic communities. When, for example, there was a large project being undertaken for new cloisters at a monastery, the *Master* may well have been the designer, and agreed the design with the abbot, who in turn had consulted his monastic brethren. The *Master* would not have had the financial resources to undertake the project in his own right with the objective of making a profit. He would have been an agent of the monastery, paid by them, and would have orchestrated every aspect of the work, from sourcing the materials to ensuring the appropriate number of skilled people to do the work. He would have been architect, surveyor, project manager, materials manager, personnel manager, accountant, payroll manager, and so on. In the seventeenth century, where there were major projects, designs would have been increasingly developed by architects like Inigo Jones, who devised a scheme, drew it, agreed the concept with the client and would then oversee the construction to completion. Again, there would have been a requirement for one person to have had the liaison between the architect and the men doing the work. He may even have been consulted on the best way to approach the construction, drawing on the skills and knowledge of the *Master* craftsmen. Equally, the *Master* would have also been responsible for the hiring of labour and ensuring skills.

In earlier times, the king may have required specific works to be undertaken, such as building a new castle for defence of his kingdom, and that needed one person to have a responsibility for ensuring that the work was carried out. Hence, we find the use of the terms, King's Master Mason and Surveyor-General. Such men were usually required to supervise and ensure construction of a variety of different civil works.

The common theme is that the *Master* was a person who was chosen, because of their knowledge, skill and organising ability, to get the job done

This is little different to the role of the Master in the lodge today.

## The Wardens

The role of the Warden also has links to the guild system, but in the lodge, it seems to have adopted a further role, developed out of another custom that may be thousands of years old.

As far as the title Warden is concerned, Bernard E. Jones notes that it may well have been derived from a Latin concept that would have created a derivative word of guardian, a person who had a responsibility to guard. In the Middle Ages, it seems that when a major project was undertaken, there was a Master, who was also a Master Mason, and a deputy, who was Warden. As the guild system developed, the wardens had the responsibility for ensuring that the work practices were upheld, the right skills were being used, and the number of individuals admitted to the trade as apprentices wasn't being undermined. The wardens were the guild enforcers – the guild police. So, they deputised for the Master and ensured the rules were obeyed.

In the era after the restoration of Charles II, and especially after the Great Fire of London, there were lots of building works taking place simultaneously. Because of the extent of the disaster, there were many individuals from other areas of the country, often unskilled, who travelled to London and claimed experience of various trades with the intention of making money from the misfortunes that had befallen the city. In the case of the stonemasons, they had sole right to all stonework within the City of London and Westminster and within a seven miles radius. It became the role of the Wardens to ensure that only properly trained craftsmen, who were members of the Company, were undertaking the work, and that those who were not qualified to participate, were kept out. This was very much the enforcer role through which they were the guardians of the work and the Company responsibility.

In the modern lodge, the Wardens are an important part of the management structure, whose duties include checking to make sure that only those who are suitably qualified individuals enter the lodge and participate in the work/ceremonies – which is akin to checking the credentials of workmen in former times. They were the guardians of the lodge.

There is one other attribute – that of marking the sun at its meridian.

The meridian is described as being a great semicircle on the globe, passing through the North and South poles.[53] In theory, this imaginary line could be anywhere. In Britain, it is the imaginary line that passes through Greenwich Observatory to the east of London and has become the centre from which global time has been established – Greenwich Mean Time, GMT. It is, therefore, the point from which every new day is started, and from that, each new month, year and millennium. In former times it was a place where the position of the sun was monitored to be at its highest above the horizon, which corresponds with the twelfth hour of the twenty-four hour day - midday. At that time a cannon would be fired so that everyone in the City of London and Westminster, and the ships moored along the Thames, knew it was midday and could set their time-pieces accordingly. It also represents the point from which longitude is measured and thereby other meridians. Greenwich observatory was founded in 1675 by Charles II, some forty-two years prior to the Grand lodge of England.

The role of the Warden in a modern lodge is to mark the sun at its meridian and is asked by the Master, what time it is. The Warden replies that it is high twelve. This does not necessarily mean that this phrase is a reflection of the purpose of Greenwich or the Greenwich Meridian. The process of marking the position of the sun at its highest point the sun reached in the sky, is thousands of years old.

To our ancestors there were certain times of the day when marking the position of the sun was important, and was usually a function of priests/ sages (learned and wise men). In the absence of calendars, as we have today, they kept a check on the passing of the seasons by noting the position of the sun along the horizon at sunrise. Through the course of a year, the sun has four primary movement positions that we still note; the spring equinox, the summer solstice, the autumn equinox, and the winter solstice. This variation is caused by the Earth's axis being tilted.

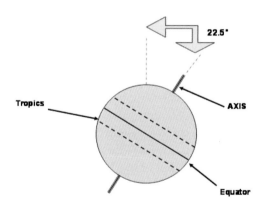

This tilt remains in the same plane as the Earth orbits the sun. Thus, when the Earth's axis is tilted towards the sun it is mid-summer in the northern hemisphere and the point of the Summer Solstice, typically 21st June each year. The sun rises and makes a pronounced arch in the sky.

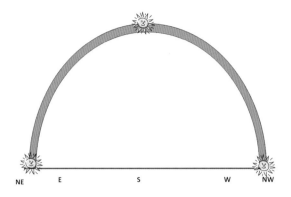

The path of the Sun - Summer

When the sun is at its lowest point, it is mid-winter – the winter solstice, typically 21st December each year. These are the two extremities and are characterised on maps as the two tropics of Cancer and Capricorn.

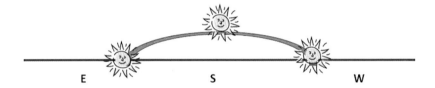

There is however, a further point, the equinox. This is when the sun is over the equator as it seems to travel from summer to winter, and the reverse, and is the position of the sun at the autumn and spring equinoxes.

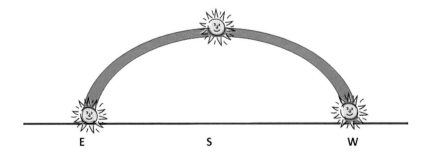

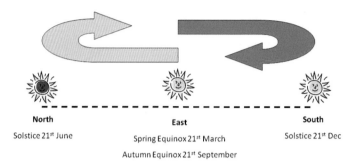

| North | East | South |
|---|---|---|
| Solstice 21ˢᵗ June | Spring Equinox 21ˢᵗ March | Solstice 21ˢᵗ Dec |
| | Autumn Equinox 21ˢᵗ September | |

The way our ancestors saw it all

The way our ancestors observed this seasonal variation was by monitoring the position of the sun along the horizon at sunrise.

There would therefore have been a necessity for two people to work together in such monitoring, every day; the senior of the two who would observe the position by using a sharp stick or spear that was always at the centre of the marking place, and the junior who would move a second stick to align it between the centre position and that where the sun rose in the east. The alternative would be to mark the position at sunset.

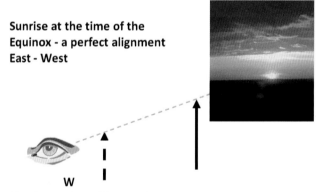

Sunrise at the time of the
Equinox - a perfect alignment
East - West

W

Marking the Sun at its meridian – Sunrise, precession & seasons
Marking the Sun at its meridian – Mid-day, time and seasons
Marking the Setting Sun       – Sunset, stars & moon lunar calendar

This process could be simplified by marking the position of the sun at midday using a shadow. If, for example, an obelisk with a pointed top was placed in an open position, and the highest point the sun reached in the sky monitored by constantly marking out the shortest shadow on any one day, then over time it would be possible to draw a line from the centre of the base of the obelisk, through the point of the shortest shadow, and that line would represent the position of the sun at its midday meridian. By marking the length of the shadow along the line would provide an indication of the movement of the seasons and thereby the dates for specific religious festivals.

Marking the position of the sun has been an important religious requirement for many centuries. In the Islamic religion, created in the early seventh century, there are five major times for prayers, and these have always been governed by the position of the sun. They are; around dawn, just after noon, in the afternoon, just after sunset and about nightfall. There would therefore be an important task needed within the priesthood, to mark (monitor) the progress of the sun to denote the time for calling people to prayers.

Likewise the same happened in many cities across Europe, often associated with the church, for many centuries. In the city of Prague, for instance, once the centre of the Holy Roman Empire, there is a square that marks the main centre of the historic town. Around 1650, a statue was raised to the Virgin Mary on the southern end of the square, with a shape that, when a shadow was cast, provided a pointed shadow in much the same way that an obelisk would. From the base of the statue, a copper line was inserted into the pavement of the square to indicate midday – the sun at its meridian. At the end of World War One in 1918, Czechoslovakia declared independence, and as a sign that it had broken free from Habsburg domination, the column was destroyed, but the line remains.

*The remains of the midday marker in the Old Town Square – Prague. K.L.Gest*

It would therefore seem logical that the position of the Junior Warden is in the South, the position of the marker for determining the sun at midday, and the Senior Warden in *the west* for determining the season based on the movement of the sun along the horizon. It also explains why the Junior Warden lowers his column, as he is marking in the horizontal plane, whilst the Senior Warden has his column erect to signify the observer's position with a fixed marker.

## The Deacons

If one thinks in terms of freemasonry being connected with the craft of stonemasonry, then there is no record of deacons being associated directly with that trade. It may have originated in the religious guilds, however.

There is a suggestion that the role of deacons was created in Scottish lodges in the time of William Shawe and the introduction of the Shawe statutes in 1598/99. In this instance, and particularly during the late seventeenth century, the role of the wardens and deacons was sometimes merged, depending on the size of the lodge, and in others the deacon is effectively the Master. Hence it has been suggested that Dr Anderson used the Scottish lodge definition of the deacon when compiling the constitutions of 1723, noting that the union of Scotland and England had taken place in 1707, just sixteen years earlier.

Notwithstanding that, the word *Deacon* is described in the Oxford Concise Dictionary, as being *a layman attending to church business in Nonconformist churches.* This would again, aptly describe an interpretation in a religious guild, including being a *layman.* Yet a better understanding of how and why the role might have come into being is found in the Catholic Encyclopaedia:

> *"The name deacon (diakonos) means only minister or servant, and is employed in this sense both in the Septuagint (though only in the book of Esther…) and in the New Testament …But in Apostolic times the word began to acquire a more definite and technical meaning. Writing about 63 A.D. St. Paul addresses "all the saints who are at Philippi, with the bishops and deacons" (Philippians 1:1). A few years later (1 Timothy 3:8 sq.) he impresses upon Timothy that "deacons must be chaste, not double tongued, not given to much wine, not greedy of filthy lucre, holding the mystery of faith in a pure conscience." He directs further that they must "first be proved: and so let them minister, having no crime", and he adds that they should be the husbands of one wife: who rule well their children and their own houses. For they that have ministered well shall purchase to themselves a good degree, and much confidence in the faith which*

*is in Christ Jesus." This passage is worthy of note, not only because it describes the qualities desirable in candidates for the diaconate, but also because it suggests that external administration and the handling of money were likely to form part of their functions."*[54]

This definition is a very apt description of the role of the deacons. A servant would be expected to run errands and act as a messenger –this is one of the roles of a deacon in a lodge. The comment that *they must first be proved* also fits, for it is in this position that the member is prepared for the role of being a warden. And the further comment ...*for they that have ministered well shall purchase to themselves a good degree, and much confidence...* is a reflection of their roles in supervising candidates in ceremonies, and inspiring confidence in the other members of the lodge, such that when the time arrives, they will be well equipped for their role as Master. This is added to by ...*This passage is worthy of note, not only because it describes the qualities desirable in candidates...But also because it suggests ...the handling of money were likely to form part of their functions...*and it does, in their usual role of alms collections.

If freemasonry is descended through the religious guilds, then it would be logical that they would know the biblical references. Furthermore, in earlier times the people that collected the dues as part of the membership of the related guild, as part of their burial fund, may have been termed *deacons* as a reflection of the connection with the description from the bible. It would have been a role akin to being a treasurer. In this role, they would demonstrate trustworthiness, and be acting as messengers. Hence in the period of Charles II when other developments occurred, the role became more logically established within the structure of a Society of Free-Masons.

### The Tyler and the Inner Guard

Masonic historians show that there is no direct relationship between these roles and anything in the stonemasons' craft that might require such a title. The titles of these roles do not occur in Anderson's Constitutions of 1723. Quite what their origins are, and their purpose, is purely speculation.

It is also noted that in 1717, Anthony Sayer, Gentleman, was the first to occupy the Chair of the newly formed Grand Lodge and later became Tyler. The first mention of a Tyler in Grand Lodge is in 1732 nine years after Anderson's Constitutions were published. Just six years later in 1738, the second edition of Anderson's Constitutions was published, and the term Tyler is used. This suggests that the term was not known in 1717 or in 1723, which raises a question as to what happened between 1723 and 1732 that saw this position created. Although speculation, the answer may be quite simple. There was no Freemasons Hall at that time and meetings were held in rooms in Public Houses, like the *Kings Arms, Strand, London.* With what, to strangers, may have seemed a strange meeting taking place, in a building where doors didn't fit tightly as they may do today, where there was only one thickness of floorboards that didn't fit together tightly, one could understand merrymakers being curious as to what was happening on the other side of the door. It would soon be necessary to have at least one person holding the door on the inside, the Inner Guard. But, even if the door had a bolt or lock, this arrangement would have quickly changed as it was realised that it was better to have someone on the outside to keep off unwanted intruders rather than let them get to the door in the first place. There had to be a means of communicating from the inside of the lodge room to the guard on the outside without unbolting the door. A simple code using knocks on the door would solve that problem.

So where does the term Tyler originate? There is no clear answer to this question. Most dictionaries don't list the word, and some of those that do, mention that it is used in freemasonry. Trying to trace the etymology of the word is not very revealing either: A typical definition is that it was the person who tiled a roof to give it a covering, hence tiler. At first glance this seems entirely inappropriate – there is no direct connection with one who places tiles on a roof and someone who is guarding a door, except, that is, that the roof provides a covering and the guard is in effect, covering the lodge. It does not explain either why the (i) in tiler was changed to a (y). Dictionaries of old Anglo-Saxon words are not helpful either, except through one word, *tigel,* which describes several things from an earthenware pot to a roof tiler. A variation of *tigel* is an *Olde English* word of *tigele* (pronounced tie-lay) which apparently also meant *to cover.* Keeping in mind that the first Masonic use of the term *tyler* was some three hundred years ago, the word *tigele* would probably have been more widely known than it is today, and as such be an ideal word to use for someone covering or protecting the entrance door. Even so, it is possible that this definition has been copied several times by well meaning compilers of dictionaries and we cannot rely on it, as it might not have been a correct translation in the first instance.

There is one other reference and that is to the French term for describing a stonemason or stonecutter – tailleur de Pierre[55]. Pronunciation of the word *tailleur* could easily translate into *tyler,* but this raises questions as to why one would use a French word for this one position. Thus, we are still left with the conundrum of where the word came from.

## The Entered Apprentice, Fellow, Free-man and Mysteries

In the modern world of the twenty-first century, it is not uncommon for an individual to work for a company or local government institution for many years, residing in a stable community, having obtained an education at university or college which forms the basis of their knowledge. They become, employees. For many people entering the workplace their employer is a source of steady income and they can rely on a steady income for most of their working lives. In mediaeval times through to the eighteenth century, nearly everyone was self-employed, they lived by their own effort. Those that were unskilled were the poorest. To have a skill recognised by a guild was a passport to a modest living. Weavers might work a loom in their home and take their produce to the market in the town and sell it, and thus they became part of that town and may have lived and worked there all their lives. There might be several weavers working in a single town. Candle making may well have been a family business handed from father to son, but a small town would only be able to support perhaps a few such businesses.

The stonemason went where the work was. A large town might have enough work to support twenty stonemasons on a regular basis, and the guild controlled who was permitted to set up a business in a given town. It ensured there was just enough work for every mason that was a member of the guild. There were times when a major project was being undertaken, as in the building of a large abbey church, a bridge or an extension to a monastery. A large abbey church might take one hundred masons five or six years to build and when completed, most would have to travel elsewhere looking for work, hiring themselves out, selling their labour and their skill. The craft of the stonemason was a very special skill and as such rates of pay were good for their times, but when the work stopped, the pay stopped, and the only way to become an accepted craftsman in the trade of the stonemasons was by apprenticeship.

The term apprentice is well understood. It was a young person who would be sent to a master craftsman to learn the trade of that craftsman, such that ultimately they could earn their living by the skills that were imparted to them. It has been a recognised system of learning for over one thousand years, but probably existed well before that time in an informal sense as fathers taught sons, mothers taught daughters, and passed on skills and knowledge they had accumulated, such as carpentry and tallow making.

It was in the reign of Elizabeth I that the value of apprenticeships was recognised in an Act of 1563 known as the *Statute of Artificers and Apprentices*. It was devised to protect the apprenticeship system after the guild structure had been abolished during the main period of the reformation, some years earlier. As well as providing a means of regulating the system, it also protected the skills that were learnt, by forbidding anyone from carrying on a trade or craft unless they had served an apprenticeship of at least seven years with a person that was a *master* of that trade or craft. In many respects the *statute of Artificers and Apprentices* also gave stature to the *master*, and hence the means by which one achieved recognition of that status. The Statutes formed the basis of the system of learning trades and crafts that held sway through the period that the Grand Lodge was formed in 1717, and for many years thereafter.

It was during the period of the industrial revolution that some changes were made, largely for economic reasons, and apprenticeship periods for some trades were reduced to five years. The industrial revolution also saw the development of new trades and skills, the evolution of the trading company, and the necessity for apprentices to *live-in* the business with the master, was no longer appropriate, so minor changes were made to the system. Until the late 1960s in Britain, serving an indentured apprenticeship with a reputable employer was the university system of the trades and crafts; it declined in importance in the latter part of the twentieth century, but has, as we entered the twenty-first century, had a revival, albeit in a modern context, with shorter periods of training and starting at a later age.

In the Middle Ages, the guilds had strict codes of governance of apprentices. To become an apprentice one had to be around fourteen years of age, usually a boy, and parents or guardians paid a sum of money to the craftsmen to take the boy on for training. The typical minimum length of apprenticeship was seven years. Hence someone joining a trade at age fourteen was twenty-one years of age when they finished, twenty-one being the then age of majority. In return for the payment, the master provided board and lodgings for his apprentice, though the conditions were often harsh. The apprentice was totally under the control of the craftsman who probably treated them more like slaves in the early years, fetching, carrying and being given all the dirty tasks the masters didn't want to do themselves. Yet it did teach the youngster that there were other aspects to earning a living than merely making whatever the finished goods were that the craftsman produced. Through the course of his apprenticeship the young man would be taught the *secrets and mysteries* of that craft, which in the case of the stonemason, might cover everything from how to handle tools for best results, how to make certain tools, because every craftsman needed his own tools and there were no speciality shops to buy them in. The apprentice would also be shown how to choose different types of stone for different types of work, digging foundations and the importance of ensuring they were firm and how to achieve it, how to size a lintel over a door, and many other related aspects of the trade or craft. These were the elements of knowledge that collectively made up the *secrets and mysteries* of that trade and set them apart from all others. Taking on an apprentice meant notifying the guild to which the master belonged, and in latter times their name would be entered as an *indenture* into a register at the *Guildhall*. He became an *indentured apprentice*. The information would record the date, apprentice's name, name of the master, the value of the fee paid, the trade he was entering. The *indenture* became a record of the obligation that the master owed to the apprentice and the apprentice to the master. Completing one's apprenticeship was extremely important as it was the passport to ultimately being accepted for and entering the guild and thereby being designated as a recognised craftsman, and later, a free-man who could take on projects for his own account. Thus, at the end of the apprenticeship period a note would be added to the indenture, in the register that originally recorded it, that the apprentice had completed his time. There were times when a master might fall ill, die, or was otherwise unable to continue to train the apprentice, in which case, the guild would appoint another of their number from the same craft, to take over that responsibility.

All qualified craftsmen of the time had passed through the same system and recognised its significance and that they owed something to the craft from which they derived their living. At the end of the indentured period, and a suitable time to solidify his skills by working on other projects with other craftsmen from the same guild, the craftsman could apply to become a free-man. This involved swearing an oath, having his name entered into yet another register along with the signatures of endorsement of other free-men of that town/city. This provided him with the opportunity to take on work in his own name rather than only working for someone else.

Many previous writers have turned to the records of The London Company of Masons when seeking information, but many of their records were destroyed in the Great Fire of London, and are not necessarily indicative of what might have happened in other areas of the country. Rochester in Kent was the second location after Canterbury, where St Augustine established a church, so too the following is from their records.

A typical page from a record book of apprenticeships maintained at the Guildhall in the City of Rochester, Kent, in the year 1667. It clearly shows the name of the apprentice in the left hand column. Together with the detail of trade, master, fee paid and other obligations.

Below is a later entry that records that the apprenticeship was completed.

*Reproduced by kind permission of Medway Archives, Kent*

A further entry in a record book of apprenticeships maintained at the Guildhall in the City of Rochester, Kent, in the year 1667. It is for one John Tayler who was apprenticed as a bricklayer to a Thomas Patton.

The top part is an agreement that Thomas Patton will accept John Tayler as an apprentice.

The lower part is the Indenture record, which is detailed below.

*Reproduced by kind permission of Medway Archives, Kent*

## The Indenture record for John Tayler reads:

*This Indenture made the first day of May in the eighteenth year of our Sovereign Lord Charles II, between John Tayler son of John Tayler late of Frinsbury in the County of Kent Bricklayer on the one part and Thomas Patton of St Margarets in the City of Rochester Bricklayer on the other part witnesseth that the said John Tayler of his own free will and consent of his friends hath put and bound himself an apprentice with and after the manner of an apprentice with him to dwell conform and abide with and to the said John Patton from this date thereof for the full and term of seven years from this day to be compliant[and viz]*

*And the said Thomas Patton for himself and executors and [assignees] doth covenant promise and grant to the said John Tayler his said apprentice that the said Thomas Patton his executors and [aforesigned] and some of them shall and will after the best and speediest manners that he or they […] may teach instruct inform or cause to be taught instructed or informed his said apprentice in the art trade mysteries and corruptions of a bricklayer and in the manner chastise him finding providing and giving unto his said apprentice during the said [period] sufficient and [warm] linnen and woollen host shoos apparel washing and all other vestments in fitt and [state] for an apprentice. And in the end of the said term shall and will give unto his said apprentice his good suit of apparell for all parts of his body fitt for his doing and wearing that is to say for holy fairs and other for washing days and fitt and convenient for his wearing on [Sundays].*

*The mark of the said John Tayler*

*Sealed and solemnized in the presence of*
*James [Doy]*
*Abraham Pindor*
*Rv Heath*

Words and areas of the Indenture that are unclear have been included in [brackets].

Very similar text applies to all indentures of that era.

What is noticeable is how close to certain phrases in the modern ceremony of being made an *Entered Apprentice* in freemasonry is, with some of the terminology that is used in the indenture. The apprentice entered into the arrangement of his *own free will;* that he would be taught the *art trade mysteries and corruptions* of the craft, and that the apprenticeship lasted for a *full seven years.*

Having completed his apprenticeship, the young man would be expected to become a *journeyman*. That may well have been within his own town/city but also included going to work in other regions. It was not unusual for an employer to *turn out* his apprentice the day after the apprenticeship period ended; that way he had no further obligations to him, like feeding him and giving him lodgings without payment. The purpose of the *journeyman* period was to gain experience in a range of different applications of the skill and knowledge he had gained. It was quite common for an apprentice to be *turned out* to become a journeyman, even in the mid-twentieth century, especially in the building trades, or speciality skills like welding.

It is probably from this *journeyman* period that we gain the term *fellowcraft*, a craftsman whose knowledge and ability is *superior to an entered apprentice* but *inferior to that position we trust you will hereafter attain,* that of being a Free-man of the town/city and admitted to the guild as a *master craftsman.*

In Scotland this process of turning out a mason on completion of his apprenticeship was literally described in the Shawe Statutes of 1598/9 in that it was agreed that after serving their time as an apprentice, a stonemason could not be permitted or accepted fully into the craft until he had worked at the trade for a further seven years as a minimum, *seven years and upwards.*

At the end of a further period, usually of not less than a further seven years, fourteen years in total, the former apprentice could apply to be fully admitted to the guild and be recognised as a master craftsman. In England that also entitled him to become a free-man. The following is the text of a description of the responsibilities of being a free-man, as it applied within the City of Rochester, Kent.

> *"Being a freeman entitled both privileges and obligations. The privileges included exemption from duties for loading and carrying goods on ships, rent payable for erecting stalls in markets and fairs, for anchorage and wharfage, and for tolls for carrying goods through the city. They were also granted the right of foremarket. This enabled freemen to buy and sell goods in markets and fairs in priority of those not free or 'foreigners', as those living outside the city were called. Only freemen were to exercise or use any trade or business within the city, become civic officials or vote for members of either local or central government."*

There were two ways in which one could become a freeman, and for which the Corporation made no charge for the endowment of the status:

- Apprenticeship
- Patrimony – by birth, being the son of landed or titled gentleman, or a person who was a freeman.

In the case of a major city, like Rochester, Kent, there would be individuals who migrated to the city having been free-men in other towns. They were granted freemen status, usually on payment of a fee and proof of their status elsewhere; in the mid-1700s it was £20.

Rochester was an important city built on the banks of the River Medway, with traceable roots that extend back beyond Roman Times. It is on the main route between Canterbury and London. By comparison with many towns in England, it had a vibrant commercial centre with a modest population. Nevertheless, the number of freemen of the city at any one time was limited to a very small proportion of the population, hence the status was upheld.

The image on the left is a declaration of individuals admitted to the freedom of the City of Rochester on 28th February 1712, and 4th March 1712, having sworn their oath. The signatures are of the freemen also in attendance to witness the occasion.

*Images are reproduced by kind permission of Medway Archives, Kent*

*The image to the right is from the register of those granted Freedom of the City of Rochester during a period of nearly one year in 1767/8. Of the twenty-eight listed, eleven received freemen status by serving a registered apprenticeship. In that period, on 30th January 1768, William Patten, Mason, became a Free-man having served his apprenticeship with William Pile and Francis Smith Patten. He was thus a free-mason.*

| 30th January 1760 | John Murton | Carver | Apprenticeship to Richard Chichely |
| 30th January 1760 | William Patten | Mason | Apprenticeship to William Pile and Francis Smith Patten. — |
| 30th January 1760 | Owen Skinner | Marriner | Birth from Henry Skinner. |

*m.*

*ey.*

In Rochester, the duties and obligations of a freeman were set out in the freeman's oath that was sworn at the time his freedom was granted and entered into the register.

> *"Ye shall be true and faithful to our Sovereign Lord King...and to the heirs of our Sovereign Lord King; obeysant and obedient shall ye be to the Mayor and Ministers of this city; the Franchises and Customs thereof ye shall maintain and this Citty keep harmless you that in you is. Ye shall be contributory to all manner of charges within the City, as summons, watches, contributions, lot and scot, and all other charges, bearing your part as a Freeman ought to do. Ye shall implead or sue no Freeman out of this City. Ye shall also keep the King's peace in your own person; Ye shall know no gatherings, conventicles or conspiracies made against the King's peace but ye shall warn the Mayor thereof, to let it to your power. All these points and articles ye shall well and truly keep, according to the laws and customs of this City, to your power. So help you God."[56]*

As we have seen in the *indenture* document for John Tayler, he was to be taught the mysteries of his craft. These were the *tricks of the trade*, those things that not only resulted in a good job well done, but those little tricks that enabled it to be done quickly and without undermining the integrity of whatever was being constructed; and of course those small tricks that hold a structure together for many years, as opposed to a structure erected by someone who did know the tricks of the trade and found that it fell down a few years later.

There is one sensitive aspect of apprenticeship in the Middle Ages that probably has a connection with the Masonic ceremony of initiation. It relates to a statement that is made by the Master shortly after the candidate has entered the lodge room for the first time. He is paraded in front of all the assembled brethren and the Master states:

> *"The brethren will note that ...is about to pass in view before them to show that he is a fit and proper person to be made a mason."*

In the Middle Ages, a person could only be taken on as an apprentice if they were whole in body and mind. A man who had any form of deformity, however slight, would not be admitted. Even the loss of perhaps, the top of a finger in a hunting accident, could be enough to result in exclusion. The work of the stonemason involved lifting heavy stones, climbing ladders with them, working at heights, from dawn to dusk. So a person who had a disability could not perform the full extent of the demands of the work, and were therefore not admitted.

Through the twentieth century, there were many Masonic researchers who indicated that when Dr Anderson first compiled his Constitutions, he included a number of elements of the Scottish Lodge traditions within them. This is not surprising. It was only ten years prior to the formation of the first Grand Lodge, that the union of crowns and Scotland and England took place, creating the United Kingdom of Great Britain and Ireland, and the palace of Westminster ceased to be the home of an English Parliament but became the seat of government for the entire union. It would not have been unreasonable, therefore, for freemasonry to be formalised using practices that were established in both kingdoms.

In the era following the creation of the United Grand Lodge of England in 1813, freemasonry grew, and many lodges had well over one hundred members. It is interesting to note that in the era of the nineteenth century through to the late twentieth century, a typical period of time between being admitted as an *entered apprentice* through to being the *master of the lodge*, and thereby being accepted as a *past master* who was expected to be, and had demonstrated proficiency in all the levels and functions of the lodge, was fourteen years. This is the same time period between a person being admitted to an apprenticeship in the late Middle Ages, completing their training, enhancing their knowledge by being journeymen, to being fully accepted into the craft/guild. Even in smaller lodges today, and assuming progressing to one new office in each subsequent year, it will still take seven years before one becomes a *past master*.

# Chapter 12

# WHAT IS THERE TO BE LEARNT
IN THE DEGREES?

The fact is, that we have absolutely no idea where the contents of the various degrees in Freemasonry came from or what motivated their structure. At the time when Dr Anderson was compiling the first book of Constitutions published in 1723, there were only two degrees formally in place in England; in Scotland there appear to have only been two degrees; yet in Dublin in 1723, there were three used in the two premier lodges of that city.

Over the past one hundred years there have been many eminent men who have researched and produced a great deal of information about which lodges were operating where, and which men of title and fame were members of which lodge. When it comes to the subject of why we have three degrees, or where they came from, the information is less helpful. In fact, it's not very helpful at all. There are those that believe there was originally just one degree, namely that of the Entered Apprentice, used only when a new member was admitted; there are others that suggest that there were two degrees that might have been used in a single meeting, one after the other – one for the admission of a new candidate, and one that embraced what later became the second and third degree. There are yet others that suggest that over time the second of the two degrees was broken down into a third. Many earlier writers quote reference documents that have been assembled by Ars Quator Coronati, the premier research lodge, or have interpreted various old manuscripts, but when it comes to explaining exactly how and why there were changes, there is no real conclusion. This is even the case in the use of the word *degree;* why not level or step? There might be a simple answer to that question, which also provides a reason for why we have three degrees.

If one looks at our ceremonies, the words and actions, across the three degrees, it is difficult to imagine that anyone sat down and deliberately contrived every part. We know that something existed well before 1717, and that it was more widely based than just London. In the previous section there is a reference from Dr Plot, published in 1686, that states…*the Society of Free-Masons…I find the custom spread more or less all over the nation…*Many of what we now see as major towns and cities were little more than villages when Dr Plot wrote his comment, so the main centres where such societies existed were likely to have been some distance apart. With the limitations of transport and communications in that era, it is difficult to imagine that they were all operating in a regulated and consistent manner. Thus when Dr Anderson put together the first edition of the Constitutions the chances are that he picked those items that seemed to have a regular theme and moulded them into the ceremonial content we now know. Part of that knowledge came from the *old charges* that he was able to reference, but was also the type of information that a building designer/architect/stonemason was likely to know, especially in the period after the restoration. It was also possibly the type of information that been taught to apprentices, and learnt by journeymen, so that the sum of the knowledge qualified them for admission to the guild.

There is a time span of nearly 300 years since Dr Anderson compiled the first Constitutions. It is not impossible that at that time most of the men who were freemasons knew and understood exactly what the ceremonies were about, and any logic that existed within them. Over time, however, the fraternity attracted an increasing number of individuals who came from professions that were not associated with the building trade, and so the knowledge became known to fewer and fewer individuals, so that by the time the United Grand Lodge of England was created, it was almost totally unknown. After, UGLE was formed there was the rise of insurance companies and banks, friendly societies and other financial institutions, along with the growth of large companies that grew with the industrial revolution. Interest in freemasonry grew and the number of lodges multiplied. This meant that entire lodges could have had a membership where there was no understanding or connection with the ceremonies in any way. This enabled all manner of innovations to creep in, especially towards the end of the Victorian era when archaeology, especially in the Holy Land and Egypt, began to produce some fascinating new finds, and with them a whole new culture of beliefs, some of which found their way into the Masonic culture. With the passage of yet further time leading to our current era we have reached the stage where many lodges have members that learn and say the words and actions, have absolutely no idea what they are saying or doing, but get praise from the Masonic hierarchy for getting it right. Yet, there seems to be sufficient information within the ceremonies, plus some external information that is now generally available, that enables us to piece together what that original knowledge and structure would have been.

## The term degrees

It is generally believed that several thousand years ago, there was a civilisation that developed in the area of fertile plain at the junction of the

Tigris and Euphrates rivers. It was known as *Sumer* and was later absorbed into the Babylonian empire. It is today part of Iraq. This civilisation is believed to have developed a counting concept that was based on the number 60, and that it also formed the basis by which a circle came to be considered as 360 degrees. To ancient peoples there was also a symbol known as the six-spoked wheel. The six-spoked wheel was a symbol of the sun, the horizontal line representing the position east – west of the sun at the time of the spring and autumn equinox, whilst the other two lines represented the extremity of the movement of the sun, east-west, at the time of the summer and winter solstices.

# The Labarum

An interpretation of it has been associated with the Emperor Constantine and the adoption and use of Christianity as the unifying religion of the Roman Empire, the symbol of the Labarum. Constantine is known to have previously favoured the Roman sun god – Invictus.

By virtue that the wheel has six segments, then under the Sumer counting system, if each segment represented 60, then 6 divisions of 60 = 360. It is believed that this is the origin of the circle having 360 degrees. Half 60 is 30; half of 30 is 15; therefore if you divide the circle of the Earth into easily manageable portions of 15 degrees, then you have 24 sections, the basis of the unit of time that we call an hour; one hour is the equivalent of the earth rotating on its axis by 15 degrees.

The Entered Apprentice is taught that the *Earth constantly rotates on its axis in its orbit around the sun.* When opening the lodge meeting we note that *the sun regularly rises in the east to open and enliven the day,* and when we close the lodge we note *as the sun sets in the west to close the day* in other words, the sun rises in the east and sets in the west. What most people fail to realise is that this is one of Mother Nature's clever illusions, created by the rotation of the Earth on its axis in a counter-clockwise direction. Thus, when the sun appears over the horizon in the east, we are in the west, relative to it. As the Earth rotates we pass in front of the sun and in so doing, this creates the illusion that the sun is the item that is moving towards the west from the east.

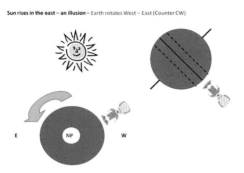

Sun rises in the east – an illusion – Earth rotates West – East (Counter CW)

*The sun rises over the horizon, so we are in the west relative to it.*

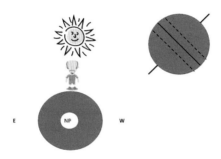

*By midday the sun is directly overhead.*

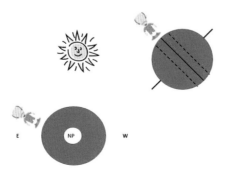

*At sunset, we are in the east relative to the sun.*

Furthermore, the lodge-room is set out so that the Master is in the east and his Wardens are placed, one each, in the south and west. When we perambulate around the lodge-room we do so in a clockwise direction, East – South – West. We are therefore moving in the direction that the sun appears to travel when viewed from Earth. Interestingly, there is no ceremonial office positioned in the north of the lodge-room; the sun never circles through the north. Thus each complete perambulation around the lodge-room is replicating the circle of 360 degrees. Hence, the word *degree* has a practical association in freemasonry, rather than expressions such as level or step, and the three degrees of attainment are, in part, illusions to the three primary compass positions that the sun appears to travel through, East, South and West.

There are of course the other three positions of the sun that might also have formed the basis for the three-degree system. It was the movement of the sun to the three primary positions on the horizon; the spring equinox, the autumn equinox and the summer/winter solstice, of which, until shortly after the period of the *enlightenment*, the spring/vernal equinox was one on the most important events in the solar calendar and for many centuries was the starting point for each new year.

It is also worthwhile noting that when Dr Anderson set out the Constitutions, the Royal Society had only been in existence for sixty years, the Greenwich Observatory for a little over forty years, and the period of the *Enlightenment* was just gathering momentum. All angular measurements of the Earth and elevation in the sky, are measured in degrees.

So against this background, what is the knowledge that a builder/architect/stonemason of old would have needed to understand, that is still reflected in the degree of an Entered Apprentice today, and we expect them to know before they move on to being the journeyman/fellow?

### The Entered Apprentice knowledge

We are told that on being admitted to the *mysteries and privileges* of freemasonry, the Entered Apprentice (his name having been duly *entered* in the minute book of the lodge, a residual element of the days when the name would have been registered at the Guildhall) learns several things; first that *the Earth constantly rotates on its axis in its orbit around the sun;* second, he has some basic tools to work with, a maul/mallet (referred to as a gavel), a chisel, and a means to measure. He learns that he was admitted on the *square,* which could imply that he was made aware of certain aspects of the term *square* that formed part of the *arts and mysteries* of his craft.

Are these merely words or do they perhaps stem from the stonemasons craft? To answer this question, let's take an imaginary apprentice of the post restoration era and look at what he might have been taught, and how that fits with ceremonial content.

One can imagine that in the late Middle Ages and through the seventeenth century, for the first year of the apprenticeship, the apprentice probably spent most of his working day running errands for the master, fetching and carrying his tools, clearing away debris, fragments of stone, and other general jobs. He might have been taught to recognise different types of stone. One thing is certain that would not have happened in his first year; he would not have been given a beautiful piece of stone of substantial proportions and been invited to create a Corinthian column from it. He would have not have known what tools to use, how to start, how to measure, and so many other factors. There were many things he needed to learn before he could ever hope to be entrusted with fashioning such a column. Nearly all apprenticeships, past and present, use the first years for the apprentice to become proficient in the use of the tools of the trade, starting with a very limited selection. And, every craftsman needed his own tools.

One can image the apprentice being given a piece of rough stone of reasonable size and with very jagged edges, and being told that his first task is to create one face that is flat. For this, he would need two tools; a chisel and a maul/mallet, both of which he would have to make himself. His master might give him a piece of metal acquired from the blacksmith, and a couple of pieces of hard wood, like oak, obtained from friendly carpenters, and the apprentice would spend nearly every spare moment he had during evenings and at occasionally quiet times in the day, whittling the wood with a sharp knife, into the shape of a maul head and a separate handle. He would quickly be made to realise that the handle of the maul would probably be in his hands all day when working the stone, so shaping the handle so that it fitted comfortably in the hand would be important. He would probably go to the blacksmith and be shown how to heat the metal to be white hot, how to handle it, and how to shape it, and the apprentice would be expected to hammer out and make his own chisel. Then again in the evenings he would sit with a sharpening stone, grinding one edge of the chisel to be sharp before taking it back to the blacksmith who would give it a final treatment to make it hard so that it didn't blunt with the first blow, and tempered (de-stressed) so that it didn't shatter when being used. Only then was he able to start to prepare one face of the stone. In the meantime, he had probably watched his master and other craftsmen if they were available, on how to hold the tools, and position the stone so that he could work with an element of comfort and access to the stone that would enable him to produce quality work. So, by the end of the first year he probably had two tools he had made himself, and a lump of stone with one flat side.

> *Point: The working tools of a maul/mallet and chisel are tools of the first degree. The Maul is to knock off all superfluous material and the chisel is to smooth the stone.*

Now the master tells him he has to render the rest of the block to be, for example, two cubits long and one cubit square, where every surface was flat and square to each other. For that he needed two new tools; a measure, easily created from a length of wood or a reed; a square formed into the shape of a letter 'L'.

This now leads him to ask a question. How do you make a square that is set at an angle of exactly ninety degrees? Enter the works of the Greek philosophers, translated from Arabic into Latin that had been collected and compiled by Islamic scholars in the ninth century. In particular, Euclid's geometry.

The master tells the apprentice to remember three numbers, 3, 4 & 5. He then draws the outline of a triangle in the dust of the workshop or the ground and shows the apprentice that if you have three pieces of stick cut to length in regular units, and arrange them in a particular pattern, you can create a square with an angle of exactly ninety degrees – a right angle. Using some flat wood or metal, he can now arrange the pieces around the triangle and secure them, thereby making a perfect square. This the apprentice does, and when completed, he now has yet another tool and a key piece of knowledge - the numbers 3, 4 & 5 and how useful they can be. Again in evenings and his spare time, he can now use his maul, chisel and square to form the other three sides and ends of the stone block so that they are flat and square, using the first face as a reference point.

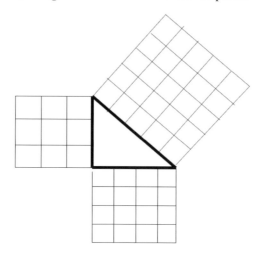

*The 3, 4, 5 triangle features in Masonic jewels.*

At the end of the first period of training the apprentice has two working tools, knowledge of one of the first principles of geometry, a square, how to make a measuring stick, his first block of stone shaped as the master wanted, calloused and bruised hands. He is now ready to learn the next *mystery* of the art of the craft.

Let us now also imagine that the master has received a contract to build a new church in stone to replace one originally built in wood that is now beyond repair. It is the decade following the great fire of London. By this time, around 1675, Copernican theory was at last being accepted. Some twenty-five years earlier, Galileo Galilei had died, having a few years previously been tortured by officials of the Roman Catholic Church for expounding Copernican ideas, that maintained that the sun was the centre of the universe and that the Earth orbited around it.

For the building of this new church, a local landowning gentleman has donated a small piece of land for the purpose, land that had previously been open farmland belonging to a monastery that has long since been demolished. The church, he is told, is to be dedicated to St. George.

The master agrees a design with the clergy and churchwardens and provides an estimate of cost. This being accepted, the master then contacts carpenters to organise timber for roofing struts and scaffolding, a tiler to tile the roof when the main structure is finished, and then begins to assemble the stone and other materials needed at the site, all of which the apprentice is aware of. They have to wait until 23rd April before they can commence any work, because the orientation of the building has to be marked before the foundations can be set out and the work begin.

The master explains to the apprentice that there are four cardinal points to the measure of Earth, north, south, east and west, and that these four points have been known to masons since time immemorial; that the sun rises in the east each day and sets in the west each day, but that each day the sun rises in a slightly different place as it moves along the horizon with the progress of the seasons. He explains that one of the secrets of church building is that the altar is in the east, and there is a large window so that the first rays of Gods' sun can illuminate the church each day. But the real secret is that on the feast day of the saint to whom the church is to be dedicated, the sun, as it rises over the horizon, shines a beam of light directly down the centre aisle. To do this, they have first to *mark* that orientation; it will be the centre line of the building from which everything else will be developed. Thus, they wait until the 23rd day of April, St George's feast day. They have chosen the area of ground on which the church will be built. They have two pointed sticks, one of which is stuck firmly in the ground, at what will be the western end of the church, and made vertical by use of a plumb-line attached to it. Whilst it is still not yet dawn, the other stick, also with a plumb-line attached to aid ensuring the post would be vertical, is taken by the apprentice to a point beyond where they estimate the eastern end of the church will be. They wait until the first beam of light appears over the horizon. The master peers over the point of the fixed stick and instructs the apprentice to move to the place where a line of sight exists that passes through the two points and to the place on the horizon where the sun rose. By fixing pegs in the ground at the base of the pointed sticks, and running a cord between them - a skirret would be ideal for this purpose - they now have the centreline through the intended church that corresponds with the rising sun on the day dedicated to the saint. They have also done something else. *They have marked the sun at its meridian*, and fixed the position of that imaginary meridian line, as it passes through the north and south poles, on 23rd April, St George's Day.

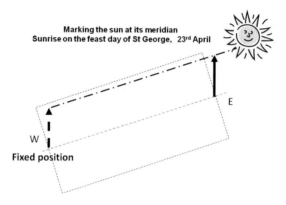

Marking the sun at its meridian
Sunrise on the feast day of St George, 23rd April

E

W

Fixed position

Note: The centre line marked out in 1675 would not correspond with a similar process today; the orientation would be at least ten days out of alignment. In 1675, the Julian calendar, created in the time of Julius Caesar, still held sway over dating systems in Britain. During one thousand five hundred years of its use, a small error in the system had resulted in the spring (vernal) equinox not occurring on the date it should, 21st March, but had drifted to the 11th March. This affected other key dates in the religious calendar as well. The Vatican believed the time had come for the calendar system to be updated. This was done in 1582 and in the papacy of Gregory XIII, a new system came into being, known as the Gregorian calendar. It is still the calendar that we use today, although it is now more widely known as the Western calendar. All the countries that were dominated by the Holy Roman Empire moved to the new system, but in 1582 England was still in the aftermath of the Reformation, and so did not accept the new calendar at that time because of its connections with the Catholic faith. It was 1752 before Britain harmonised the calendar system. This meant it had to lose eleven days from the calendar for that year. This was done in September 1752, the dates running 1st, 2nd, 14th, 15th and so on. This resulted in a number of riots across the country as people realised that the day on which rent would be due, would be eleven days quicker coming round, and that they may not have the money to pay the landlord.

From the centre-line marked by the master and apprentice, and with the use of a square, some pegs and some cord, they can now mark out the position of the inside of the outer walls and therefore prepare the foundations, which is a shallow trench all round. The master points out, that if one stands looking east, and with the west to one's back, then north will be to the left and the south to the right. This is important, because traditionally the first stone to be set in the foundations is always in the northeast corner, this being the furthest place on the horizon to which the sun travels and gives us the summer solstice. As they are ready to set the first stone the clergyman and churchwardens appear. In the foundations, below where the first stone is to be set, they lay several gold sovereigns, the currency of the day. It is a tradition handed down from the ancient Egyptians and Romans, that a treasure is buried under the foundation stone in anticipation that the building may prosper for all who use it. The foundation stone is set, and the building work can then commence.

The apprentice has something else to learn. Having set the foundation stones, the building superstructure is usually commenced by building up the northeast corner first, ensuring that it is square and perpendicular. It becomes the point from which the rest of the building is developed, and unless it is sound the rest of the structure may be weakened.

The apprentice has now leant that the Earth orbits the sun, how to orientate a building to coincide with a specific celestial event, the four cardinal points of the Earth and how to remember them, and the traditions associated with laying the first stone, the foundation stone, and the importance of having the first corner square and perpendicular/upright.

*Point: After the first-degree ceremony the candidate being admitted to freemasonry notes that '…the earth constantly rotates on its axis in its orbit around the sun…'.*

*During the first degree ceremony the candidate stands in the northeast corner of the pavement, the outer edge of which symbolise the foundations, whilst he symbolises the foundation stone. There is also the statement made that 'You…are placed in the northeast part of the lodge to represent that stone…may you raise a superstructure, perfect in its parts and honourable to the builder'.*

*Towards the end of the ceremony the candidate is placed on the centreline of the lodge, facing the east (the sun) and on a line between the master and the senior warden, which symbolises the centreline of the orientation.*

At the end of each working day when master and apprentice return home, the apprentice still has his first block of stone that is twice as long as it is square, a double cube. The master explains that in the new renaissance architecture that has been inspired in England by Inigo Jones, there are often ornate pillars, and the pillars stand on plinths that are either in the form of a double cube or single cube, but more about that will come as his training continues.

The master instructs him to separate the double cube into two blocks of equal size. How, he asks, will the apprentice be able to measure the point that is the centre of the length of the block which he will use to mark where the block is to be split into two without a standard measure? The apprentice having no idea, the master shows him the following method.

The master takes a piece of straight wood, and a stick, and draws a straight line in the dirt. He then points out that the apprentice needs to find the centre of the line, but he has no idea how long the line is. The master takes a pair of compasses and stretches them so that when he places the point on one end of the line, the other point of the compasses is longer than the approximate centre of the line. He then draws a circle with its centre at the end of the line; goes to the other end of the line and does the same thing. Now he has a line with two circles that cross one another. By drawing a line through the two points where the circles cross and through the line we want to divide, then the point where the second line crosses the first is the middle of the first line. What is more, the junctions of the lines create a perfect square of ninety degrees that can be used to create a mason's square for checking his work.

From Euclid dividing a line

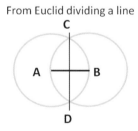

The apprentice can now take a piece of wood, or maybe a straight reed, and cut it to a length that is exactly the length of the block. He lays it on the ground and in the dust marks the length of a line corresponding to exactly the length of the block. Using the compasses and the system he was shown, he can now mark the exact centre of the line and use that to cut a reed or other suitable material to that exact length and transfer it to the block of stone. From that mark and using a square, he is now able to score a line right round the block. The master then shows him how to separate it into two blocks of equal size. Thus separated, one block is set aside for later.

The apprentice has learnt another simple piece of practical geometry and a use for a pair of compasses.

The master also points out something else whilst the apprentice has the pair of compasses in his hand. If he now draws a circle from a point where the horizontal and vertical lines cross, then the circle is divided into four equal parts, and that each fourth part forms a right angle of ninety degrees; thus, four sections of ninety degrees adds up to 360, so a circle is measured as 360 degrees. This is important to remember when producing certain tracery in church windows.

The fourth part of a circle

*Point: In the passing ceremony, there is a point where the candidate is asked what a square is? '…an angle of ninety degrees or the fourth part of a circle..'*

Using the block of stone that has not been set aside, the apprentice is about to learn yet another of the *secrets and mysteries* of the craft. He is about to learn the *secret of the square, it is* one of the most treasured secrets of the craft of the stonemason.

The master tells the apprentice that his next task is to reduce the block of stone to exactly half its size without using a standard measuring stick. He requires his chisel and something rigid, straight and flat, a piece of wood will do. The master instructs the apprentice to score a straight line on the stone, using the sharpened edge of his chisel, with the line running from one corner to the opposite corner, and the same for the other two corners. He now has two diagonal lines that meet in the centre. This is a way of finding the centre of a work face. Sometimes a hole may have to be cut or a recess made and the centre has to be found first. The apprentice now takes a piece of straw or reed, or something similar, and places it at the centre and breaks it so that its length is the exact distance between the centre and the edge of the block, and now uses that stick to mark the halfway point along each edge. The master thinks this is cumbersome and tells the apprentice to use his square, which he does.

He now scores a further set of lines on the stone using his chisel, linking the four points on the edge, so that they too, form a square. Where the first lines across from corner to corner, meet the lines that go from edge to edge, he scores another four lines parallel to the outside edges. The result is a square in the middle that is exactly half the size of the outside square of the block. This method of reducing any square of any size to exactly half that size, is one of the great secrets of the master mason.

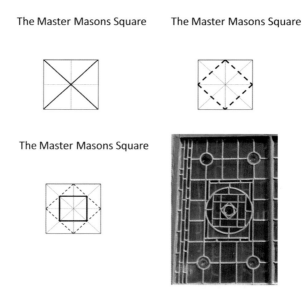

The Master Masons Square  The Master Masons Square

The Master Masons Square

*The Master Masons Square in a church window. K.L. Gest*

By now the apprentice is nearing the mid point of his apprenticeship and through all the shaping and reduction of the stone that he has done, he has mastered how to use the basic tools, and some of the basic geometry and methods he can easily remember that are key to his craft. The master notes that his apprentice *has made such progress in the craft* that he is now ready to know another secret of the square. He shows him some drawings of the type of classical architecture that Inigo Jones has now made famous. He points out that one of the important considerations in doing a good job is making a building look right, by making everything look balanced. This can be done, he says, by using the geometric shape of a square. Inigo Jones, he notes, copied the system from the Romans, and the Romans copied it from the Greeks and the Greeks copied it from the Egyptians. It was a system called perfect proportion.

It starts, the master says, with a square. The point of a pair of compasses is placed at the centre of the bottom line, and then extended to the top corner. An arc is then drawn down to the bottom line, and the extended part is called the golden ratio. This, he says, is used for making a building look balanced in terms of the width versus the height.

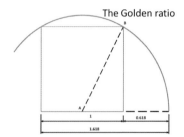 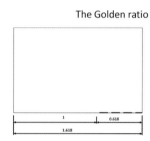

One of the first buildings that Inigo Jones built in England using this geometry was The Queen's House, Greenwich. One can see that the use of the square ends of the building means that the golden ratio extends the square to the centre of the front of the building, whilst a square around the centre of the building sets the position of the outer windows. There are many other areas in the building geometry where this concept was used when creating the design.

 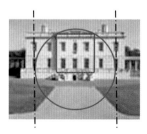

*The Queen's House, Greenwich*

*The images of the Queens House are reproduced by kind permission of the National Maritime Museum, Greenwich*

The apprentice now notes that the *square and compasses* are key tools in the development of designs for building in stone, but he still has much to learn. When he has finally completed his apprenticeship it would have been impractical to take the Guildhall book showing a record of his indenture, with him everywhere he went as proof of his being a time served craftsman. It was an era long before individual certificates of such status were introduced. One can therefore speculate that a method of signs and symbols evolved that the craftsman could use to demonstrate his proficiency and that such methods of proof were only conveyed to him once he had completed his time and the entry as such was recorded in the Guildhall register. But, he was only a time served apprentice, there was still much to learn and experience to be gained before he could be accepted into the guild.

What we see from examining the Entered Apprentice degree contents, in the context of an apprenticeship of three hundred years ago, are the remnants of information an operative mason/builder of that era is likely to have acquired. Through our ceremonies, we are continuing to convey that knowledge.

### The fellow/journeymen degree as an extension of the apprentice

At the start of this chapter, it was pointed out the at the time Dr Anderson compiled the Constitutions for the Grand Lodge of England, there were only two degrees that were worked in England and Scotland. It was further believed that the first was merely a ceremony of admission, and as such, may have been quite short. The second degree was held to have been a combination of what today we define as two separate degrees.

At first sight, the degree of a fellow/journeyman contains very little knowledge, and seems to be based more on Old Testament doctrine, borrowed to fit in with a ceremony. But that is misleading, especially when considered in its entirety, including the tracing board. It seems, in part, to be a continuation of the apprenticeship process, followed by an introduction to the architectural features of the renaissance, classical characteristics of that architecture and celestial mechanics.

The ceremony itself first deals with proving that the candidate has indeed served a full apprenticeship, and that as such, he fully understands the secrets of the use of the square. Also during the operative apprenticeship the candidate was made aware of the importance of the foundations and that one corner of a building was built up first as the starting point from which the rest of the structure would be constructed. It would have been most important to ensure that foundation stone was level in both its width and its length. This was achieved with the use of a level. This too, was a tool that the apprentice would make himself under the guidance of the master. It would comprise, as an example, a piece of wood about a cubit long that would act as a vertical element, and another that was about half a cubit long to act as a base. A simple plumb bob hung from the top of the upright would suffice. The level needed to have a mark at the base so that as the plumb bob swung it aligned with the mark to show that it was level. The level needed to be calibrated, that is to say, that the mark needed to be in a position that was guaranteed to be level. This was probably achieved with a water level during the making of the wooden version where the surface of still water in a container will always be level. Vitruvius shows methods for doing this in his books on architecture. Made of suitable materials, the same level device could also be used to ensure verticality / upright progress of a wall; the plumb bob would swing from side to side for level and forward and backwards for upright measures.

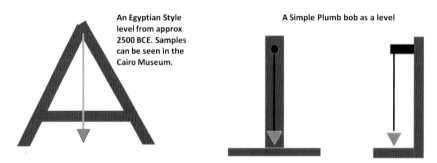

*There are several methods of creating levels and plumb rules. Interesting examples of all masons tools from antiquity can be seen on display in the Cairo Museum of Egyptian Antiquities.*

The apprentice now has several tools and a good understanding of what they are used for, and knows how to make them.

In the second ceremony, the candidate is placed in the southeast corner of the lodge pavement. Interestingly he never stands in the other two corners, suggesting there is nothing to symbolise in so doing. During the first ceremony he started off in the northeast corner, but has symbolically moved to the southeast corner in the second degree, from where he then returns to the centre which is in the east. This seems to be a record of the three primary positions of the sun, the equinoxes and the solstices, symbolising the movement from mid-summer through to mid-winter and returning to the position of the spring equinox and the end of one cycle of life and the start of another.

This involvement of the sun seems to be endorsed by another action that happens earlier. The candidate is in the west and is instructed to move to the east, which he does in a curved motion. This has all the characteristics of symbolising the rotation of the Earth, which, in counter-clockwise movement, represents the illusion of the movement of the sun that has already been noted in this chapter. But, it seems to combine this rotation of the Earth's axis with something else. There are five steps.

In the bible there are many references to the number forty. In addition, in recording that the tabernacle was built by Moses in the deserts of the Sinai, there is also reference to an event called the *shekinah* (there are many spellings for this term). Even in the Islamic religion, the *shekinah* is featured. There has been much speculation about what this was. Furthermore, the curving motion of the steps of the degree and the fact that there are five of them, suggests an illusion to the pentagram, but it may well also be an illusion to that ancient event called the *shekinah*.

In this degree the candidate is encouraged to study *the hidden mysteries of nature and science*, and one such art, and a mystery attached to it, is that of astronomy. Prior to about 1700, this would have been astrology, the main difference being that astrology was the science of predicting where certain stars and planets would be at any given time, and that of astronomy, keeping in mind that the Greenwich Observatory was not founded until 1675, is the study of the universe in all its parts. There are now many archaeologists that believe that one of the astronomical phenomena that ancient peoples, our ancestors, observed, was that of the movement of the planet Venus. This planet seems to describe the pattern of a pentagram in the heavens over a forty-year period, and returns to the same starting point. And a pentagram is a five-pointed geometric figure. If this is the basis of the five steps of the degree, then one must ask - how did it get there? Yet again, the answer may be simple.

We know that in England and Scotland at the time the First Grand Lodge was formed, there were only two degrees, but in Ireland there were three. There has in the past, been much speculation about the two/three degree system, and when they all started. We only know that the three degrees were formalised with the creation of the United Grand Lodge of England in 1813.

Ireland has a long Celtic heritage that has been usurped through political and territorial adventures by both Scotland and England. The first Christian Church in England was the Celtic Church that had originally transferred from Ireland to a base on the island of Iona, in Scotland. Celtic Christianity was usurped by the Catholic Church at the Synod of Whitby. It is not impossible that elements of Celtic belief could have found their way into that third degree. It is now well founded that the ancient Celtic site in Ireland known as Newgrange may well have been an astronomical observatory, and, amongst other things, one of the astronomical cycles recorded there was the *shekinah*.

Just before the Grand Lodge of England was formed, a man was born in Scotland by the name of James Ferguson (1710 – 1776). Ferguson went on to become a renowned Scottish astronomer. He made studies of the orbits of the then known planets, but paid particular attention to the planet Venus. In 1756, he published a book entitle "*Astronomy explained upon Sir Isaac Newton's principles, and made easy to those who have not studied Mathematics*". In that book, he published the following diagram of the orbits of Venus, and indeed confirmed the ancient belief that Venus did have a forty-year cycle and return to its starting point in the sky. It is possible that the pattern described by Venus, which we have come to know as the pentagram, was in fact inspired by the *shekinah*.

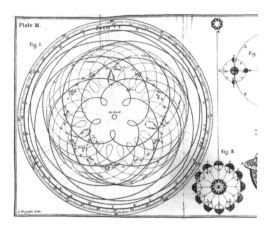

*This image is reproduced by kind permission of the Royal Astronomical Society.*

It seems highly possible that the *shekinah* and the associated image of the pentagram both found their way into our ceremonies. The publication of the Preston's Illustrations of Masonry, another highly acclaimed reference work long before the United Grand Lodge was formed, took place around two decades after James Ferguson had published his work, and is just the type of material that former freemasons might have consulted.  Hence, it found its way into the ceremony in England, and may well have been part of the third degree already used in Ireland by virtue of ancient Celtic traditions.  It was then globally reinforced through the second degree ceremony after 1813.

Whether or not the *shekinah* is actually the focus of reference in the ceremony, has to be speculation, as there are no records that confirm it, one way or the other. Equally there is nothing to suggest it would have featured in the operative apprentice knowledge except that having knowledge of certain aspects of celestial mechanics would have been known. Irrespective of this, it is a fact that geometry played a part in the knowledge of the operative mason and it is highly likely that the symbol of the pentagram did feature, for the reasons associated with window tracery. It is also a fact that there is an illusion to part of a circle in the ceremony of the second degree, and the number five.

The period we are considering is around 1675. This was a period when religion was still a major influence of life. If, as previously suggested, freemasonry was descended from the religious guilds, then one would expect the knowledge of the stonemason to be able to reflect it. They did – in window tracery. What is more, the pentagram has links with the circle and the *golden ratio* mentioned earlier.

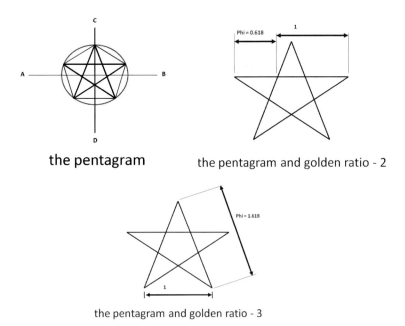

the pentagram            the pentagram and golden ratio - 2

the pentagram and golden ratio - 3

In religion, the five points of the pentagram are associated with the five wounds of the crucifixion, and is an image frequently found in the tracery of windows in churches. There are also many plants in nature that feature this configuration, as well as other geometric relevance.

*The image of the pentagram in a church of a college of Cambridge University. K.L. Gest*

Having looked at the content of the ceremony itself, there is another area to be considered - the tracing board.

The tracing board is based on several aspects of the Old Testament, but in particular, the building of Solomon's Temple. The detail recorded in the Books of Kings and Chronicles is usually read and passed over without much thought. The ecclesiastical community use it to emphasis what a magnificent effort was made in praise of the deity. Yet the information seems to expose yet another secret. This is revealed in the alignment of the description of the temple, its furnishings and the position of the pillars. This is further endorsement of the ancient concept relating to the alignment of important buildings with solar and celestial events. One such significant structure where this can be seen is the Temple of Abu Simbel in Egypt.

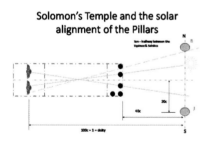

Solomon's Temple and the solar alignment of the Pillars

The Temple of Abu Simbel was built to reflect various elements of solar cycles and hence provided a calendar. It was cleared of sand in 1817 by a man named Giovanni Battista Belzoni. He had spent a considerable amount of time in England before going to Egypt. Artefacts of ancient Egypt recovered by Belzoni are on display in the British Museum. A little

known fact is that he was a freemason and member of the Royal Arch.
*Author's note: In an earlier book – **The Secrets of Solomon's Temple** – I examined
the attributes of the dimensions of the pillars of Solomon's Temple, as recorded
in the tracing board text, in some detail, and came to a number of conclusions
and demonstrated solar alignment akin to that experienced in the Temple of Abu
Simbel, based on that information.*

There is yet one more item in the second-degree ceremony to note. There
is a reference to a winding staircase and this is alluded to in the associated
tracing board. To be *winding* it obviously curves. If one takes a stick and
winds a piece of string on it, then the string has gone round and round the
stick. Likewise, a *winding* staircase can go round and round, in other words,
in the form of a spiral. A spiral can be created on the principles of the *golden
ratio* as was shown earlier with a square, relating to the concept of balanced
proportion. It is created using a series of squares, each one doubling in
size and rotating around a centre in a counter-clockwise direction. As
one looks up the centre of the spiral is in proportion as the centre moves
further away. As mentioned earlier, one of the first buildings that Inigo
Jones was commissioned to build was the Queen's House in Greenwich.
It is recognised as being the first to be built using the Renaissance style
classical architecture based on the principles of geometry of the type that
were known to Euclid and the ancient Greek and Roman philosophers.

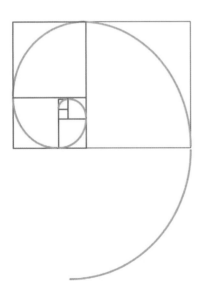

Image by Getty Images

Thus we can see that far from being an empty ceremony devoid of meaning, the second degree contains very considerable information that is similar to that which would have needed to be known and understood by the operative mason. It is this information that may have completed part of the training of the apprentice of former eras.

The tracing board contains a great deal of information relating to architecture, built into a story that draws on events and characters from the Old Testament. Through the story, one is informed that there are five noble orders of architecture, Tuscan, Doric, Ionic, Corinthian and Composite. These derive from the era of classical architecture erected in the Roman Empire during the life of Vitruvius. The diameter of a pillar of each style was also proportionally related to the length. This is yet more information relating to the craft of the operative stonemason – a bit more for the Journeyman/fellow to remember.

## The degree of a Master Mason

The first degree seems to be about the square, and how this geometric figure could be used by an operative mason to achieve certain processes without elaborate tools to do so. It also includes information about the movement of the sun to enable building orientation. The second degree seems mainly concerned with the principles of celestial mechanics and the geometric figure of the pentagram, a figure that regularly features in tracery work produced by operative masons in churches and major civic buildings, and has the added attraction of relating to the winding/spiral in that both are regarded as being geometrically created using the *golden ratio* of balanced proportion.

When it comes to the third degree, it seems to be a mixture of several events; first we are expected to know something about the square and compasses, and indeed, in the previous consideration of the first and second degrees, we note how they can be used to good effect, although by no means the limits of their practical use to the operative craftsman. The square and compasses are not mentioned again. In the next stage of the ceremony we have some directions where one person goes east and the other west, in search of some discovery they hope to make. Then we are told about a circle, and in particular it is the point at the centre which is highlighted, though neither the circle or the centre are mentioned again in the ceremony.

A point within a circle, is the point from which so much geometry used in elements of the creation of a design involving classical architecture, commences. Yet it also has another meaning that was well known to our ancestors of long ago. It was a symbol used to represent the sun.

Notwithstanding that, the two elements of circle and the centre are the key to a geometric configuration that, in ancient times and since, has been regarded as most sacred – *Vesica Piscis* – also known as the *Mandorla*. It is highly probable that in the third degree, the foundations were laid for this very special geometric character to be further explained in both the installation ceremony of the Master, and its relevance to other Masonic symbolism, as we shall see.

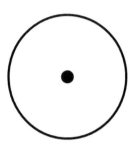

There then follows a story known as the Hiramic Legend. This legend is supposedly based on the character mentioned in the Old Testament, who was sent by the King of Tyre to assist Solomon in the building of the Temple in Jerusalem. There is no mention in the Old Testament books of Kings or Chronicles that during the building process Hiram was murdered, but that is the basis of the legend. A trawl through many of the old papers and books in the Library of Freemasons Hall, all written by eminent men of their day, including clergymen, hypothesise about who Hiram was, how his name might have been spelt in old Hebrew and how it might relate to current English, but do not present any plausible argument for how this story developed or came to be part of Masonic ceremony. The vacuum has led to many speculative suggestions.

Various researchers of former days point out that although a character that might be interpreted as Solomon's helper, with the name Hiram, was known in the Old Charges for at least two hundred years prior to Grand Lodge of England being formed, there is considerable doubt that any operative masons prior to that time would have known anything of the legend. There is a reference recorded in the Cooke MS of around 1450 CE, which apparently states, *And yr Kyngis sone of Tyry was his [Solomon's] maist. Masen.*[57]

In the absence of any real substantiating information about where the legend started it has been speculated that either the legend somehow developed in the sixteenth and seventeenth centuries and then was gradually assimilated into Masonic ceremony prior to 1717, or, that it was specifically written and used to create a ceremony after the Grand Lodge was formed.  Of these two ideas, the first has nothing to support it of any substance. In the case of the second, why or what may have inspired someone to compose and write it *and* it be seen to be of such significance that it was included as a major item of the key degree of a master mason? One document lists no fewer than fourteen different suggestions as to what the legend might really be about and who it might involve.  These range from the murder of Thomas à Becket in Canterbury cathedral; the murder of Jacques de Molay in Paris when the Knights Templars were finally suppressed; the execution of Charles I; and, *is it an allegory for the death of the sun in winter and its coming to life again in the spring*?[58] In view of the reference to the circle, and that it could be considered the sun, then the last suggestion might have more relevance, and it would fit with other similar references in the other ceremonies. But, perhaps not so that it should form the centrepiece of a major step in ones Masonic career. There is also the suggestion that is a moral tale to remind us all that death is the final curtain of life on this Earth. Hence, when the end comes, we each wish to leave, having given a good account of ourselves and our actions and whether or not we did good by others. Thus, the living of a wholesome and virtuous life is essential.

There may actually be another reason, not only for the legend, but also why it was included after the formation of the Grand Lodge of England in 1717.

# Chapter 13

## A NEW SOLOMON;
## A NEW TEMPLE;
## A NEW HIRAM:

At the end of the last chapter, we were left wondering where the Hiramic Legend may have come from, what and who it was about, and why it was suddenly included in the third degree ceremony without there being any great proof to substantiate that it had existed prior to 1717.

When the Grand Lodge of England was formed, there was no fourth degree, now known as the Royal Arch. That was included from 1813. Thus, the inclusion could not have been inspired by the contents of that degree.

So, to what does it possibly allude?

Between 1600 and 1717, Britain had been through some fundamental and wide-reaching changes. A Scottish king and his heirs had taken the throne of England following which James I approved the translation, printing and circulation of the King James authorised version of the bible; there had been a murderous civil war that ravaged England, Scotland and Ireland followed by the execution of the monarch, and establishment of an early form of republic called the Commonwealth; there had been the plague and great fire of London; the restoration of the monarchy; the union of the crowns and parliaments of England and Scotland in 1707.

Between these great events of history, there was a group of other developments and evolutions that, whilst they were also major landmarks of history, were in more limited spheres of influence, but they were absolutely key to the future success of Britain. Inigo Jones had introduced the renaissance style of classical architecture. The wife of James I, Anne of Denmark, had commissioned Jones to build a pavilion – the Queen's House. It was regarded as revolutionary in its design when completed, and the Queen's House at Greenwich was regarded as so impressive that across Britain, many of the wealthy and noble families incorporated classical architecture in their own stately homes. The style also spread to include many new fine buildings for state and civil function. The Royal Society had received its Charter and was conducting research into aspects of science and nature through which the period known as the *enlightenment* had commenced. A new Royal Exchange had been built in London, also incorporating classical architecture, and merchants spread their interests around the globe. An Observatory had been built at Greenwich to study the heavens. There had been wars against the Dutch, but then England had a Dutch king, William III, to replace another king who had fled. And rising from the ashes of the great fire of London, was a new temple – St Paul's Cathedral.

Prior to many of the above events however there had been a slight change in the affairs of London masons. In 1654, the London Company had styled itself in its accounts, and presumably for some years prior, as the *Company of ffremasons of the City of London*. Yet, the following year, 1655, it became the Company of Masons. There is a view, extended by a former Master of the Worshipful Company of Masons of London, that:

> *"It has been remarked that this Company had no connection at any time with the "Society" of Free Masons, which before the time of the Reformation had members termed freemasons in most parts of the country, working upon the various religious edifices there in progress. But, as I have said before, it is my humble opinion that ever since the masons of London formed themselves into a brotherhood, or gild, for their mutual protection and assistance, so long did they number among their members certain masons who were also members of the "Society".[59]* What is being expressed is an opinion that there were operative masons who were members of a society or fraternity of free-masons. He also notes that in Masons Hall London, there was a cabinet on a wall, kept under lock and key, in which there was a list of several names of *accepted* members. This, it is stated, seems an anomaly, as it suggests that these people had some importance to the Company and yet the term *accepted* had never been used within the Company to describe any level of membership. Thus, around the mid-1600s, there were men who were members of the Company but not operative masons, and that there were probably members of the craft of operative masons who were members of another society. Perhaps this other society was a continuation of the religious guild system, and through membership, one was entitled to certain charitable opportunities and funeral rites.

**The old and new temple**

As stated earlier, one of the main events of the latter 1600s was the rebuilding of St. Paul's Cathedral. The records indicate that the current cathedral deigned by Sir Christopher Wren, is the fifth major church to be built on the same site, with the first having been built around 604 CE.

Fire, it seems, had been a great hazard in London, and as the City burnt, each time, the church dedicated to St Paul went with it. In 1087 CE there was one such fire and the third such church was destroyed. Another new building was commenced. It was after the Conquest of 1066, in a period when great building work was being undertaken by the Normans. Far from completion, this fourth cathedral/church caught fire yet again and much of the new building work already undertaken was ruined. It took 225 years, from the fire in 1087, to complete the fourth building, in 1314. This building was totally destroyed in the great fire of 1666 and has since passed into history as *Old St Paul's*.

Sir Christopher Wren had studied architecture in France and Italy. In 1668, two years after the fire, Wren was commissioned to design a new cathedral. When he set about designing a replacement cathedral he apparently used St Peter's Basilica in Rome as a source of inspiration but the first few designs he submitted were rejected. It took eight years before he produced a plan that finally achieved a royal seal of approval in 1685, and rebuilding could commence.

According to records, the foundation stone was laid on 21st June 1675, by Thomas Strong, Master Mason. This date is usually one celebrated each year as the summer solstice. Other claims are that the stone was laid on 25th or 28th June 1675. This discrepancy in dates may well be due to miscalculations associated with both astronomical measurement and the change in the calendar system from the Julian calendar to Gregorian calendar in the next century. Another record from the London Company of Masons, states that *Thomas Strong, having made the first contract with the commissioners appointed to superintend the work, laid the foundation-stone with his own hand the 11th June 1677.*[60]

St Paul's took 33 years to build - *when the last stone on the top of the lantern was laid by Edward Strong on 26th October 1708.*[61] It was another two years before it was completed in all its parts, and reported as such in 1710, to parliament.

The second degree tracing board is a tale that centres around the building of Solomon's Temple. The key component is a *winding* staircase, which has fifteen steps in the combinations of three, five, and seven. It is accessed via an entrance on the south side. It just so happens that on the south side of St Paul's Cathedral there is an entrance, now not used, and was originally known as the Dean's Door. Just inside that entrance, is a winding staircase in exactly the same geometric golden ratio proportions as that at the Queen's House.

*The south side of St Paul's Cathedral, London and the Spiral Staircase*

It took thirty-three years to build St Paul's Cathedral, ten years and upwards. In the main steps leading upwards from the road to the main entrance there are, first, ten steps, the tenth being a platform step, followed by a further fourteen steps to the door, twenty-four steps in all. In those thirty-three years that the fifth St Paul's cathedral was being built, an immense number of masons were employed, and as we have seen earlier, several of those that met with Elias Ashmole in 1682, were the Master and Wardens, and those aspiring to be master and wardens, of the Worshipful Company of Masons of London. This meeting was seven years after the approval of the design for St Paul's receiving royal approval. Building work for the cathedral had started.

It is also worth noting that as part of the façade of the building, there are at each end, two pillars incorporated on either side of the classical portal.

Sir Christopher Wren lived to see his great achievement finished. He died thirteen years later, in 1723, at the age of ninety-one years. His death was in the same year the Anderson Constitutions were first published. As a lasting testament to his vision it remained the tallest building in London for over two hundred and fifty years, until around 1984 when the skyline of the City began to change with high-rise developments. Set on a hill, St. Paul's had hitherto been a dominating feature on the skyline, which worshippers would have had *continuously before their eyes whilst going to and coming from, divine worship.*

When the *Old St Paul's* was destroyed, very little was left. There are, however some curiosities. One is a small statue.

## John Donne

Through the late Elizabethan era and the seventeenth century, poetry, drama and satire, had become new literary interests. One of the great exponents of that time was William Shakespeare, and a great contemporary of Shakespeare's was John Donne. In his early life, Donne was a poet, lawyer, and Member of Parliament. He later turned to the church, and became an Anglican priest in 1615. Six years later, in 1621, he became the Dean of St. Paul's Cathedral, a position he held until his death in 1631.

He seems to have had a fascination for death. A month before his own

demise, he delivered a sermon to Charles I at the Palace of Whitehall, a sermon that is now regarded as one of his finest and often quoted. There is some speculation that he actually prepared the sermon to be used at his own funeral. The text of the sermon has survived and it has some links to masonry. It is called *Death's Duell, or a Consolation to the Soul, against the dying Life and the living Death of the Body.* In it Donne draws parallels of life with great buildings, the foundations, the strength of the walls, and the buttresses that prevent them from collapsing.

In the months prior to his death, Donne also commissioned a statue to be made, so that he could see what he would look like wrapped in his shroud. After the great fire of 1666, this small statue was one of the items that was recovered. It is now on display in St. Paul's Cathedral. As a poet, he left us with one memorable line, so often used:

*…any mans death diminishes me, because I am involved in mankind; and therefore never send to know for whom the bell tolls; It tolls for thee…*
*John Donne, Meditation XVII*

*The statue of John Donne, complete with shroud wrapped round.*

## The Masons

There is an old saying that *it is an ill wind that doesn't blow somebody some good.* That was certainly true for the London Company of Masons. Like so many others, Masons Hall was destroyed in the fire. Not only did it need to be rebuilt, but across the City, there was suddenly a lot of work to the benefit of the operative masons, which improved the prestige of the London Company. Not least for which was the support it now gave to the other Worshipful Companies that had prided themselves as being the superior guilds.

> *"After the fire of 1666 the Court of Common Council order that the twelve great Companies should provide themselves with fire-engines, buckets and ladders, the smaller Companies also to be provided with buckets and ladders. The Masons Company, with certain others mentioned, was to provide two master workmen, four journeymen, eight apprentices, and sixteen labourers, (thirty men in all), to be ready on all occasions of fire to attend the Lord Mayor and Sheriffs for extinguishing the same."*[62]

London wasn't the only place where there was a demand for the skill of the masons. Over a long period, the British navy had been allowed to decline in strength. The Civil War had resulted in virtually no new developments and the seagoing forces were most neglected. In the same time frame, a series of conflicts had broken out that are known as the Anglo-Dutch Wars. In the past, coastal towns like Dover, Portsmouth and Plymouth had been fortified in the expectation that trouble, if it came, would be from the south, where Spain and Portugal had impressive naval capability. Now the problem was coming from just across the sea in the Low-Countries. London was easily threatened. The Thames estuary was wide open, and the main dockyard was in a river just off that estuary at Chatham, a river that was strongly tidal and narrow. It had been decided that a new dockyard and fort should be built on the Kent coast, at the junction of the rivers Medway and Thames. The town of Sheerness, on the Isle of Sheppey, had been chosen as the site for this dockyard, in 1665. The work was regarded as so important that in the years immediately after the fire, building the dockyard had some priority, requiring the skills of a large number of masons. These skills were, numerically, well short of requirements, and the government wanted every mason available. This meant that their skills were now in very short supply in London to deal with the aftermath of the fire.

After the great fire, rebuilding work in London commenced, and it is known that many unscrupulous individuals travelled to London in the hope of rich pickings, by preying on the discomfort and loss of the London inhabitants. As a result of the shortage of skills, the City saw a large number of such individuals claiming to be masons, with the intention of securing work they were not qualified to undertake. In 1677, Charles II granted a Charter of Incorporation to the Company of Masons. The following extract notes:

> " Charles II…grant them such privileges as should seem requisite …and willing and intending the support and continuance of the Company and the improvement of the art and mystery of masons, and to the end they might be empowered to suppress and reform all abuses practiced by persons who took upon them, without sufficient skill and knowledge, to work at a mason's trade, and that the art and mystery of masons within the City of London might from henceforth be artificially and truly exercised. His Majesty ordained and granted that all and singular masons, freemen of the City of London, and all other subjects that should thereafter use the art in London or Westminster, or within seven miles compass of the same on either side, should be one body incorporated politic by the same master, wardens, assistants, and commonly of the art and mystery of masons of the City of London…"[63]

From this we can see that the London Company of Masons had, through this charter, the sole rights in respect of any work that was to be undertaken by masons. It also charged the Company to police the trade, keeping out those not qualified to undertake such work, and to ensure that stone to be used was of a good quality and correct measurement, and that if wasn't that it should be corrected at the cost of those who had supplied or formed it.

One can only imagine that against such a background of authority, there were some individuals, who were attempting to claim themselves to be masons, who did not have the training or skills to perform such work, were found out and banned from the City of London and Westminster for not having appropriate qualifications. And one can equally imagine that there may have been some violence when unauthorised individuals were caught.

Notwithstanding the above comment, it is sad to note that the man who was the principal Master Mason at the start of the building of St Paul's, and credited with having laid the foundation stone, died during its construction.

**Hypothesis:**
**New Solomon; New Temple; New Hiram Abif; New legend**

From everything that has been noted from the previous pages, it is suggested that:

1.  When Inigo Jones created his revolution in architecture, and the gentry of the day saw that the classical style had been accepted by the royal court, many noble families wished to have the same. Many of the wealthy and noble gentlemen were merchants and based in London to be close to the royal court or the centre of business, and as such had connection with the London livery companies. Thus when they wished to have a property built, they turned to the London Company of Masons. This resulted in not only a demand for the skills of the mason, but that certain of these wealthy gentlemen should be members of the London Company to keep an eye on the plans and expenditure. They may have been encouraged to join the *Society* of Free-Masons to enable that to take place. Thus, by 1700 there were several such members of the Company, and the *society* had also grown in membership in London.

2.  As suggested earlier, the Society of Free-Masons may have developed within the religious guild system as opposed to the operative mason guilds of the middle ages, and existed as a fraternity. At the time of the reformation, the guilds were banned, and the country entered a long period of religious and political turmoil. The fraternities of free-masons kept a very low profile for fear of reprisal by the relevant authorities. After one hundred and fifty years of such uncertainty, in the early 1700s the political and religious outlook was now more settled and the former fraternities could be more open.

3.  By 1710 when St Paul's Cathedral was officially completed and recorded as such before parliament, there was a move to formally distance the *speculative freemasonry* of the Society of Free-Masons, from the operative London Company of Masons, and form a completely separate organisation with its own constitutions that could not interfere with the business of the Company. This resulted in the formation of the Grand Lodge of the City of London and Westminster, before it became the Grand Lodge of England in 1717.

4.     After St Paul's Cathedral was completed, its true magnificence came to realised. In between the formation of the Grand Lodge in 1717, Dr Anderson and others, used the *Old Charges* of the London Company, and any other, plus the knowledge they had in respect of the operative masons who were also members of the new Grand Lodge, to develop the first constitutions that were published in 1723. During this period, the new Grand Lodge wanted to do something to mark the excellence of Sir Christopher Wren's great achievement. Wren died in 1723, and afterwards it was realised that there were a number of attributes of the cathedral that were compatible with the Old Testament text in respect of Solomon's Temple. Thus a story was deliberately created, based on St. Paul's Cathedral, but interwoven with biblical content.

5.     Through the building of St. Paul's Cathedral, and the connection with Solomon's Temple, Charles II became David, who in the Old Testament, designed the temple - Charles approved it; Sir Christopher Wren became Solomon – who built it; Thomas Strong (he died during the building) became Hiram Abif; The Master and the London Company of Masons, became King of Tyre through which *an immense number of masons were employed* and materials to build the project, were channelled.

6.     The statue of John Donne, discovered in the ashes of the fire of the *Old Cathedral*, along with his sermon to Charles I, and his now memorable line – *for whom the bell tolls*, became a centrepiece of the third degree, along with other attributes of St Pauls.

7.     The five points of fellowship are derived from the five cathedrals built on the site, all a basis of religious and personal fellowship through the ages.

8.     Items 4, 5, 6 & 7 above, all became the structure of the third degree until 1813, by which time freemasonry had expanded, along with trading routes, to other parts of the globe. In Europe this expansion included families / members of the old Hansa, and as a result some attributes relating to the new customs of those overseas territories, became fused with the original degree, and are what we use today.

9.     Attributes of the cathedral already mentioned (there are more) include:

a.    The two pillars at the sides of the main portal.
b.    The entrance on the south side.
c.    The winding staircase
d.    The number of steps
e.    The ability to have had it before the eyes (in the 1700s) whilst going to and coming from worship.
f.    The geometry used in its construction.
g.    The setting of the last stone in the lantern by Edward Strong (reflects in Royal Arch)
h.    Clearing the debris from the fire and *Old St Paul's*.
i.    The number of pillars in the cathedral.
j.    Being lowered into the vault under *Old St Paul's*.
k.    etc. etc. etc.


*Author's note: I respectfully suggest all this connection with St. Paul's was generally known not only in the eighteenth century, but well into the nineteenth, especially by those in the Grand Lodge. By that time, other esoteric devices and distractions were attracting the interests of eminent members of the organisation, such as with the arrival from Egypt of Cleopatra's Needle and its installation on the bank of the River Thames in London. The background awareness gradually drained and died.*

To quote the text of a plague in the wall of St. Paul's Cathedral, London,

**"Remember the Men Who
Made Shapley the Stones
Of St. Paul's Cathedral
1675 – 1708"**

*There is, I accept, one item missing. That is the murder committed by three ruffians.*

*Several years ago I was researching something else in London, and chanced on a book in the Library at the Guildhall, that dealt in detail about the fire of 1666, and in particular, the details of those that were killed or died as a result. There was a section about criminals who had swooped on the City remains, looting personal treasures. I have no doubt that during the years after the fire, there were all manner of rouges that sought profit from the disaster, some of whom tried to pass themselves off as masons, and were caught by the London Company of Masons in accordance with their Charter. Perhaps in desperation to obtain work, two or more seized a mason working on something other than St Paul's, and tried to persuade him to show them 'how to do it', but he refused, as they were not members of the Company.*

*For his bravado, he was killed, perhaps being hit about the head with a maul or some other implement. I have tried, in casual moments, to locate such a story, but it has so far eluded me. Perhaps there was such a major event that became a memory amongst the London Company members, and it found its way into the Hiramic legend, and is still to be found.*

One last observation. When the clearance of rubble and debris from the burnt out remains of *Old St. Paul's* was completed, and the design for the new St Paul's had been agreed, new foundations were needed on which to construct the new cathedral. As shown earlier, the foundation stone was laid by the Master Mason for the project, Thomas Strong. There is some documentation that suggests this was done with great ceremony and that Sir Christopher Wren and many dignitaries, representing the great and famous of the day, were present. This one event may well have been the inspiration for the Masonic Foundation Stone ceremony that followed and was a regular feature in towns and cities across Britain for the next two hundred and fifty years.

# Chapter 14

# THE ROYAL ARCH

When considering the Royal Arch degree, we should remember one thing; if historical information is correct, then official freemasonry in all its parts is a reflection of the *art, secrets and mystery* of the stonemason's craft, the fruits of which we can see around us, and in ancient monuments around the world. It is an *art* that has been exercised with incredible ingenuity and skill for at least the last six thousand years.

The Royal Arch position in freemasonry, as defined in the early declarations and Constitutions of the United Grand Lodge of England, notes that.

> *Ancient Masonry consists of three degrees and no more…those of the Entered Apprentice, The Fellow Craft, and the Master Mason, including the Supreme Order of the Holy Royal Arch.*

Based on this form of declaration of 1813, it is clear that the Master Mason and the Royal Arch were considered one and the same degree. What is more, the word *Ancient* has been used, as opposed to *Antient* which was a means of distinguishing one of two brands of freemasonry from another in the eighteenth century, the other being the *Moderns*.[64]

When it comes to the history of the Royal Arch, there is a notion of its existence in some form back to the 1720s. In the late nineteenth century and early twentieth, many papers were produced that languish in the archives of Freemasons Hall, London, that attempt to provide a definite trace on the origins, but, with the value of what we know of so many aspects of history today, let alone freemasonry in general, it has to said that much of it is a catalogue of dates, places and names that mean very little. Much of the work is highly speculative but well meaning. Because of the word *Holy* appearing in the title of the Order, there is a reasonable spread of opinion from those who were members of the ecclesiastical establishment, and there is some debate as to whether it was a separate degree in Ireland, Scotland, America, or the Continent before it reached England. Every piece of work has been undertaken with the best of intentions of all those who contributed, within the constraints, beliefs and paradigms of their times. Yet, if one browses through them one emerges with no clearer idea about what the Royal Arch is about, than when one started.

One thing that does emerge is that in the eighteenth century, there was some hostility that existed between the *Antients* and *Moderns*. The *Antients* claimed to practice only the ancient rites, whilst the Moderns disapproved of it on the grounds that it was an innovation. The reason for this dispute is unclear except that the Moderns saw themselves as being, well, the more modern.

To one quote one source:

> *"Whereas the 'Antients' regarded it [Royal Arch] as the 'Root, Heart, and Marrow of Free Masonry', the Grand Secretary of the Moderns in 1759...said 'we are neither Arch, Royal Arch, nor Antient'"*[65].

With that kind of retort, one gets some sense of the hostility of one to the other, yet on 22nd July 1766, The Excellent Grand and Royal Chapter of Jerusalem, was formed, the first such Grand Chapter in the world. So much for sentiments expressed just seven years earlier. It became the Supreme Grand Chapter from 1813 with the merger of the Antients and Moderns, as had taken place with the craft structure.

Although written in the mid-twentieth century, there is the following observation in one, intensely-researched book, that notes:

> *"..Some writers...have said that the Royal Arch was 'concocted' by the 'Antients'...but in truth the 'Antients' did not themselves invent or fabricate the Royal Arch Degree. They found it waiting for them..."*[66]

In other words, it was a ready-made *package* they picked up and ran with. This only raises the question of where did that *package* originate from? Yet again, there has been much conjecture with suggestions that it was *mutilated* out of the third degree, whilst there was also the suggestion that it was a degree that was known only to Masters and Past Masters. This latter position seems to have been accepted by both sides. As that common ground seems to have been the meeting place of the protagonists, it seems a good place to leave the anguish of the 1700s.

What might the Royal Arch be about? As stated at the start of this chapter, we should remember one thing; if historical information is correct, then official freemasonry in all its parts, as defined in 1813, is a reflection of the *art, secrets and mystery* of the stonemason's craft, the fruits of which we can see around us, and in ancient monuments around the world. So, when looking at the Royal Arch we perhaps need to look with those eyes. In the past six thousand years, the craft will have passed through several generations of religious belief; Islam was created one thousand five hundred years ago; Christianity, two thousand years ago; there was a pantheon of gods and beliefs in ancient Rome, Greece and Egypt; there were the influences of the religions of the east, including Mithras, Buddha and Hinduism, plus many other smaller religions, and every single one of them has believed that their brand of religion was the favoured one. Through all that time and all those channels, we are advised, knowledge was collected and passed on through the generations, and some of that knowledge, undoubtably, became reflected in ancient monuments and the information that was needed to enable them to be created.

There are three symbols that identify the degree of the Royal Arch from the other official degrees; the triple tau, Solomon's Seal and the Catenarian Arch.

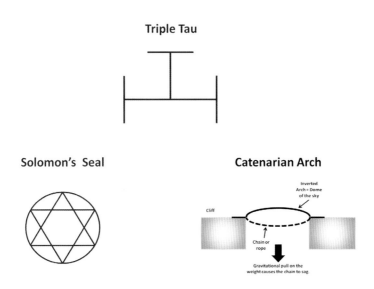

**Triple Tau**

**Solomon's Seal**

**Catenarian Arch**

## The Tau

The Tau has many uses today, especially as a symbol in scientific formula, or to symbolise various mathematical functions. Originally it was the nineteenth letter of the Greek alphabet, but it has also been used to represent the cross in Christianity. It also seems to have a connection with ancient building, and in particular, proportion. It is an ancient symbol for the golden ratio with its twin values of 0.618 and 1.618. Today however, to distinguish it from use in science and mathematical formula, the value of the golden ratio is usually shown by another symbol, the 21st in the Greek alphabet, that of *phi* – $\phi$.

It has been mentioned and demonstrated earlier, in respect of the Entered Apprentice degree, how the *square* forms the basis for geometrically creating a dimension that is 0.618 of the length of a side of the square, using a pair of compasses. In important buildings, such as the temples of ancient Greece, this proportion was paramount in a desire to please the gods. Indeed, it is also known by the term – *divine proportion.*

Every building has three dimensions, length, width and height. To fully comply with being *in proportion* then the rules of the golden/divine ratio need to apply to all three planes.

There is a suggestion, but it should be stressed, no more than a suggestion, that the original "T" (Tau) that was used to define this proportion, when written down or sculpted, had a ratio that symbolised that feature, a matter we will return to in due course:

**0.618**

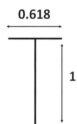

1

The ratio of the horizontal element compared with the vertical, probably makes the "Tau" look rather out of proportion by comparison with what we are sometimes used to seeing in our twenty-first century world. We are conditioned from the time we start to learn to write on how we should present certain characters of the alphabet. That difference is a problem that seems to have developed from the invention of the printing press, which resulted in the "T" being reconfigured to satisfy the size of printing character blocks, the printers having no previous knowledge of its value in building. Thereafter, and having lost its proportions, it was gradually replaced by the letter phi.

From this it will be seen that the *triple tau,* in appropriate proportions, is a symbol for a building that comprises the dimensional benefit of the golden / divine ratio for each of its planes. This is the type of information the stonemasons of the Middle Ages probably knew, and incidentally recorded on the face of a stone, at ground level, just above the foundation stone.

### The Catenarian Arch
The Catenarian Arch is the basis for setting out the Chapter meeting room. If one stands on the top of a hill, or an open plain, especially on a clear day without cloud, the sky will seem to be a large dome that folds down to the horizon in every direction and embraces everything on Earth. That is the way our ancestors envisioned it. Thus, in architecture, it was a *divine* attribute to be copied, and hence was replicated as the dome in cupola's and for religious buildings. Some of the oldest surviving structures in the world, identified by archaeologists, are dome-like structures in the Nubian desert, that are believed to have been constructed around 1300 BCE.

If one takes a strong and heavy rope, ties it securely to one tree, places the rope over a stout branch and pulls down with the intention of pulling the rope out straight, one will note that it invariably sags in the middle. This can be seen in pictures of rope bridges, or those used as walkways. This is because the weight at the centre of the length of the span is being pulled down by gravity – but our ancestors may not have appreciated that aspect of science. If this is done with a chain anchored to two cliffs that form a gorge, then the same effect will apply. If the chain is now lengthened, the character of the curve will change.

**Catenarian Arch**

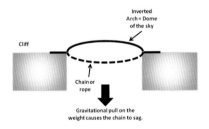

**Catenarian Arch - modified**

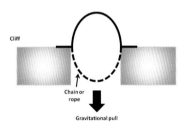

Thus, the Catenarian Arch can have a number of profiles. The shape of the curve in the above illustration is not untypical of that used in some ancient buildings in the Middle East. It also provides the former for domes on many buildings. As a tool for the use of the builder's of the Middle Ages, two stout timbers, or stone walls, of the distance apart they would be in the structure, and a strong piece of rope, could be used to create the pattern for the dome, by allowing the rope to sag until it reached a curve that they found met the requirements.

Inverted, the shape also comprises a useful profile that has considerable compressive strength, so ideal for use in underground vaults and chambers. By shaping the stones like shallow wedges, the weight above forces the stones together, and the one at the top of the arch becomes the locking piece, or keystone.

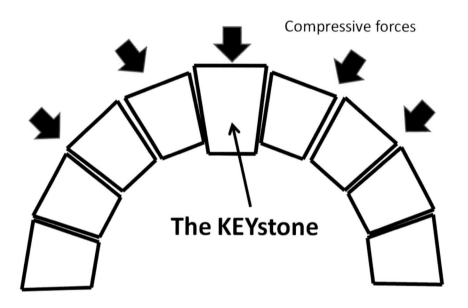

Compressive forces

The KEYstone

**Solomon's Seal**

In the Entered Apprentice degree, we saw how the square could be used in simple, effective and different ways for design, and to shape stone, as well as a means of regulating the finish of the work. In the Royal Arch degree, we now make use of two other geometric figures, the circle and the equilateral triangle.

We must assume that Solomon's Seal, as it has sometimes been called, was known to the stonemason builders of the Middle Ages. In fact we can be very certain that it was - it features boldly as a window in the north face of Chichester Cathedral, Sussex, and can be found in many other cathedrals and large churches, in different locations, such as at Bristol, Chartres and Notre Dame to name a few.

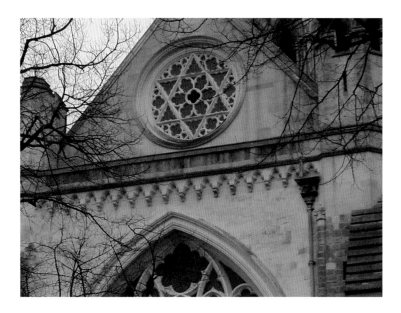

*The 'Solomon's Seal', complete with circle in Chichester Cathedral, Sussex. It is directly above another window formed in the pointed arch style. K.L. Gest*

We should remember that our ancestors only had a few fundamental tools, with which they achieved a great deal. When is came to geometry, and the use of that geometry to solve problems, not just those of a building nature, the three key figures were the Circle, Square and Triangle.

The symbol of the overlapped or intertwined triangles hides an image that has been most sacred for hundreds of generations in various parts of the world. It starts with a process that was used in the Entered Apprentice degree description, developed by Euclid, for separating a line of unknown length into two equal portions. But, it has one difference. This time the circumference of one circle touches the centre of the other, and it is important that the diameter of each circle is exactly the same size. This produces a configuration known as *Vesica Piscis*.

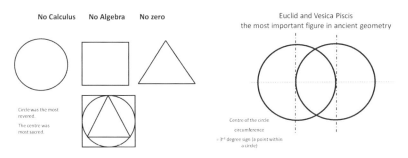

At the centre of the two overlapping circles is the shape of a pointed oval. This shape is known variously as the *vesica, almond* or *mandorla*. It is this shape of the vesica which is probably the most sacred of all geometric configurations. It seems that in ancient times it was venerated as the source of creation, because its shape has a close resemblance with the female vulva of all animal life, the source of creation of all human life.

In the Middle Ages, the vesica took on a very different role, as the basis of architecture that influenced construction for hundreds of years thereafter - the pointed arch that was originally known as the *French style* but more often referred to as *gothic*. It can be seen sculptured into cathedral and abbey walls, cloisters, senate chambers, and many other places with a religious connection; Canterbury cathedral, Peterborough cathedral and Romsey Abbey are just a few of the sites.

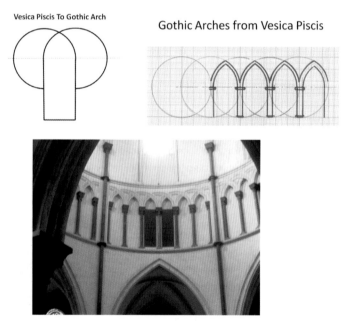

*This Vesica Piscis pattern can be found in the gallery of the Knights Templar Round Church in London, beautifully carved by expert hands of stonemasons.* K.L. Gest

Vesica Piscis has much more to offer to the builder of the Royal Arch. This simple configuration of two touching circles contains some remarkable properties. The width the vesica at its widest point is equal to the radius of the circles that created it, so half the width of the vesica is half the radius. A vertical line drawn down through the centre, from top to bottom, produces √3 as a ratio to half the radius of the circle.

Producing √3 in Vesica Piscis

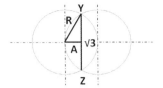

The vesica also has another wonderful characteristic associated with Royal Arch. The junction of the triangle formed at ABC in the diagram, is 60°, therefore, that at BAC is 30°. It therefore follows that if one replicates that triangle in the other half of the vesica, the angle at BAC will become 60°. And from that, plus a circle with a radius drawn from the centre to the top of the vesica, we can develop a perfect *Solomon's Seal.*

Producing **30°** in Vesica Piscis

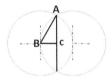

Royal Arch Symbol
Solomon's Seal in Vesica Piscis

One more secret of the vesica is that it geometrically produces the golden/divine ratio with the numerical values of 0.618 and 1.618. The distance across the width of the vesica is 0.618 of the length through the vesica, and can be represented by a "T" - tau.
We now have all the characteristics to make another well-known Royal Arch symbol.

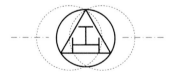

*Author's Note: I believe that all the basic geometric images used in Royal Arch, and the background knowledge that created them, was that of the Antients. It is the knowledge of the pre-reformation period when the predominant architectural style was French/gothic. This in turn has many similarities to the catenarian arch, a style of arch used prominently in the Middle East and probably particularly noted during the religious wars known as the crusades.*

## The legend and the Double Cube

The legend that accompanies the ceremony of Royal Arch, relates, for the most part, in the setting the keystone in the top of a dome. In many respects it reflects a key moment in the building of St Paul's cathedral, London - St Paul's took 33 years to build - *when the last stone on the top of the lantern was laid by Edward Strong on October 26ᵗʰ 1708.*

The legend is built around the building of the second temple by the Israelites on their return from their Babylonian bondage, the first, Solomon's Temple having been destroyed. In clearing away the debris, some curious items are found, by the Israelites, and reflected in the furnishings of the Royal Arch ceremonies.

One item found is a *Long-lost volume of the Sacred Law.* There is only one such event recorded in the Old Testament, in 2 Chronicles 34:14,15, and takes place some years *before* the Babylonian attack, and is not mentioned again. Depending on which version of the Old Testament used, it happened when a priest was scurrying around in the dark recesses of Solomon's Temple and discovered the document.

> *While they were bringing out the money that had been taken into the temple of the LORD, Hilkiah the priest found the Book of the Law of the LORD that had been given through Moses. 15 Hilkiah said to Shaphan the secretary, "I have found the Book of the Law in the temple of the LORD." He gave it to Shaphan.*⁶⁷

Keeping in mind that freemasonry is an allegory, illustrated by symbols, one can't help believe that this is a record of the rediscovery of Vitruvius' book of architecture that was rediscovered languishing on a shelf in a monastery where it hadn't been looked at for several centuries.

The next item discovered when clearing the debris, is "a pedestal, a block of white marble, wrought *in the form of* the altar of incense, a double cube." On the front of the pedestal is an engraving of a circle and triangle. White marble is a building material that is not found in the Middle East, but, until recently, was available from only two sources, Italy and the USA. As North America was still 2,500 years away from being discovered by Europeans, it would not have been the source of supply for Solomon's Temple, and there is no knowledge of it being quarried in Italy at that time either. The only *altar of incense* mentioned in the Old Testament, is one that was part of the furnishings of the first temple; it was where the spices were mixed and the incense burners were filled. There was an instruction that absolutely nothing else other than the incense was ever to be placed there. The following notes the passage in Exodus that refers:

In Exodus 30:2 altar was square 1c x 1c x 2c high - acacia wood.
In Exodus 30:3 wooden box 'overlay the top and sides with pure gold'.
In Exodus 30:6-9 altar, where the incense was mixed, fired, lamps filled
and don't put anything else on it.

It is from the text of Exodus 30:2, that we find the mention of a double cube. This implies that at the time the scribes were writing the text that is now the Old Testament, this geometric configuration was well known. So, why is it mentioned in the legend in a different form to that in the bible, and why does it feature in the furnishings of a Royal Arch Chapter? And, why the engraving of the circle and triangle? Yet again, we start by going back into history to the time of the ancient Greeks.

As will have been realised by the observations thus far, the ancient Greek philosophers had a strong mastership of geometry, and discovered most, if not all, the basic principles that we know today. There was very little they did not understand, except, that is, for one thing - how geometrically, with the basic forms of square, triangle and circle, could one create a double cube? By this they meant doubling the volume, but keeping it as a single cube. It was a puzzle they never solved. Hippocrates (c 460 – 377 BCE) suggested the double cube problem could be solved by doubling the vertical length thereby effectively placing one cube on top of another - but doubling the length is not a geometric constant (standard) like Pi or Phi. It creates a major distortion of volume.

Hippocrates (c 460 – 377 BCE) suggestion for the double cube

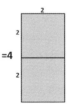

If one takes a cube of 2 x 2 x 2 units then the volume is 8 units, and to double that volume, one is looking for a single cube of 16 units. If one doubles the length of the sides of the cube, we now have 4 x 4x 4 units which produces a volume which is 64 units, four times more than what we are looking for.

Mathematically the answer is that if we have a cube with sides that are 2 units long, then the formula to provide the length of the sides of a cube that will be double the volume is:

**Length of side A = $\sqrt[3]{2}$ = 1.25992105…x 2 = 2.52**
**2.52 x 2.52 x 2.52 = 16.003.008…**

Sir Isaac Newton (1643 – 1727) was not only alive when the new St Paul's cathedral was being designed and built, but also when the first Grand Lodge was being formed. It was also the time when the Renaissance architecture of the Greeks and Romans was attracting a lot of attention, and columns featuring the five noble orders of architecture, were being erected. The columns not only have unique capitals to distinguish them, but their diameter is dictated by the height. This was a very clever visual idea on the part of the operative masons, because if one measured the diameter, one knew how high it was without actually erecting scaffolding and climbing up to measure it. The architect may have wanted a building with a large impressive portico. That would require a lot of chunky stone, and a lot of weight to be born by the pillars. Instead of having large heavy round pillars that would then spoil the aesthetics, it might be better to place two thinner pillars close together in place of one very large pillar. Irrespective of this, there was a need for ensuring it was undertaken with appropriate proportions. One large pillar might be supported on a single stone block with double the volume of the circle that defined the diameter of the pillar. If it was to be two smaller pillars, then they might be supported on a stone block, that was formed into a double cube, and positioned horizontally. And in some cases a single column might be supported on a vertical double cube.

Nearly all such pillars have one thing in common, that they terminate at the ground end, with a circular collar that provides an aesthetically pleasing way to interface the column to the base.

*Author's Note: Perhaps you'd like to test the ratio. The above column is of a pillar at the church of St. Martin-in-the-fields, London, built in 1721. Measure the width of the column as printed on this page and the dimension is "y". Take $\sqrt[3]{y} = z$ multiply by y = measured width of the base. K.L. Gest*

Sir Isaac Newton apparently became fascinated by the unsolved problem of the double cube, left by the Greeks, and it was a problem for the stonemasons as well. Accordingly the great scientist and mathematician came up with an answer, although it has to be said, that it did not produce a standard value, such as we have for phi or pi.

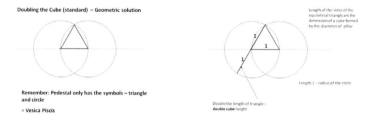

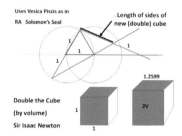

It starts with vesica piscis (circle) and an equilateral triangle.[68]

The geometry of the circles in vesica piscis, were, it seems, another tool in the stonemason/builder armoury. It provided a means for an operative mason to create a tool (square) that incorporated the basic angles he would use, 90 degrees, 60 degrees, 30 degrees. It wasn't only the architectural gothic style that benefited from the use of this geometry. By superimposing the use of the circle onto the famous library at Ephesus, a major city of the Roman and Byzantine periods, now in Turkey, we get some idea as to how this geometry might have been used in its design to set key features (making allowance for the angle at which the picture was taken). This is speculative and not intended to be definitive proof that this was the way in which major structures in ancient Greece and Rome were developed, but it does fit in with the concepts of Vitruvius, and then reflected in the geometric symbols of Royal Arch.

It will also be noted that there are elements of this same geometry that were used in what we often refer to as the architectural style of the Georgian period, mainly in the 1700s.

*The above images are of the remains of the great Celsus Library at Ephesus on which, geometric imagery has been added. Originally the library had a wonderful statute of the goddess Athena – the goddess of Wisdom. K.L.Gest*

The following statement appeared at the start of the book:

*The mandorla is a symbol with a secret.*

The mandorla has now revealed some of its secrets.

It is ancient wisdom that most freemasons have had before them for generations, - and haven't realised it.

**Platonic Solids**

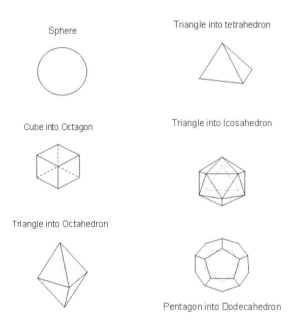

Another aspect of the Royal Arch degree, is a study of the platonic solids. In platonic theory, there are five solids. Although in the diagrams above, the sphere has been shown, it is, strictly, not a platonic solid. They are created when one takes a shape like a triangle and then bringing them together, equal side to equal side, until one creates a solid object representing the original. The creation of these solids is often credited to Pythagoras, but this doubted by some scholars. Irrespective of that, the solids were studied quite intensely by the Greek philosophers. Around 360 BCE, Plato attributed certain elements to the solids, for example, earth, air, water, and fire. This philosophy is often found in another geometric figure, not seen regularly in freemasonry, but nevertheless recorded. It is the octagram, representing the four cardinal points of the Earth, and the four elements:

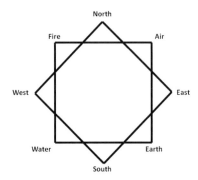

### The Master and Past Master degree

At the start of this chapter it was noted that at the time the Antients and Moderns merged to create the Supreme Grand Chapter, the Royal Arch degree was considered as part of the repertoire of the Masters and Past Masters. There seems to still be traces of it.

For example, there is a point in the ceremony of installing a new Master, when one scoops up water, starting from a crouching position, to one standing upright, rotating the arm at the same time. If one remained erect and rotated the arm about the shoulder, one would create a circle. However the nature of this *scooping* movement dictates that the shape created by the action, is one side of, and probably symbolising, a vesica.


Author's Note:

*There is a small phrase used in Royal Arch that is rather strange:*

*"If thou canst comprehend these things, thou knowest enough. Nothing is wanting but the key."*

*I believe that the key and the knowledge both rest with vesica piscis. When you know how to identify and use it –*

you comprehend and know enough.
The secrets of the key are revealed.

Chapter 15

# THE ANTIENTS V MODERNS

We saw in the last Chapter that in the 1700s there was no love lost between the Antients and the Moderns. Which leaves one wondering why that should have been the case, why one felt that they were using original and ancient rites, whereas the other was seen as an innovation. There may be a simple answer.

It has been suggested in this book, that freemasonry descended, not from the craft of the stonemasons of the Middle Ages, but from a separate Religious Gild that was associated with the stonemasons. At the time of the reformation, the religious guilds were disbanded, but many changed their name and mode of operation to prevent accusations of anti-religious activities of the wrong kind, depending on how the political wind was blowing. However, through the stormy period until Charles II became king, the ceremonies were kept as gentlemen's gatherings, meeting very infrequently. By the early 1700s, the political climate had become more settled, so that, when the Grand Lodge of England emerged in 1717, and the Constitutions were published in 1723, it was felt that the old ceremonies and knowledge could gradually be revealed. The knowledge was that which had developed in the time from around 1200 CE to the reformation, dominated by the gothic period, and known within the stonemasons' craft. Thus, the Antients came into existence.

Inigo Jones had kicked off the Renaissance in England, and introduced the classical architectural style. As this gathered momentum, there was an interest that developed within the wealthy gentry and merchants of the era, to know more about the classical period, and hence came into greater contact with the works of Euclid, Pythagoras and Plato, as well as the other major Greek philosophers. These were, in the main, men who had no direct contact with stonemasonry, other than that they had houses built in the classical style. They were accepted into the new Grand Lodge structure. With their knowledge of Greek language and mythology, plus the Platonic solids, they became the Moderns.

This then, would represent two different routes, two different backgrounds and two different philosophies. If this is so, then it would explain why they were so antagonistic, one to the other.

The following table is a suggestion for the key events and possible route of the development of the Antients and the Moderns.

| Era | Stonemasons | Religious Guild | | Classical |
|-----|-------------|-----------------|---|-----------|
| 1100 | **Pointed Arch used in St Denis Cathedral** | Religious guilds are known in Europe | | Euclid rediscovered. Translation Arabic to Latin |
| 1200 | Gothic building style used in cathedrals in Britain | Charity Guild of gentlemen, aldermen and masons free of the Guild | | |
| 1300 | First Charter for Guild of Stonemasons | | Black death and Peasants revolt | |
| 1400 | | | | **Vitruvius rediscovered.** Leonardo da Vinci. |
| 1500 | Gothic era stops. Demolition not new build | Guilds banned, becomes Fraternity of Free-Masons. Mainly gentlemen and regional | Reformation | Palladio, classical architecture. **Renaissance** |
| 1600 | New Charter for London Company **St. Paul's started.** | Fraternity has members from the London Company and create Society of Free-Masons | Great Fire. Period of enlightenment commences | Inigo Jones Queen's House. Stately Homes in Classical style Interest in |
| 1700 | **St Paul's completed** | **Antients** | First Constitutions and Grand Lodge/Chapter | Classical Greece - Plato **Moderns** |
| 1800 | | | **United Grand Lodge/Chapter** | |

| Year CE | Commissioner | Structure | Type of work | Work location | Masons Involved | Guild influence |
|---|---|---|---|---|---|---|
| 1000 | Church Monastic communes | Churches + Living accommodation | New build Modification Extension Repair | Large towns + Rural | Few per town + Saxon settled | Low |
| 1050 | Church Monastic communes Community | Churches Living accommodation Fortifications | New build Modification Extension Repair | Large towns | Few per town + Saxon settled | Low |
| 1100 | Church Monastic communes King/Barons | Churches Living accommodation Fortifications | New build Modification Extension Repair | Large towns and New entres | Norman + Increased itinerant | Post conquest |
| 1150 | Church Monastic communes KingBarons/Lords Knights Templar | Churches Living accommodation Fortifications Regional Castles | New build Modification Extension Repair | Towns Rural and New centres | Norman + Increased itinerant | Merchant power grows Templar influence |
| 1200 | Church Monastic communes King Earls/Lords Knights Templar Community | Churches Living accommodation Fortifications Regional Castles Barns/Bridges Preceptory | New build Modification Extension Repair | Towns Rural and New centres | Norman + English Increased itinerant | Craft and merchant guilds share power |
| 1250 | Church Monastic communes King Earls/Lords Knights Templar Order St John Community | Churches Cathedrals Living accommodation Fortifications Regional Castles Barns/Bridges Preceptory | New build Modification Extension Repair | Towns Rural and New centres | English + Norman Itinerant + settled | |

| Year | Clients | Building types | Work | Location | Masons | Events |
|------|---------|----------------|------|----------|--------|--------|
| 1300 | Church<br>Monastic communes<br><br>King<br>Earls/Lords<br>Knights Templar<br>Order St John | Churches<br>Cathedrals<br>Living accommodation<br>Fortifications<br>Regional Castles<br>Barns/Bridges<br>Preceptory | New build<br>Modification<br>Extension<br>Repair | Towns<br>Rural and Regional centres | English<br>Itinerant and settled | Templars disbanded 1307<br>Guild Charters issued |
| 1350 | Church<br>Monastic communes<br><br>King<br>Earls/Lords<br>Order St John<br>Other Orders<br>Corporations | Churches<br>Cathedrals<br>Living accommodation<br>Fortifications<br>Regional Castles<br>Barns/Bridges<br>Preceptory<br>Mansions | New build<br>Modification<br>Extension<br>Repair | Towns<br>Rural and Regional centres | English<br>Itinerant and settled | |
| 1400 | Church<br>Monastic communes<br><br>King<br>Earls/Lords<br>Order St John<br>Other Orders<br>Corporations | Churches<br>Cathedrals<br>Living accommodation<br>Regional Castles<br>Barns/Bridges<br>Preceptory<br>Mansions and country houses | New build<br>Modification<br>Extension<br>Repair | Towns<br>Rural and Regional centres | English<br>Increased Itinerant | Post black death |
| 1450 | Church<br>Monastic communes<br><br>King<br>Earls/Lords<br>Order St John<br>Other Orders<br>Corporations<br>Merchants | Churches<br>Cathedrals<br>Living accommodation<br>Regional Castles and palaces<br>Barns/Bridges<br>Preceptory<br>Mansions and country houses<br>Civic Buildings | New build<br>Modification<br>Extension<br>Repair | Towns<br>Rural and Regional centres | English<br>Itinerant and settled | |

| Year | Patrons | Building types | Work type | Settlement | Occupation | Events |
|---|---|---|---|---|---|---|
| 1500 | King<br>Earls/Lords<br>Corporations<br>Communities<br>Wealthy Merchants | Regional Castles<br>Palaces<br>Mansions and country houses<br>Civic Buildings | Demolition of monasteries.<br>Modification<br>Extension<br>Repair | Towns<br>Rural and Regional centres<br>Cities | English<br>Itinerant and settled | Reformation |
| 1550 | King<br>Earls/Lords<br>Corporations<br>Communities<br>Wealthy Merchants | Mansions and country houses<br>Civic Buildings | Demolition of monasteries.<br>Modification<br>Extension<br>Repair | Towns<br>Rural and Regional centres<br>Cities | English<br>Itinerant and settled | Reformation |
| 1600 | Church of England<br>King<br>Earls/Lords<br>Corporations<br>Communities<br>Wealthy Merchants | Churches<br>Fortifications<br>Mansions and country houses<br>Civic Buildings | New build<br>Modification<br>Extension<br>Repair | Towns<br>Rural and Regional centres<br>Cities | English<br>Itinerant and settled | Civil War<br>Renaissance |
| 1650 | Church of England<br>King<br>Earls/Lords<br>Corporations<br>Communities<br>Wealthy Merchants | Living accommodation<br>Barns/Bridges<br>Mansions and country houses<br>Civic Buildings and works | New build<br>Modification<br>Extension<br>Repair | Towns<br>Rural and Regional centres<br>Cities | English<br>Itinerant and settled | Civil War<br>Renaissance<br>Plague<br>Great Fire of London |
| 1700 | King<br>Earls/Lords<br>Corporations<br>Communities<br>Wealthy Merchants + traders | Living accommodation<br>Bridges<br>Mansions and country houses<br>Civic Buildings | New build<br>Modification<br>Extension<br>Repair | Towns<br>Rural and Regional centres<br>Cities | English<br>settled | Renaissance<br>Rebuild London + St. Paul's |

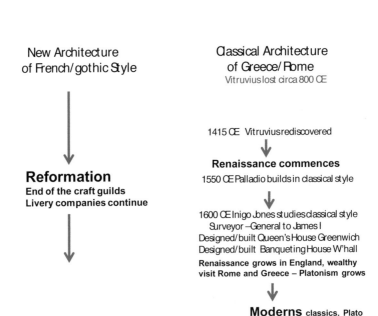

800 – 830 CE      Islamic Scholars translate Ancient Knowledge into Arabic

1100 CE – Crusades – Capture of Jerusalem – ANCIENT Knowledge sent to ROME

1110 – 1135 CE     ANCIENT knowledge translated from Arabic to Latin = Euclid

1135 CE  Gothic Arch
designed and Used

1150 CE  Gothic Arch
moves to England to
around 1485 CE

## Reformation

**Antients**  Euclid, geometry

New Architecture
of French / gothic Style

Classical Architecture
of Greece / Rome
Vitruvius lost circa 800 CE

1415 CE  Vitruvius rediscovered

**Renaissance commences**
1550 CE Palladio builds in classical style

1600 CE Inigo Jones studies classical style
Surveyor – General to James I
Designed / built Queen's House Greenwich
Designed / built Banqueting House W'hall
**Renaissance grows in England, wealthy
visit Rome and Greece – Platonism grows**

## Reformation
**End of the craft guilds
Livery companies continue**

**Moderns** classics, Plato

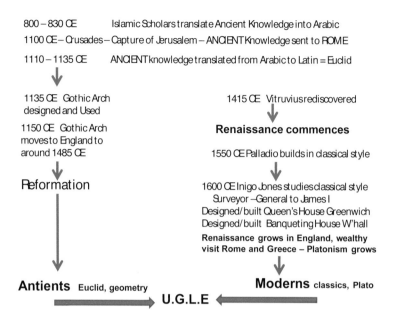

800 – 830 CE    Islamic Scholars translate Ancient Knowledge into Arabic
1100 CE – Crusades – Capture of Jerusalem – ANCIENT Knowledge sent to ROME

1110 – 1135 CE    ANCIENT knowledge translated from Arabic to Latin = Euclid

1135 CE  Gothic Arch
designed and Used

1150 CE  Gothic Arch
moves to England to
around 1485 CE

Reformation

1415 CE  Vitruvius rediscovered

**Renaissance commences**

1550 CE Palladio builds in classical style

1600 CE Inigo Jones studies classical style
Surveyor –General to James I
Designed/built Queen's House Greenwich
Designed/built  Banqueting House W'hall
**Renaissance grows in England, wealthy
visit Rome and Greece – Platonism grows**

**Antients** Euclid, geometry        **Moderns** classics, Plato

U.G.L.E

# Roots of Freemasonry

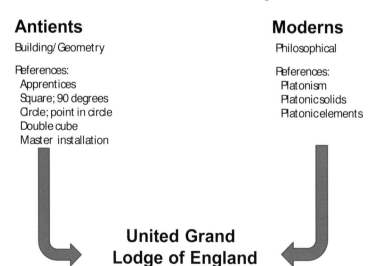

## Antients

Building/Geometry

References:
 Apprentices
 Square; 90 degrees
 Circle; point in circle
 Double cube
 Master installation

## Moderns

Philosophical

References:
 Platonism
 Platonic solids
 Platonic elements

# United Grand
# Lodge of England

# Section 3

## Chapter 16

### THE FOUNDATION STONE,
### PLUS THE MYSTERY OF THE LIGHTED TAPER

**Foundation Stones**

Following the formation of the United Grand Lodge of England, and for most of the next one hundred and fifty years, one of the great events undertaken in the name of freemasonry was the laying of foundation stones for new civic and public buildings, such as hospitals, town halls, schools and British Government offices in other countries. The practice declined in the mid-twentieth century when architectural concepts were the subject of a radical shift away from, what until then had been traditional building styles, using materials like bricks and stone, to high-rise towers of concrete, steel and glass.

Laying the first or foundation stone of important buildings is still seen as an important custom throughout the world. There are a range of local, national and tribal customs that exist, from killing an animal, like a sacrifice so that the blood spills onto the stone, sprinkling it with holy water and burying all manner of articles under it, with ceremonies taking place at sunrise, sunset and mid-day. In more recent times, the stone has become a *commemorative* stone, set in a wall at eye height, on which is engraved the date, names of those who laid it, the architect, surveyor, and so on. Others have cavities carved in them and articles deposited in them as time capsules. These ceremonies all have one thing in common, and that is to give some kind of communal blessing to the construction of the finished building, with an expectation that it will serve the community well.

The Masonic ceremonies for laying foundation stones have been extremely grand affairs, amongst much pomp and ceremony accompanied by grand parades of freemasons, in order of their Masonic rank, and in full regalia.

One of the earliest such parades following the formation of the United Grand Lodge of England, took place in Lincoln, and was recorded by the Reverend George Oliver, who was a keen freemason, a member of the clergy, avid writer, and who became the Deputy Provincial Grand Master for that Province.

In 1841, Oliver published a small pamphlet entitled:

*"A brief history of the Witham Lodge No 374 (now 297) Holden in the City of Lincoln, with a description of the ceremonial used at the levelling of the foundation stone of a New Masonic Hall, and sermon preached on that occasion by the Rev. Geo. Oliver DD, Deputy Prov. Grand Master; Domestic Chaplain to the Right Honourable Lord Kensington, member of the Society of Antiquaries".*

Oliver notes that the oldest Minutes book at that time available for that lodge, was one that commenced on 5th December 5th 1732, but also suggests that an older one had existed but been lost. He states that the membership of the *lod*ge at that time consisted mainly of men "who were in the highest class of gentry in the county". The lodge had enjoyed a fairly buoyant existence, but had then entered a period of decline in membership so that meetings became irregular, with meetings held at an inn. By 1840 it seems to have either stabilised or grown again because in that year, the Master and Wardens sent a letter to the Corporation of Lincoln, seeking to rent and restore a building next to the Guildhall (known as the Stonebow), that had been used as a gaol and had fallen into disrepair.

*"The lodge offered to refurbish the building and create a suite of rooms appropriate for public purposes". The Corporation agreed, and "the levelling of the foundation stone was laid with Masonic honours on Thursday the 15th April 1841".*

This event was clearly quite an occasion, not just for the members of Witham Lodge, but for the families and the city in general and is described in some detail by Rvd Oliver.

It was started, he says, by the Lodge being opened at the Lion Hotel, and after a simple ceremony to ensure the proceedings were lawful and to be carried out with dignity, a procession was formed. Leading the procession was The Union flag, borne by the son of a Master Mason. They were followed by:

Band of Music
Marshal with baton
Visiting brethren, according to the seniority of their lodges.
Officers wearing their collars and jewels, with their respective banners.
Rough Ashlar, borne by the son of a Master Mason.
Entered Apprentice
Tracing board of the 1st degree
Corinthian Column, borne by the son of a Master Mason.

Brethren of Witham *Lodge*, not being in office
Tracing Board of the 2nd degree

Ionic Column Doric Column

Borne by the son of a Master Mason Borne by the son of a MasterMason

Perfect Ashlar on a platform
Trowel – Inscription plate – Mallet

Junior Deacon with pillar Senior Deacon with pillar

Director of Ceremonies
Salver, with Corn, Wine, Oil and Salt, Borne by the son of a Master Mason.

Secretary with Book of Constitutions Treasurer with coins to be deposited

Junior Warden with Plumb Rule
Banner of Witham *Lodge*
Senior Warden with Level
The Provincial Grand Officers
Past Master and P.P.G Superintendent of Works with the plans
The covenant with Square and Compasses, Borne by the son of a Master Mason

Steward with Wand Steward with Wand

Deputy Prov Grand Master
Master of Witham *Lodge*, with Square
Prov Grand Sword Bearer

Steward with Wand Steward with Wand

Union Flag, Borne by the son of a Master Mason
Prov Grand Inner Guard
Marshal with Baton

The Rvd Oliver describes the scene:

*"The effect of the procession was imposing; and the crowds of people of both sexes, who thronged the windows throughout the whole line, viewed the display with admiration and delight. The spectacle was indeed of a superior character. The banners of the several County Lodges, disposed with much taste in different parts of the procession. The Master Mason sons, to the number of eighteen fine youths, from 8-12 or 14 years of age, decorated in an uniform manner, with sky blue scarfs and rosettes, and bearing the emblematical furniture of the lodge…"*

Rvd Oliver goes on to note that he then delivered a sermon - some ten pages of printed text which would have taken fifteen to twenty minutes to deliver, so one must hope that the ceremony occurred on a calm warm day.

The stone had been delivered in advance and raised on an "A" frame derrick, supported by rope and pulleys. A raised platform had been erected around the site where the stone was to be laid, primarily so that the wives and children associated with freemasonry on that day, along with other dignitaries, could view every aspect of the event.

> *"The treasurer…then produced a phial, containing a quantity of silver and copper pieces of the present reign [this would have been Queen Victoria], to which, the boys who had assisted in the ceremonial, added a copper coin of the present year. It was deposited in a hollow of the lower stone, and the Worshipful Master, having spread the mortar, the stone slowly descended, the band playing the National Anthem."*

The stone being set in place:

The Worshipful Master applied a square to ensure that the stone was good.
The Senior Warden applied the level to ensure the stone was level.
The Junior Warden applied the plumb rule to ensure the stone was upright.
The Prov Grand Master, taking the mallet, gave the stone three knocks.
The Worshipful Master then approached the stone again and slewed some grains of wheat over it, sprinkled it with wine.
The Prov. Grand Master scattered salt on it.
The Worshipful Master poured a quantity of oil over it, pronouncing the benediction:

> *"As Jacob making himself a pillow of stones, on which sleeping he dreamed he saw the gates of heaven, and when he awoke, he anointed the stones with fresh oil, praying..that in the building which may arise from it, none but good men may be admitted, and men that fear God and love the brotherhood".*

There was a short oration, the procession reformed and progressed back to the Lion Hotel, from whence it had started, followed by a good dinner attended by over one hundred invited brethren and guests.

The pattern used in this ceremony was very similar to that which was subsequently used in all Masonic stone-laying ceremonies. The Grandness of the occasion cannot be understated, and must have created a great deal of public interest whenever, and wherever, they were performed.

*These old photographs show not only what a wonderful spectacle a procession leading to a stone laying ceremony must have created, but also the stone laying itself, especially surrounded by so many women and family members of those taking part. The same basic practice was used in British dominions around the world.*

Left: Foundation stone at Government House, Perth, Western Australia. The inscription on the plate reads:
*"This foundation stone was laid on 17th March 1852 by Worship Brother Francis Lochee of Lodge of St John No 712 of the United Grand Lodge of England of Antient, Free and Accepted Masons"* K.L. Gest

Right: The stone marked the foundation of a new regional hospital specialising in Eye and Sight treatment. It was laid in 1933. K.L. Gest

It is interesting to note the mention of the small cavity into which the coins were inserted during the ceremony in Lincoln. There are very few instances recorded where stones have been removed and the *treasures* or time-capsules examined to find out just what was inside at the time the stone was laid. One such recovery was from the Royal Mint in Perth, Western Australia, in which a time capsule was inserted. The foundation stone was set on 23rd September 1896 by Sir John Forest, who had been an explorer in Western Australia prior to becoming the State Governor. The Mint had been under the control of the Royal Mint in London until 1970 when it reverted to the control of the State Government. The stone was laid despite the fact that the plans for the building had still not been approved by the authorities in London.

Gold had been found in three major locations of Western Australia, namely Kalgoorlie, Coolgardi and Murchison, and the mint served to refine the gold as well as the issue of coinage for local use.

When the time capsule was opened on 26th May 1999, it was found to contain:

- Seventeen newspapers dated just prior to the date the stone was laid, and from several major towns of that era, spread around the south west of the State.
- Three different West Australian government directories.
- A sealed envelope containing postage stamps and postcards of the era.
- A sealed envelope containing plans of the colony of Western Australia.
- A list of coinage enclosed in the time capsule; a glass jar with cork stopper containing nine coins of different denominations, all dated in close proximity to the stone laying event.

With the exception of the time capsule, which is a later innovation, one can envisage that the rest of the ceremony may well have been based on that undertaken by Thomas Strong, and witnessed by numerous dignitaries', for the laying of the foundation stone of the current St Paul's Cathedral.

## The Mystery of the Lighted Taper

For the past one hundred years, much of Britain, Europe and North America, and territories that they have been associated with, have enjoyed the benefit of electric lighting. Over the past few hundred years, we have moved through lighting by tallow oil, candles, kerosene, gas and electricity. This makes one wonder why, most lodges in this modern era, still light candles and do so ceremonially, with a lighted taper that is carried around the lodge.

*Author's Note: Having pondered this for some time, and not finding a satisfactory answer, other than it was a recognition of the times when freemasonry was being formed, I had dismissed it as a quaint custom. Once I had identified a possible connection of modern freemasonry with St Paul's cathedral, I wondered if it had anything to do with the lighting of the candles in that church. Accidentally I came across what I believe may be the real connection, but stress that this is my conjecture.*

The story starts just after the reign of Henry V. Henry V died in 1422, and his son inherited the throne as Henry VI, but was still an infant. The country was therefore run by regency, of which the Duke of Gloucester, the young brother of Henry V, was a key member. The Duke annulled his first marriage to the Duchess of Hainault and married Eleanor de Cobham a year after the young Henry VI was born.

Eleanor had been persuaded by a chaplain from Worcester, Richard Walker, who also apparently dabbled in sorcery, that her husband, Duke of Gloucester, would one day be king, and with it, she would be queen. She therefore spent a considerable amount of time with the chaplain/ sorcerer attempting to bring this about by witchcraft. Her efforts were discovered, and in 1441, she was seized, tried and convicted of her crimes. Her punishment was that she was taken to *Old St. Paul's cathedral*, from where, and dressed only in a white sheet, she was made to walk the streets of London for three consecutive days, carrying a lighted taper, and visiting a number of churches on route, the whole punishment to purge her of her crimes and, to do penance. The Duke annulled the marriage the following year. Richard Walker was also punished, in 1422.

Edward IV (1445 – 1483) is described as having been a very able king. He was never defeated on the field of battle, and increased his wealth substantially through shrewd investments made with merchants who were members of City of London Companies (later to become the Livery Companies). Edward also had two sons, who, shortly after his death, disappeared from the Tower of London and were believed killed on the orders of their uncle, Richard III. During the reign of Edward IV he had a group of mistresses that he favoured. One of these was a lady known as Jane Shore (1445 – 1527).

Jane had been born to a wealthy merchant, who had a shop in London that served the ladies of the nobility and wealthy gentry. Jane apparently, grew up to be quite a beauty and was known as the *Rose of London*. Her reputation, and her connection with ladies of nobility and wealth, resulted in her becoming the desire of many wealthy suitors. Her father, eventually encouraged her to marry William Shore, another wealthy merchant, who was some years older than Jane. The marriage didn't last. Jane obtained an annulment in 1476, citing as grounds that her husband was impotent.

It was in the same year that her marriage was annulled that she apparently came to the attention of Edward IV and became his mistress. Records suggest that he was devoted to her, and she to him, and she remained with him until his death in 1483.

Jane became the mistress of two other high-ranking noblemen, such that when Richard III became King, she was charged with conspiracy because of her liaisons, and imprisoned. As penance, Jane was taken to St Pauls Cross, outside of *Old St. Paul's,* where she was *divested of all her splendour*, clothed in little more than a petticoat, made to walk barefoot around the streets of London, carrying a lighted taper and visiting many of the churches, as had Eleanor de Cobham some forty years previously.

On completion of her penance she was sent to Ludgate prison, but was later released, married well, and lived to a reasonably old age.

*Author's Note: Both of the above instances involved Old St. Paul's. In both cases, the carrying of the lighted taper was a penance for the wrongs that the individuals had been perceived to have committed. It was, what the church would call, an act of repentance and remission of sins. In carrying the lighted taper around the lodge, it seems to me to be an enactment of that same process on behalf of all the members present.*

# Chapter 17

## THE OLD INITIATION

There had been disclosures. A mysterious and secretive world was open for all to see. The shockwave sent a ripple of disquiet, and fascination, through the drawing rooms of polite society, at dining tables, amongst military officers and government officials, and among those who were aspiring to be accepted into the various social groups that met in the coffee houses or those that dispensed chocolate.

The year was 1724.

It was already dark. The long, warm summer evenings, bathed in sunlight, had given way to the prelude of winter. The air was already chilly and suggested there would be frost on the ground by morning. All around him were the unmistakeable sounds of city life; the calls of the street vendors looking for their last few sales of the day; children yelling to one another and running, pushing their way through the crowds as they hurried home to who knows where; the clanking of the horses and carriages that ran through the city by day and night; the striking of a church bell denoting the top of the hour; seven of the clock, the appointed hour, and – oh yes, the unmistakable stench of the city after the purity of the country air.

The Reverend John Dene checked that he had arrived at the correct address, The Red Lyon Tavern, in the courtyard of Red Lyon Street, Holborn, next to Lincolns Inn Field in the Parish of St Giles, London. He had arrived at the tavern at exactly the appointed time. The door of the tavern was slightly ajar, and such light as there was from the few candles that were lit within, spilled out to cut a thin line across the cobbled yard outside where two horses, steam still rising from their backs as signs of their exertions, were being uncoupled from a carriage ready to be led to a stable block at the corner of the courtyard. Someone of importance, the reverend mused, someone who could afford to own a carriage and horses, was obviously visiting the metropolis. The Reverend Dene pushed the door open and stepped inside. His gaze quickly adjusted to the smoke filled gloomy interior and with one sweep of his eyes about the room, noted his friend, Dr Stephen Bland standing by the fireplace with a tankard of ale raised to his lips. Seeing the arrival of John Dene, the doctor beckoned him to his side and handed him a jug of ale that had already been purchased and awaited the arrival of the newcomer.

Bland congratulated the reverend on such a prompt arrival and pointed out that by so doing he was already demonstrating that he was a worthy man. Dene was advised to relax and enjoy his ale for he would not be needed at the start of the proceedings in the room above. When they had emptied their tankards, the doctor disappeared through a small oak door at the rear of the tavern, his footsteps then heard mounting the wooden stairs beyond that led to the small room directly above the main bar that the Reverend Dene had entered. The faint and muffled sounds of merriment and chatter descended through the floor and there was the occasional clip-clopping of hard heels of shoes or boots as someone walked across the uncarpeted wooden floor above. A few minutes later the doctor returned for his companion, escorted him up the staircase, along a short passage and into a small room, well away from the main room, a room from which the sounds of a large gathering were being emitted. The room the Reverend Dene entered was lit by a single candle, placed in a candlestick that was positioned on the floor behind a solitary wooden chair that had already been placed in the centre of the room. The Reverend was invited to take his seat. As he approached the chair the shadow his body cast from the light of the candle transformed from one that engulfed most of the room to one that merely reflected his seated posture. Even so, the shadow extended across the floor, up the wall opposite and halfway across the plaster and lath ceiling above. In due time, the doctor explained, he would come back to the room for his companion and his ordeal and test of merit would begin. The doctor left and the door was firmly closed. John Dene was left in the room with nothing but the chair, the light from the candle and his shadow for company. Embraced by these simple facilities he had time to be with his own quiet thoughts and contemplation.

In the room above the tavern bar, some forty other men had already assembled. Among their number were several men of social standing for the times; there was a bishop, a magistrate, a barrister, a lawyer, a banker, the head master of a fashionable boy's public boarding school, a senior clerk from the city administration, three highly influential businessmen, an engineer, an undertaker, and a man described as simply *a gentleman* who owned several estates to the west of the city and derived his income from the rents paid by tenant farmers.

There was the owner of several trading barges that sailed regularly between London and towns in northern England. When asked about his usual cargo he replied that it was mostly fine wine and ales. Indeed, he may have been right for his vessels were usually filled with barrels of human urine, collected from the emptying of chamber pots, *piss pots*, used for toilet purposes in most of the London residences, of all social stratas. The urine was then shipped in barrels to be used in the textile industry, for fixing dyes, in the northern mill towns where the industry was centred. As the only safe fluid for drinking in the city area, most people consumed ale when their financial circumstances permitted, while those of a more affluent social standing may well have consumed wines. Anyone who really knew the nature of the business the barge owner was involved with, knew that he was camouflaging the real nature of the cargo and instead described his unusual shipments as *taking the piss*.

The rest of the gathering in the room comprised men who were associated with various respectable trades that were registered at the Guildhall in London, where all official trades were validated. Among their number were several who were registered members of the London Company of Masons. Soon, all those gathered in the room would come to count the Reverend Dene as one of their assembly.

The meeting room had been well lit by several candles strategically placed around the walls of the room in front of mirrored glass to reflect the light. One of the men took the candlesnuffer and extinguished most of them. He began pacing up and down the room closely inspecting the floorboards. He was looking for patches where light from the tavern bar below was seeping through. It might mean that floorboards had been tampered with enabling unwanted eyes to peer up and glimpse the events taking place in the room, or for an eavesdropper to place his ear trumpet against the ceiling below and listen to the proceedings as they unfolded. This was a private occasion, not meant to be seen or heard by anyone other than those who had proclaimed their secrecy by the commitment to an oath. Had any light from below been detected, then the area of the floor would be pointed out, a strip of thick cord would be pushed into the offending area to reduce the risk that the secret events of the evening would become known to anyone who was not entitled to them. When no such gaps had been detected and his investigations had been completed, the loan wanderer took a lighted taper and relit the candles.

The Master, having removed his hat, took up his position behind a single small table that stood at one end of the room. Around his neck was a triangular-shaped ribbon from which hung a right-angled builders square made from brass, with the outside of each leg measuring some 18 inches in length. In more ancient times such a measurement would have known as a cubit, the length of an arm of a man from the point of his elbow to the tip of his outstretched middle finger. On the table were two sets of candlesticks, each being six in number, one set being slightly taller than the other. These candlesticks, each with a lighted candle, were placed in two patterns of triangles, one which interlaced with, and was inverted within, the other. The Master picked up the gavel that had been placed on the table and gave it a gentle but audible knock, sufficient to signify that he demanded the attention of all who were assembled in the room.

"We will form the lodge", said the Master. The member who had previously inspected the floor boards, moved towards the door, accompanied by another member, opened it and stepped outside, closing the door behind them. Each drew a sword from a sheath that was buckled about his torso. Their task was to prevent the unwarranted intrusion of anyone not invited to enter the room whilst the private meeting was in progress. A Past Master of the lodge stood to the left of the incumbent. He had a ribbon about his neck, triangular in shape, and from it hung an image of the sun. In his hands he held compasses and a string of cords. Two other members took up predetermined positions; one at the end of the room opposite the Master and one at the side of the room to the left of the Master. They were the Wardens. The other assembled members stepped to the sides of the room and took up positions, such that they were roughly equi-spaced, standing beside wooden benches placed around the walls of the room to be used as seats.

"Show me that there is none here that should not be so by not having been initiated as a member of our Free Maysons lodge."

All, simultaneously, provided the demonstration of proof the Master had demanded.

"Thus assured you will clothe yourselves with your badge that demonstrates the proficiency you have achieved in the knowledge of our ancient Order."

Each member retrieved from a pocket inside their coats, a thin white lambskin apron that they tied about their midriff. A quick glance revealed many different images embroidered delicately on the aprons to denote the level of knowledge attained. A common theme was the image of two pillars with an illustration of the sun above one and the moon above the other. There were also a large number of skin aprons that had nothing embroidered on them, they were bare and white.

"Brothers of this ancient Order of Free and Accepted Maysons, this lodge is open in the name of holy St John, forbidding all cursing, swearing, or whispering, all profane discourse whatever, under no less penalty than what the majority shall think proper, but not less than one penny a time and not more than six pence." The Master made three knocks on the table with the wooden hammer and replaced his hat. "Has any one of you received any communications in any manner whatsoever that might affect this lodge?" asked the Master.

Nobody responded.

"That being so I will ask the brother lawyer to read to us the details that he recorded of our last proceedings, which were on the day of the Summer Solstice."

The lawyer stepped forward holding a substantial ledger. Another brother Free Mayson held a candle so as to illuminate the pages. The lawyer read for about three minutes giving an outline of the previous meeting.

"Does anyone disagree with what our brother lawyer has recorded?" asked the Master.

Nobody responded.

"Very well, brother lawyer, you are instructed to copy it at your leisure into our book of proceedings and, prior to our next gathering, you are to submit a copy, under an appropriate seal, such that prying eyes may not become aware of the contents, to the Grand Master of Free and Ancient Maysons."

The lawyer bowed slightly, closed the ledger and stepped back to his original position.

"Today," began the Master, "our chief business is to initiate into our noble fraternity, a man who has been well and worthily recommended to us, and has passed all examination and enquiry as to his character that has been available to us. Is the Gentleman proposed last lodge night, ready to be made?" The doctor affirms that he is. "Then brother Wardens you will leave the room and ensure that the candidate is prepared for his ordeal, after which we will admit him here upon the square where he will be subjected to the time honoured ritual and pledge his fidelity to our ancient institution by the swearing of an oath of secrecy."

The Wardens leave the room and join the Reverend Dene in the room where he has been patiently waiting.

"Are you ready to continue through the trials of your initiation?" asked the Senior Warden.

"I am," replied the candidate.

"And do you come here and seek admission to our fraternity of your own free will and accord?"

"I do," came the reply.

At this stage, the candidate was asked to remove everything about him that was metallic, buckles, buttons, rings, even the money in his pockets. The candidate was blindfolded for until he had pleaded an oath of secrecy he was not a member of the ancient fraternity of Free and Ancient Maysons and could therefore neither see or hear anything of its proceedings, or identify any of those who were present. He had been left seated in this room for over half an hour with little more than his thoughts for company, to enable him to reflect fully on the step he was about to make. If he had any doubts, that was the time to change his mind. But he did not. Having been thus prepared The Wardens assisted the reverend gentleman to be seated again. The doctor, the member who had previously proposed him, joined him in the same room, ostensibly to provide protection and company whilst his friend was in his state without light, but neither was permitted speak to the other.

On their return to the meeting room, the Wardens advise the Master that the candidate had been prepared.

"Then brother Free Maysons, we will mark the square".

The two Wardens advanced to the table. When both were standing in front of it, the master removed from the ribbon about his neck, the right-angled brass builders square. It was ceremoniously passed to the Senior Warden who received it from the Master with great solemnity. The past Master held out the string of cords, passing them to the Junior Warden. Both men then turned away from the table.

The Senior Warden knelt on the floor to one side of the room and placed the brass square on the floor such that it pointed both across and down the room. With the Senior Warden holding the square firmly in place, the Junior Warden stepped forward and, using a piece of chalk he took from his pocket, drew a line along the outside edge of each leg of the square. Both men then stood and pulled a length of string from the cords. Knots had already been tied in the string with sufficient length between them as to represent about half the width of the room. With the Senior Warden holding one end of the cord, the Junior Warden took the chalk and ran it along the length of the string between the two knots. Both men again knelt on the floor. The Senior Warden placed one knot on the junction of the right angle that had already been drawn using the square. The Junior Warden pulled the string tight, and positioned it such that it ran along the line of the square marked on the floor, its exact position monitored by the Senior Warden. When the latter signalled that the alignment was correct, the Junior Warden pinged the string so that a continuous chalk line appeared on the floor representing the distance between the knots. This process was repeated three more times until a near perfect square had been marked out in chalk, with the Senior Warden positioning the brass square on the floor, the Junior Warden chalking the string and pinging it. When completed the square and cords were returned to their relative keepers. To complete the setting out, three candles held firm in their candlesticks were lit and placed in the shape of a triangle around the centre of the marked square.

Led into the room, still blindfolded, the reverend was taken to one corner of the room and positioned so that he was facing it and therefore away from the proceedings, although because he was unable to see he didn't realise the unusual stance he had been placed in. The room was otherwise silent.

"You will remove your coat, your waistcoat and your blouse, if you please, so that you are bare of chest," instructed the Senior Warden. This done, the candidate, still blindfolded, was escorted to the centre of the chalked square where he was turned to face the Master.

"Free and ancient Maysons of this lodge, this candidate for membership among us will be led past and before you so that you can see that he is a man and that you are not being deceived by an impostor by virtue that it is a woman dressed in the garments of a gentleman."

The candidate was then led around the inside edge of the square so as to be on full display to the assembly, and then returned to the centre of the square.

"What is thy full name?"

"John Sebastian Dene."

"And what is thy profession or calling in life?"

"I have the good fortune to serve God as the vicar of St. Margaret's Parish in the county of Hampshire."

"Do thou swear on thy honour that thou art of the full age of maturity, that being twenty one years?"

"I do so swear."

"And in whom do thou place thy unerring trust."

"In God, sir, for I know he is always with me and will afford me his protection."

"Good. In the certain knowledge that thou art protected by thy faith in God, thou mayest follow thy leader in confidence in the knowledge that no danger will befall thee."

And so the ceremony of the initiation, trust and obligations of the candidate continued. Only when completed was the blindfold removed so that the Reverend Dene had moved from the symbolic darkness of a lack of the knowledge retained in freemasonry, into the light of the room and symbolically to the access of such knowledge. He looked about him and the faces assembled in his honour. There are two he already knew. The doctor was one, and to his amazement, his Bishop was the other.

The newly made Free Mayson was led to the northeast corner of the square that has been marked out on the floor in chalk. The Master addressed him.

"You will stand just outside the lines on the floor with your heels together, and with one foot pointing along the line and the other foot pointing down the line." The Master waited for this movement to be completed and then continued. "In the building of any grand structure, the first stones to lay are the cornerstones. They are always placed at the northeast corner of the foundations. The foundations are most important for if they are incorrectly set, aligned or of insufficient strength, then in time the building will fall. As you stand now, your feet symbolically represent those cornerstones and your body is straight and upright as should be the corner of any building. In joining our ancient fraternity we pray that your future life will be built on the solid foundations your feet now represent, that you will be forever upright in life as you now stand, as well as in all the works that you do, being prudent, temperate, trustworthy and just in your dealings with all that you come into contact with so that you will be viewed by all those around you as an honourable man and in so doing reflect honour on this fraternity and all that are members of it. As a symbol of your innocence about our ceremonies and customs, and to demonstrate to all the brother Free Masons here present this evening, we will tie around your waist an apron of pure white lambskin. This was the colour of the apron worn by the novice stonemason, or hewer of stone, as a demonstration to the skilled craftsmen that he had entered into the craft as both a free man and an apprentice, as yet devoid of knowledge and unskilled in its practices. You will wear it whenever you meet here until time and circumstances demonstrate that you have gained sufficient confidence and knowledge of our fraternity that it may be embellished with images that represent the knowledge you will have then achieved." At this time the Master tied the apron about the waist of the newcomer, amid cheers from the assembled brethren.

At the conclusion of the business of the evening, the newest brother and Free Mayson, the Brother Reverend John Sebastian Dene, was instructed by the Junior Warden to go downstairs and obtain from the tavern owners, a mop and a pail containing water. On his return to the room, and under the watchful eye of the Junior Warden, he was instructed to mop the floor of the room to remove any trace of the chalk marks made on it. If the Junior Warden was not satisfied, Dene had to do it again and again, until satisfaction was decreed. This would be the task that would fall to John Dene after every meeting until such time that there was another new brother among them. And to be certain that no trace of the markings would remain, they placed large tables over the previously marked area, and there sat down to dine.

The above scenario is a fictitious impression of a lodge meeting some 20-60 years after the formation of the Grand Lodge of England in 1717, as are the characters, although in each case, they reflect an event that actually happened. In the eighteenth century, just fifty years after the foundation of the Grand Lodge of England, the Red Lyon tavern in Red Lyon Street, Holborn, London, did exist and was used by a Masonic Lodge for its meetings – Lodge number 57. The spelling of *Mayson* was apparently used by the antients. It seems that it referred to *May–sons*, the sons of May, who celebrated the return of life given back to the earth by the warmth of the sun and from which all goodness (fruits and food) would emanate.

The collecting and shipping of urine from London to towns like Leeds in the north of England, *taking the piss,* was a well established trade.

The process of marking out a square on the floor of a lodge room with a brass builders square, chalk and skirret, are recorded practices in a Freemasons lodge in the eighteenth century; they are contained in a description known as *Jachin and Boaz,* first published in 1762.

The positioning of a candidate in an empty side room with merely a lighted candle for company is also well recorded as is the practice of removing all metallic accessories like rings, buckles and coins, all of which were returned later.

The removal of all chalk markings on the floor using a mop and pail, and this being a duty of the newest initiate to freemasonry under the direction of the Junior Warden, is also well recorded.

Such was the nature of society in England in the mid eighteenth century that only those in the community that were of professional and social standing were likely to have had the time, means and education that would afford them acceptance into a regular Masonic Lodge. These were the same type of men that became Coroners, Justices of the Peace, Magistrates, founded hospitals and orphanages for the poor and served on the Boards of the respective administrations; that helped establish almshouses that were an early form of retirement home, and served many other organisations that helped to found and administer respectable communities as far as their abilities and resources would permit for the times in which they lived. They were honourable and charitable men, pillars of society. Bishops and clergymen were often initiated, as are men of all religions, even today.

The *work* these men were a part of, or started, and the traditions they fostered, continue to this day.

In our twenty-first century world of instant global communications, where knowledge relating to almost any subject can be found at the touch of a computer button, and career progress and the course of one's life is influenced by various grades of university degree, some of the practices of freemasons' lodges, may seem bizarre to those who are newly initiated into its secrets, and even more obtuse to those who are outsiders and view it with scepticism and suspicion. But, freemasonry was founded in a very different era, one where very few individuals could read and write, where a university education was restricted to a privileged minority of the aristocracy or those attached to the monastic houses; women were seldom educated. If one was lucky, one would learn a trade skill and be admitted to a guild that regulated the work of, and those who could be admitted to, its membership. Every trade had its specific secrets that were jealously guarded to ensure protection for the income of those in the trade. Great reliance was placed on charity towards those in the respective guilds; support of guild orphans and widows, and those who had been injured in the pursuit of the trade. Freemasonry is, in many respects, a continuation of those traditions. Yet, the passing of time has reduced an understanding of the secrets and the knowledge that it contains, knowledge that is more far reaching than just that associated with building and construction. It is a window on the world and knowledge of our ancestors. When one understands that knowledge and how it is packaged, it reveals a fascinating world that is as relevant today as ever it was.

Freemasonry cannot be considered in isolation from the world affairs, social development, and politics of the centuries past; of religion and the dark ages it spawned in Europe, and the ultimate emergence into the period known as the Renaissance and the *Enlightenment*.

*Author's Note: I would like to think that this book is not just about freemasonry. It reveals much of the background that freemasonry is built on, and uncovers some of the secrets and mythology that have built up around it. It places the world, past and present, in a different context to the one that has been shaped in our minds as the product of victorious leaders, massaging the truth for political ends.*

# Chapter 18

## THE CLOSING

**Something very different**

This book started with the statement, *And now for something different.*

I stated concern that unless we make an effort to understand what we are doing in Masonic ceremonies, then they will become empty shells devoid of meaning.

Through this book I've tried to show that, in fact, there is a richness of knowledge, some of which would have been known to our ancestors. It is *veiled in allegory.*

I had noted that, in my opinion, based on observation, there are many instances where a member of a lodge had memorised large elements of ceremony, in both words and actions, delivered them perfectly and to great acclaim, but hadn't got a clue about what he had just done or said actually meant. Thus, this book was intended to shine a light on the background to some areas of our ceremonies, symbolism and terminologies.

I've presented a thesis on the origins of freemasonry; the What? Why? When? Where? and How? of the Order. I acknowledge that some of the observations made do not sit easily with the perspective that has been created in the past.

I've included a number of details of events from history, to try and demonstrate that other momentous and historical events were occurring during the development of the institution, and may have had some effect on its evolution – it was not created in isolation to its surroundings.

It has taken me twenty years to compile the data that forms the background of this book, and I have come to firmly believe that the origins of the freemasonry we practice today are:

- descended, not from the Roman collegia and what went before it, or the *lodges* of practising operative stonemasons, but from a *religious guild* in which stonemasons and craftsmen of other major guilds associated with building, like carpenters, were financial members. This *religious guild* not only promoted the moral aspects of life as espoused through religion, but provided the burial rites for departed members and their families; was a charity that assisted those too aged to work with small pensions; helped those that were infirm or injured in the process of doing their job. The primary role of freemasonry today, is the promotion of morality and charity;

- that it is a reflection of the loss of the much cherished *Old St. Paul's Cathedral* in the great fire of London. Some of the traditions of freemasonry are based on events that involved the *Old St. Pauls,* including those between when the fire was extinguished to the foundations of the new being laid.
- that the building of that which exists today, *St Paul's Cathedral, London*, designed by Sir Christopher Wren, and the fifth such church structure on the same site, forms a key plank in the development of freemasonry as an organised entity.
- that part of the knowledge and imagery in freemasonry is based on the geometric abilities of the stonemasons through the gothic period to the reformation – the knowledge of the Antients, whilst other imagery is associated with Platonic theory and is the knowledge of the Moderns, derived from the rediscovery of the classical era defined by the renaissance.

If one accepts the above analysis, then it seems probable that the original basis for the later development of freemasonry may well have occurred around one thousand years ago, *(it is older than the Golden Fleece and Roman Eagle)*, with the rediscovery of the geometry of Euclid and use in gothic architecture in the early twelfth century. That it was not derived from the stonemasons that built the cathedrals of the late Middle Ages, but was formed out of the creation of religious guilds that became fraternities after the reformation, around the year 1550. The primary role of the fraternities was one of *charity.* And *charity* remains the bedrock of our ancient institution even today. At around that time the era known as the renaissance developed along with classical architecture of the ancient Greek and Roman styles, plus the knowledge that we know as Platonic Theory. Thus, Euclid's geometry known by stonemasons, and Platonic Theory, became intertwined to create the symbolism of the institution we now enjoy. That being so, then our institution is probably no older that about 1550 – the period of the reformation and the renaissance. In relative terms, ancient it still is.

Long may our ancient and honourable institution continue to flourish, for we live in a world in sore need of it, and the principles it espouses.

# ENDNOTES

1    National Space and Aeronautics at http://www.nasa.gov/pdf/323298main_
     CelebrateApolloEarthRise.pdf.
2    *The Secrets of Solomon's Temple*, by Kevin L. Gest. Published 2007 in the United
     Kingdom by Ian Allan-Lewis Masonic, and in the United States of America by Quayside
     Publishing – Fairwinds.
3    *Titbits* magazine for the week ending March 17th 1888. It published an account of the
     three craft ceremonies of Freemasonry
4    Information available from the Worshipful Company of Masons of London. To see a
     copy of the Charter, which refers to the arts and mistery of the craft see website http://
     www.masonslivery.co.uk/downloads/43073_Masons_Charter_Book.pdf.
5    See *The Invisible College* – Robert Lomas.
6    Ashmole included in diary materials of the time reference to his having been a member
     of a Masonic *Lodge*. The dates for these meetings are placed at 16 October 1646, and
     again on 11 March 1682. An introductory article on this person can be found in "A
     Freemasons Guide and Compendium" by Bernard E. Jones.
7    See *The Invisible College* – Robert Lomas.
8    See *The Invisible College* – Robert Lomas.
9    Bede's *Ecclesistical History of England, A revised Translation* by A.M. Sellar, Late Vice-
     Principal of Lady Margaret Hall, Oxford. Published by George Bell and Sons - 1907
10   Bede's *Ecclesistical History of England, A revised Translation* by A.M. Sellar, Late Vice-
     Principal of Lady Margaret Hall, Oxford. Published by George Bell and Sons - 1907
11   *The Story of the City Companies* [London] by P.H. Ditchfield MA FSA published 1926
12   *The Story of the City Companies* [London] by P.H. Ditchfield MA FSA published 1926
13   *English Gilds – The original ordinances of more than one hundred early English Gilds*, Toulmin
     Smith, published for The Early English Text Society by the Oxford University Press –
     1870, section on the Origins of Gilds.
14   Wikipedia – Hanseatic League.
15   English Gilds – attributed in a footnote, to Dobson and Harland's History of Preston
     Guild.
16   *English Gilds – The original ordinances of more than one hundred early English Gilds*, Toulmin
     Smith, published for The Early English Text Society by the Oxford University Press –
     1870, section on the Origins of Gilds.
17   Wikipedia - http://en.wikipedia.org/wiki/Municipal_Corporations_Act_1835
18   Wikipedia - http://en.wikipedia.org/wiki /Municipal_Corporations_Act_1835.
19   English Gilds - Religious Gilds
20   English Gilds - Religious Gilds
21   English Gilds - Religious Gilds
22   The city of Cambridge: Religious guilds', A History of the County of Cambridge and the
     Isle of Ely: Volume 3: The City and University of Cambridge (1959). This information
     can also be viewed at http://www.british-history.ac.uk/report.aspx?compid=66620
23   The city of Cambridge: Religious guilds', A History of the County of Cambridge and the
     Isle of Ely: Volume 3: The City and University of Cambridge (1959). This information
     can also be viewed at http://www.british-history.ac.uk/report.aspx?compid=66620
24   Catholic Encyclopaedia – St George
25   Information available from tourist data in Norwich.
26   Information from the City library, Norwich
27   *History of the Holy Trinity Guild at Sleaford* – Rev'd G. Oliver. Copy in the library of
     Freemasons Hall, class mark 1510 oli.

28   English Gilds - Merchant Gilds
29   *The Story of the City Companies* [London] by P.H. Ditchfield MA FSA published 1926
30   English Gilds - Merchant Gilds
31   From information provided by the Worshipful Company of Grocers
32   From material issued by the Worshipful Company of Apothecaries.
33   Marketing material published by Guildhall, London
34   English Gilds - Introduction
35   English Gilds - Introduction
36   *Hole Craft & Fellowship of Masonry. With a Chronicle of the History of the Worshipful Company of Masons of the City of London* – Edward Condor
37   *Catholic Encyclopaedia* – General Chronology.
38   *A Geological Miscellany* by Craig & Jones, Princeton University Press 1982
39   *The Hiram Key* by Robert Lomas and Christopher Knight
40   *Catholic encyclopaedia* – St Bernard
41   *Catholic encyclopaedia* – St Bernard
42   *Catholic encyclopaedia* – St Bernard
43   Information available at Bamburgh Castle.
44   Text copied word for word from http://en.wikipedia.org/wiki/Vitruvian_Man.
45   Information from English Heritage
46   Anderson's Constitutions, 1723, pages 46-48
47   From *Freemasons Guide and Compendium* – Bernard E. Jones, 1950 page 99
48   From *Freemasons Guide and Compendium* – Bernard E. Jones, 1950 page 100
49   From *Freemasons Guide and Compendium* – Bernard E. Jones, 1950 page 103
50   From *Freemasons Guide and Compendium* – Bernard E. Jones, 1950 page 104
51   *The Origins of Freemasonry: Scotland's century 1590 – 1710,* - David Stevenson and *Freemasons Guide and Compendium* – Bernard E. Jones.
52   See *Chivalry* – Kevin L. Gest
53   Oxford concise dictionary
54   Catholic Encyclopaedia - Deacons
55   *Freemasons Guide and Compendium* – Bernard E. Jones, 1950, page 188.
56   These duties and obligations were set out in the first volume of the "Admissions of Freemen" for the City Of Rochester - as provided by Medway Archives.
57   Mentioned in *Freemason's Guide and Compendium,* by Bernard E. Jones, 1950 page 304.
58   The Hiramic Tradition – a survey of hypotheses concerning it, Reverend Walter William Covey-Crump, 1935, copy in Library Freemasons Hall, London
59   *The Hole craft and fellowship of Masons* – Edward Condor
60   *The Hole craft and fellowship of Masons* – Edward Condor
61   *The Hole craft and fellowship of Masons* – Edward Condor.
62   *The Hole craft and fellowship of Masons* – Edward Condor – The Charter
63   *The Hole craft and fellowship of Masons* – Edward Condor
64   This point about the difference in the spelling was noted by Bernard Jones.
65   *Freemason's Guide and Compendium* – Bernard E. Jones
66   *Freemason's Guide and Compendium* – Bernard E. Jones
67   Taken from Old Testament, new international version, 2 Chronicles 34:14 and 15.
68   The solution developed by Sir Isaac Newton can be found in many books on mathematics and geometry, but none that I've found use the vesica to create the equilateral triangle. I used it because of my previous knowledge of its hidden characteristics.

# INDEX